Real Life Diaries

LIVING WITH
RHEUMATIC DISEASES

Inspiring true stories about managing life with
rheumatoid and other autoimmune diseases

LYNDA CHELDELIN FELL

with

BRENDA L. KLEINSASSER
LAYNE MARTIN, R.N.

Foreword by
DR. MARY ANN WILMARTH

Real Life Diaries
Living with Rheumatic Diseases – 1st ed.
Lynda Cheldelin Fell/Brenda L. Kleinsasser/Layne Martin, R.N.
Real Life Diaries www.RealLifeDiaries.com

Cover Design by AlyBlue Media, LLC
Interior Design by AlyBlue Media LLC
Published by AlyBlue Media, LLC

ISBN: 978-1-944328-69-6
Library of Congress Control Number: 2017910017
AlyBlue Media, LLC
Ferndale, WA 98248
www.AlyBlueMedia.com

PRINTED IN THE UNITED STATES OF AMERICA

Living with Rheumatic Diseases

DEDICATION

This book is dedicated to all who
live with autoimmune disorders.

CONTENTS

GLOSSARY & ACRONYMS

ACUPUNCTURE

A therapy in which thin needles are used to puncture the body at specific sites along energy pathways called meridians.

ADL

Activities of daily living.

ANALGESIC

A type of medication used to treat pain.

ANKYLOSING SPONDYLITIS (AS)

A form of arthritis that mainly affects the spine and sacroiliac joints.

ANTINUCLEAR ANTIBODY (ANA)

An abnormal protein whose presence, especially at high levels, often indicates a connective tissue disease such as lupus.

ANTI-TNF INHIBITORS

The immune system creates a natural substance called tumor necrosis factor (TNF). In autoimmune diseases, the body makes too much TNF which then causes inflammation. TNF inhibitors are lab-made antibodies that block inflammation.

- adalimumab (Humira)
- adalimumab-atto (Amjevita)
- certolizumab pegol (Cimzia)
- etanercept (Enbrel)
- etanercept-szzs (Ereizi), a biosimilar to Enbrel
- golimumab (Simponi, Simponi Aria)
- infliximab (Remicade)

ANTI-CCP

Anti-cyclic citrullinated peptide

ARTHRODESIS

A surgical fusion in which bones that form a joint are held in place with metal screws or plates, allowing them to fuse into a single, immovable unit.

ARTHROPLASTY

A procedure in which a damaged joint is surgically removed and replaced with a synthetic one. It is also called joint replacement surgery.

ARTHROSCOPY

A surgical procedure that uses a lighted scope to view a joint and perform minor repairs.

ASPIRATION

The withdrawal of fluid from the body, such as synovial fluid from the joint.

AUTOIMMUNE DISEASE

A disease in which the body's immune system turns against itself, causing damage to healthy tissues.

AVASCULAR NECROSIS

A loss of blood supply to a bone, causing the bone tissue to die and collapse.

BIOLOGICAL DRUG/BIOLOGIC

A group of medications that are derived from living sources and block the inflammation process. Biologic response modifiers are a subset of the disease-modifying anti-rheumatic drugs (DMARDs), and are used to treat rheumatoid arthritis, psoriatic arthritis, psoriasis and ankylosing spondylitis.

BIOSIMILAR

A biosimilar is an almost identical copy of an original product manufactured by a different company.

CACHEXIA

The loss of appetite, muscle mass and weight resulting from chronic disease. Cachexia is associated with rheumatoid arthritis and ankylosing spondylitis

CAPSAICIN

A pain-blocking substance derived from cayenne pepper.

CARPOMETACARPAL (CMC) JOINT

Also called the basal joint, it is where the thumb attaches to the wrist and is the joint of the hand most commonly affected by arthritis.

CARPAL TUNNEL SYNDROME

A condition in which the median nerve on the thumb side of the palm becomes compressed in the space between the bones of the wrist. It can cause tingling of the middle and index finger and weakness of the thumb.

CARTILAGE

A smooth, rubbery tissue that covers the ends of the bones at the joints, acting as a shock absorber and allowing the joint to move smoothly.

CHRONIC ILLNESS

An illness that lasts for a long time, often a lifetime, whereas an acute illness comes on suddenly and resolves in a short amount of time.

COLLAGEN

A large protein that is the primary component of cartilage, tendons, skin and other connective tissues

COMPUTED TOMOGRAPHY (CT) SCANS

An imaging technique that provides a three-dimensional picture of the bone. It also shows "slices" of the bone, making the picture much clearer than X-rays or bone scans.

CONNECTIVE TISSUE DISEASE

Diseases characterized by degeneration of collagen, a key component of connective tissue such as skin, muscles, tendons and ligaments. Connective tissue diseases include scleroderma, lupus, polymyositis and dermatomyositis.

CORTICOSTEROIDS

A group of hormones, including cortisol, which are produced by the adrenal glands. Corticosteroids can be synthetically produced and have powerful anti-inflammatory effects.

COX-2 INHIBITOR

A type of nonsteroidal anti-inflammatory drug designed to be safer for the stomach than other NSAIDs. COX-2 inhibitors work by inhibiting hormonelike substances in the body that cause pain and inflammation. Celecoxib (Celebrex) is the only COX-2 inhibitor currently available.

C-REACTIVE PROTEIN (CRP)

C-reactive protein is produced by the liver and increases in the presence of inflammation in the body.

DEXA

Acronym for dual-energy x-ray absorptiometry, a scan that measures bone density at the hip and spine.

DISC

A small, circular cushion between two vertebrae in the spine.

DISCOID LUPUS

A form of lupus that affects only the skin characterized by red skin lesions covered with scales that fall off and leave scars. Lesions are usually most prominent over the bridge of the nose and cheeks (referred to a butterfly, or malar, rash), but can also occur on other parts of the body.

DISEASE-MODIFYING ANTIRHEUMATIC DRUGS (DMARDS)

A class of disease-modifying antirheumatic drugs that can reduce joint damage and/or slow down disease progression.
- Methotrexate
- Leflunomide (Arava)

ERYTHROCYTE SEDIMENTATION RATE (ESR/sed rate)

A test measuring how fast red blood cells clump together and fall to the bottom of a test tube. A high sed rate signals the presence of inflammation, possibly indicating an inflammatory disease, such as rheumatoid arthritis.

ESTABLISHED RA

Rheumatoid arthritis disease duration of longer than two years.

FIBROMYALGIA

A syndrome characterized by widespread muscle pain, the presence of tender points and often debilitating fatigue.

FUSION

A surgical procedure in which bones that form a joint are held in place with metal screws or plates, allowing them to fuse into a single, immovable unit. Also called arthrodesis.

GOUT

A form of arthritis that occurs when uric acid builds up in the blood and deposits as crystals in the joints and other tissue.

HAMMER TOES

Toes that are dislocated and look like the hammers in a piano, often seen in people with rheumatoid arthritis. The resulting ulcers on the tops of the toes are painful when walking.

HEBERDEN'S NODES

Knobby growths of bone that commonly appear on the knuckle nearest the nail in people with osteoarthritis.

IMMUNE SYSTEM

The body's system for defending itself against bacteria, viruses or other foreign invaders.

IMMUNOSUPPRESSIVE DRUGS

Drugs that suppress the immune system which may help curb the immune response in diseases such as rheumatoid arthritis and lupus.

INFLAMMATION

A response to injury or infection that involves fatigue, fever and pain or tenderness all over the body. It can also be localized, for example, in joints, where it causes redness, warmth, swelling and pain.

INFECTIOUS ARTHRITIS

A form of arthritis that occurs when a blood-borne infection settles in a joint or joints.

IM

Intramuscular

IV/iv

Intravenous

JOINT

The juncture of two or more bones in the body. The human body contains more than 150 joints.

JSN

Joint space narrowing

JUVENILE ARTHRITIS

Any form of arthritis diagnosed in a child under age 16.

JUVENILE RHEUMATOID ARTHRITIS (JRA)

The most common type of arthritis in children. There are three different forms of JRA: systemic-onset, polyarticular-onset and pauciarticular-onset.

LIGAMENTS

Tough bands of connective tissue that attach bones to bones and help keep them together at a joint.

LUMBAR SPINE

The lower back, composed of five vertebrae.

LUPUS

An autoimmune disease that affects many organs including the skin, joints, heart and blood vessels, kidneys and brain.

LYMPHOCYTES

A type of white blood cell involved in the immune system.

MANUAL THERAPY

A range of physiotherapy techniques where the affected joint is manipulated and stretched beyond the range of motion that the person with osteoarthritis is able to use.

MCP

Metacarpophalangeal joint.

MAGNETIC RESONANCE IMAGING (MRI)

A procedure in which a very strong magnet is used to create clear, detailed images of cross sections of the body.

MTP

Metatarsophalangeal joint

MUSCLE

Fibrous tissue in the body that holds us upright and gives the body movement.

NONSTEROIDAL ANTI-INFLAMMATORY DRUGS (NSAIDS)

Nonsteroidal anti-inflammatory drugs that treat the inflammation but not the underlying cause.

- aspirin
- ibuprofen
- naproxen

OCCUPATIONAL THERAPIST (OT)

A licensed professional trained to evaluate the impact of arthritis on daily activities and devise easier ways to perform activities that reduce stress on joints.

OMEGA-3 FATTY ACIDS

A form of polyunsaturated fat found primarily in cold water fish that are known to reduce inflammation is diseases such as rheumatoid arthritis and lupus.

ORTHOPAEDIC SURGEON

A doctor who has been trained in the nonsurgical and surgical treatment of bones, joints and soft tissues such as ligaments, tendons and muscles.

OSTEOARTHRITIS

Also referred to as degenerative arthritis, it's the most common form of arthritis resulting from normal wear and tear as we age.

OSTEOPOROSIS

A disease in which bone loses density and becomes porous leading to fractures.

PATELLA

The knee cap, or bone that sits over the other bones at the front of the knee.

PAUCIARTICULAR

A form of juvenile rheumatoid arthritis characterized by the initial involvement of four or fewer joints.

PEDIATRIC RHEUMATOLOGIST

A doctor who specializes in diagnosing and treating arthritis and related conditions in children.

PHYSICAL THERAPIST (PT)

A licensed professional trained to use exercise to treat medical conditions and create rehabilitation treatment plans.

PIP

Proximal interphalangeal joint.

PLANTAR FASCIITIS

Inflammation of the plantar fascia, the tendon-like structure on the bottom of the foot.

PODIATRIST

A doctor who specializes in diagnosing and treating diseases of the foot.

POLYARTICULAR

A form of juvenile rheumatoid arthritis characterized by the initial involvement of more than four joints.

POLYMYOSITIS

A disease in which generalized weakness results from inflammation of the muscles. When muscle weakness is accompanied by a skin rash, the diagnosis is dermatomyositis.

PROTEIN A IMMUNOADSORPTION THERAPY (PROSORBA)

A treatment for rheumatoid arthritis that involves filtering the blood plasma through a special column to remove antibodies associated with RA.

PROSTAGLANDINS

Hormonelike substances in the body that play a role in pain and inflammation. Nonsteroidal anti-inflammatory drugs work by blocking the production of prostaglandins.

PSORIASIS

A skin disease characterized by thickened, inflamed patches of skin covered by silver-gray scales. Up to 30 percent of people with psoriasis develop psoriatic arthritis.

PSORIATIC ARTHRITIS

A form of arthritis that is accompanied by the skin disease psoriasis.

RANGE OF MOTION (ROM)

The distance and angles at which joints can be moved, extended and rotated in various directions. Range-of-motion exercises helps improve mobility and function.

RAYNAUD'S DISEASE

A condition in which the blood vessels in the fingers and toes spasm in response to stress or cold temperatures, resulting in pain, tingling and numbness.

REACTIVE ARTHRITIS

A chronic form of arthritis that often occurs following an infection of the genital, urinary or gastrointestinal system. Features of reactive arthritis include inflammation of the joints, eyes and structures within the gastrointestinal or genitourinary tracts, such as intestines, kidneys or bladder.

REMISSION

A period when disease symptoms improve or disappear completely. Sometimes remission of rheumatic diseases, such as rheumatoid arthritis, is permanent. More often, however, it is punctuated by flares the disease.

RESTLESS LEGS SYNDROME

A condition in which legs feel uncomfortable when sitting or laying down, and is common among people with rheumatoid arthritis and fibromyalgia.

RHEUMATOID FACTOR (RF)

An antibody that is present in the majority of people with rheumatoid arthritis.

RHEUMATOLOGIST

A doctor who specializes in diagnosing and treating arthritis and related diseases.

SAARD

Slow-acting antirheumatic drugs.

SC/sc

Subcutaneous.

SCLERODERMA

An umbrella term for several diseases that involve the abnormal growth of connective tissue.

SELECTIVE ESTROGEN RECEPTOR MOLECULES (SERMS)

A group of medications that work much like the natural hormone estrogen to slow bone loss but lack estrogen's side effects on uterine and breast tissues.

SERONEGATIVE

Characterized by a negative test for rheumatoid factor. Up to 25 percent of people with rheumatoid arthritis test negative for RF. Therefore, their disease is called seronegative.

SEROPOSITIVE

Characterized by a positive test for rheumatoid factor. The majority of people with rheumatoid arthritis test positive for rheumatoid factor.

SEROSITIS

Inflammation of the lining of some of the organs, such as the heart and lungs.

SJÖGREN'S SYNDROME

A disease in which the immune system attacks the moisture-producing glands of the body causing dryness of the eyes, mouth and other tissues and can occur in conjunction with rheumatoid arthritis or lupus.

SPLINT

Devices that support or stabilize a joint or position a joint in a way that prevents further irritation or injury.

SPONDYLARTHROPATHY

The collective name for a family of musculoskeletal disorders that primarily affect the spine and include ankylosing spondylitis, psoriatic arthritis, reactive arthritis and arthritis that accompanies inflammatory bowel disease.

STEM CELLS

Immature cells in the body that have the ability to develop into specialized cells. Stem cells are used in experimental therapies aimed at some autoimmune diseases because they have the capacity to repair damage.

SYNOVECTOMY

The removal a diseased joint lining.

SYNOVIAL FLUID

A slippery liquid that lubricates joints and reduces friction between bones.

SYNOVITIS

Inflammation of the synovium, the membrane that lines a joint. Synovitis is a common feature of inflammatory forms of arthritis such as rheumatoid arthritis.

SYSTEMIC

Refers to a disease that affects organ systems of the body, rather than one specific joint. An example is rheumatoid arthritis, in which inflammation can occur in joints, but also in the heart and blood vessels of the cardiovascular system and the lungs of the respiratory system.

TENDER POINTS

Specific areas of the body that are particularly painful to pressure and may indicate fibromyalgia.

TENDINITIS

The inflammation of tendons.

TENDONS

Thick connective tissue that attaches muscles to bones.

TJR

Total joint replacement

TRANSCUTANEOUS ELECTRICAL NERVE STIMULATION (TENS)

TENS is a nerve-stimulating device connected to the skin via electrodes. Used to treat pain, it sends electrical currents of varying frequency and intensity.

TUMOR NECROSIS FACTOR (TNF)

TNF is a natural chemical in the immune system that can also cause inflammation and tissue destruction in diseases such as rheumatoid arthritis. Biological drugs known as TNF inhibitors block natural TNF and ease symptoms of autoimmune diseases.

UA

Undifferentiated arthritis

UPA

Undifferentiated polyarthritis

SELF-MANAGEMENT

A term used to describe what a person can do for themselves.

STEROIDS

Steroids are drugs that blunt the immune response but are insufficient to slow down the progression of the disease.

VECTRA DA BLOOD TEST

Vectra DA measures 12 markers in the blood called biomarkers that are linked to inflammation caused by rheumatoid disease.

UA

Undifferentiated arthritis.

UPA

Undifferentiated polyarthritis.

UVEITIS

Painful inflammation of the uvea, the pigmented layer of the eye, that can occur by itself or associated with autoimmune diseases.

VASCULITIS

Inflammation of the blood vessels. Vasculitis can occur by itself or be associated with autoimmune diseases.

VERTEBRAE

The individual bones that form the spinal column.

VISCOSUPPLEMENTS

Products injected into osteoarthritis joints to replace the natural hyaluronic acid that usually gives joint fluid its viscosity.

X-RAY

A procedure in which a high-energy radiation beam is passed through the body to produce a two-dimensional picture of bones.

FOREWORD

By Dr. Mary Ann Wilmarth

We have a group of diverse, talented, transparent, passionate, and loving individuals who took part in this book. They have willingly opened themselves up to share some of their innermost thoughts and feelings. If you've struggled with such feelings or watched a loved one go through such a process, then you know it can be difficult at best for most everyone.

This is far more than a book, though. You are entering into an almost sacred space where we are willing to share such intimacies. Not unlike the Divine Secrets of the YaYa Sisterhood or the Sisterhood of the Traveling Pants, there is an almost spiritual connection among the writers here, bonded by a force known as autoimmune disorders, multisystemic and multifaceted disease processes that affects about one percent of the world population.

The other common thread we share is the chronic illness component we all deal with day in and day out. ChronicLife, as they often name it, knows no discrimination. By sharing our challenges of living with chronic disease, we found a club where we are all welcome. As a group—a team—we never have to say, "I don't have anyone to talk to," or "No one understands." Because our team does. Isn't that a great feeling? All you have to do is reach out.

With any autoimmune illness it's very important for you to take care of yourself. Unfortunately, I was not always good at that. Once upon a time, I was more concerned with taking care of everyone else and being everything to everybody. I knew I was pushing the envelope and not taking care of myself very well. But it was getting to be too late when I started to do more self-care. I also had extenuating circumstances requiring me to work additional jobs, coupled with increased stress piling up in my life from all sides. My body became the perfect storm. I made the mistake of neglecting to take care of myself in places I needed to.

This happens for many, but I've since learned we have to fill our cup first before we're able to fill the cup of others in order to remain healthy—both for the short and long term. Remember that this is a marathon, not a sprint. And you have plenty of team members to call upon along the way. All you have to do is reach out.

Respectfully with cheers,

DR. MARY ANN WILMARTH, DPT, OCS

PREFACE

By Layne Martin, R.N.

Health is something most cherish but when we get the occasional cold or seasonal flu, most take it for granted that we'll soon be on the mend and don't think more about it other than glad to feel well again. But some of us get thrown into the unknown abyss of chronic disease. Facing a world that's wholly unfamiliar, our routine is interrupted by countless doctor appointments, scary procedures, and more. This is the life of rheumatoid diseases.

When diagnosed with an autoimmune disease, many of us scour the internet and pour over books in a frantic search for answers, only to learn that there are over one hundred different kinds. Most have heard of rheumatoid arthritis, lupus, and gout. But others sound foreign, like Sjögren's syndrome, polymyalgia rheumatic, and scleroderma. Just as the names sound baffling, so too are doctors. Sometimes it's a long process of elimination and months of testing before a proper diagnosis can be made.

Living with rheumatoid disease means we juggle an illness that can plateau—even go into remission. Those days are cherished because we know that the future holds far more days riddled with joint pain, stiffness, fever, strange sores, and even stranger rashes. Anxiety finds us grasping—desperate at times—for answers, and a treatment plan that helps.

Rheumatic illnesses can rob a person of their self-worth, identity, and sometimes even family and friends. Some of us lose our independence which forces us into accepting early retirement coupled with financial burdens from the rising cost of healthcare and medication. Faced with social isolation, depression is a common threat. It becomes a vicious cycle as we fight to regain control and balance over the life we once had.

If you are one of millions who live with rheumatoid disease or love someone who does, the following true stories are written by courageous people who share your path. Although no two journeys are identical, we hope you'll find comfort in these stories and the understanding that you aren't truly alone. For we walk ahead, behind, and right beside you.

LAYNE MARTIN, R.N.
Regional Outreach Manager, CreakyJoints
Certified Health Coach, Take Shape for Life
martinlym12@gmail.com

CHAPTER ONE

The Beginning

It's hard to explain to someone who has no idea. Feeling pain and sickness on the inside while looking fine on the outside. -ANONYMOUS

Autoimmune disorders are indiscriminate. They affect millions of men and women, yet no two journeys are the same. To fully appreciate the unique perspectives throughout this book, it's helpful to understand each writer's journey from the very beginning.

*

CHRISTINA AMES
Christina was diagnosed with rheumatoid arthritis
in 1987 at age 20 and fibromyalgia in 2011 at age 43

My journey officially began in the summer of 1987. I was home from college, and during the course of the summer, pulled a muscle. I saw a doctor, but upon my return to school, it was still bothering me so I saw a physical therapist. During one session, I mentioned that I must be taking many more notes than usual, as my middle finger was aching badly. She examined me briefly, and suggested I see one of the clinic doctors. I made and appointment for the next day, and after a check-up, a preliminary diagnosis was made: rheumatoid arthritis. I was twenty years old.

I feel fortunate, because even though I had an initial diagnosis, my official one came just a few months later. I must bring up a pertinent point: I have a birth defect of my left hand which has required over fifty surgeries. Because I was feeling pain in my hand, the clinic doctor suggested I see my hand surgeon, which I did, and referred me to a rheumatologist he worked with. That doctor made the actual diagnosis, and I saw him for several years.

I entered the new world of rheumatology, and began extensive treatment immediately. I had several joints involved, and because it came on fairly rapidly, the doctor felt aggressive treatment was best. In spite of all my hospital stays, I was reasonably healthy, so this was all new. I started some strong medicines, and with them came strong side effects, the major one being ulcers. The stomach pain was worse than any other, and I lived on plain tap water and crackers during my last year of college. I also had several endoscopies and a colonoscopy for good measure. With buffer medications, the pain eventually became less severe.

As time went along the disease leveled off. When I was pregnant with my first child, I was thrilled to go into a remission state, which can happen with women. After delivering, disease activity remained fairly low, and again I enjoyed remission during my second pregnancy.

It wasn't until several years later when I began to have more symptoms which were completely different. One day, I suddenly couldn't pull my leg up into our SUV. I thought perhaps I had strained a muscle, but it quickly grew worse. I began to have trouble walking. I was very sore but it wasn't always joint pain; it felt more muscular. I saw my primary physician, who tested me for Lyme disease. Twice it came back negative.

Within a month I couldn't dress myself and needed help tying my shoes. I couldn't hold a hairbrush and needed help showering. The lowest point came when I needed help to use the toilet.

I will admit that I hadn't seen a rheumatologist since just after my youngest was born. My first doctor had moved away. I went to another who confirmed my remission symptoms and felt I didn't need to see her unless I had pain. When I struggled, I saw a different doctor in the practice, but he didn't believe I had rheumatoid arthritis because my hands were in too good of shape for someone with a crippling disease. He grudgingly did lab work, but felt I had fibromyalgia instead, as I did have terrible pain in every pressure point. He refused to even treat me for rheumatoid arthritis, which I had. He just didn't want to admit he was wrong.

After four months of excruciating pain, I went to a new doctor. I simply couldn't stay with a doctor who would not believe me, and was basically a jerk. My new doctor initially gave me prednisone which helped. Gradually we tried more therapies including DMARDs before introducing biologics, which is my current therapy.

*

J.G. CHAYKO
J.G. was diagnosed with
rheumatoid arthritis in 2010 at age 38

Rheumatoid arthritis slipped into my life in the early days of spring, just as the blushing cherry blossoms were beginning to bud. It arrived in the night, silently creeping in while I slept, and in the morning I woke with a puffy right elbow, swollen and raw, like the salty bite of marine air on a winter's day. My doctor called it tennis elbow and after a few weeks of discomfort, it simply vanished. A few weeks later my left elbow followed suit. Believing it was the same problem, I let it run its course, and like the right elbow, it too disappeared, fading out with the withering petals on the boughs.

All was quiet over the summer. I rose at sunrise, exercised, went to work, and spent my evenings in dance classes and theatre rehearsals. I walked on pebbly beaches, hiked the lush west coast trails, swam and traveled. I watched the blushing summer evenings cool into the deep crimson sunsets of fall, and one November morning I awoke swollen and feverish, the rain pounding against my window. My joints were puffy and sore; I was weary, my eyes thick, as if I was awakening beneath the fog of a heavy anesthetic. My joints burned and my skin was hot to the touch. I was sore and stiff in the mornings. Clearly I had a caught a virus, perhaps that seasonal flu that had already begun its rounds. I carried on, but after six weeks I couldn't seem to shake it. I went to see my family doctor and he referred me to a rheumatologist. Thus began my new journey with rheumatoid arthritis.

4

My vibrant life underwent an unexpected shift as I tried to find my way through the new territory of chronic illness. My morning workouts stopped, I quit dancing, and I took a break from theatre while I tried to muddle through the new world of RA. I weaved myself a cocoon built from the threads of my own frustrations. Little did I know, my incubation was preparing me for a new transformation. I used the time to figure out how to shift the particles of my life to work within my new limitations. I couldn't approach my activities in the same way. I had to abandon a few of them. I learned to slow down, listen to my body and take a step back. My world got smaller but somehow more focused. I discovered the smallest triumphs contained the most power. It took time and patience but I found a way to restore pieces of the life I had begun to build by making simple adjustments.

Ironically, the onset of my disease inspired me to try my hand at aspirations I had postponed. I finally had the opportunity to revisit and take a chance on another passion I had embraced in childhood—writing. Writing became my new theatrical world, but now I could tell my own stories. I always believed I'd have all the time in the world to pursue a writing career. It's funny how a diagnosis of chronic illness can bring all that time to a screeching halt. I asked myself, what was I waiting for? Now was as good a time as any.

I focused on the little steps that would lead me back to the life I knew, even if it was on a smaller scale. I learned to value each success and failure. I concentrated on the positive aspects of life beyond my disease. I took care of myself. I went to physiotherapy and learned exercise techniques to keep moving and reduce pressure on my joints; I started a treatment regime that helped to reduce inflammation and stiffness; I attended sessions with occupational therapists and learned about tools to help me with everyday tasks. I discovered and mastered smaller achievements that had been overshadowed by larger, almost, unattainable goals. I gave myself permission to take time just for me it and not feel guilty.

Nobody expects to deal with chronic illness. Medication could go only so far in managing my disease, so it was up to me to figure out the rest—to be proactive, choose my own path, and not allow rheumatoid arthritis to dictate the course of my life. And that leads me to here and now—I am back on the stage again, I've returned to the dance studio on a lesser scale in weekly dance classes with my partner; I immersed myself into the wonderful world of writing. I became an advocate for living with arthritis and met a whole community of remarkable people. I learned to curb my expectation of what I believed life should offer me and instead found something to bring to my life.

"There are things I may not be able to do well or ever do again, but that doesn't mean there's nothing I can do. There are always new goals that replace the old ones. And even when I try and fail, I can still find some small consolation in the effort. The world is full of possibilities and I won't let chronic disease stop me from exploring— because I know I can." –J.G. Chayko, The Old Lady in My Bones.

*

JUDITH FLANAGAN

Judith was diagnosed with rheumatoid arthritis in 2012 at age 32,
and fibromyalgia and polymyalgia rheumatic in 2014 at age 34

In 2010, I was attending a training institution in Bega, New South
Wales, to earn certificates in business administration, and then web
technologies the following year in 2011.

During 2010, I had an unexplained injury. I had a really severe
muscle strain in my leg, and had to use crutches for about two weeks
before I was able to walk properly again. I then continued my studies
and didn't think much more about it.

Over the first six months of 2011, I did the web technologies
course without any real concern or issues. But over the next six
months I was doing web design and computer maintenance which
involved handling a lot of computer parts and lifting hard drives. My
hands began to swell and ache which meant that every time something
had to be lifted, I needed the teacher to do it for me. I also had other
symptoms. My feet were swelling and my shoulders and neck were
always very painful, and remain painful to this day. I was unable to tie
my shoes or even put them on by myself without the help of someone
else, and struggled to put my trousers on as well.

I was on the phone talking to my foster mum when she heard the
struggle in my voice and asked what was wrong. I said, "I'm trying to
get my trousers on. I'm really hurting and something's not right. I can't
put my shoes on. I just don't know what's wrong."

My foster mum said, "Right. We are going to the doctor. I'll come with you." She called the Pambula Medical Centre and arranged an appointment for me the next day. I saw the doctor and he ordered blood tests which revealed rheumatoid arthritis. I needed to have x-rays done and was sent to a rheumatologist in Canberra. I saw the rheumatologist who confirmed that I had rheumatoid arthritis. He explained all the medications I was going to start such as methotrexate, Pyralin EN, Megafol, steroids and Plaquenil.

I now live on disability. I focus on what I can do, not on what I can't. I find online writing projects, and am a health advocate for my condition, because I believe together we can all make a difference. I belong to many Facebook groups, and have made many new friends. They have been awesome connections, and I hope to make many more. I also made a special friend in the rheumatoid community, but sadly she is no longer with us. I will always continue to be an advocate for myself and others in her honor. I will continue to raise awareness and provide information from reputable sources to educate the world about these diseases, and be a voice for those who can't speak up.

*

SHELLEY FRITZ
Shelley was diagnosed with
rheumatoid arthritis in 2012 at age 42

They say forty is when your body starts to ache a little more, but I knew my aches and pains were more than just age-related. The first time I felt like something was really wrong was while I was driving to work and my swollen, stiff hands hurt to grip the steering wheel. My right foot throbbed as it pressed down on the gas. I had never felt pain like this before. The pain was so intense it brought me to tears. For the next two years, I faced unexplained daily fatigue and swollen, painful joints in both hands, wrists, elbows, knees, feet and toes. I woke up each day feeling like I had the flu, making it very difficult to move. The joints in my feet and hands were affected the most, causing daily struggles to get out of bed and turn on the shower. Swollen, painful feet stirred me to awaken throughout the night. Throbbing fingers had somehow curled up during the night resulting in extremely stiff and painful joints in my hands. Some days it took a full five minutes to hobble just fifteen feet to the bathroom. My body collapsed on the toilet with a huge sigh of exhaustion and frustration, as if I had just climbed ten flights of stairs. Sometimes I cried right there in the bathroom. There were days when no matter how hard I pulled, I could not turn the shower handle on, and I was forced to call out for help. My family treaded water with me trying to figure out when I would need support and when I could be independent.

My primary care doctor suggested I increase vitamin D and B_{12} then referred me to various specialists for my symptoms. I visited the cardiologist for my fatigue levels and shortness of breath, a physical therapist for joint pain, and a gastroenterologist for intestinal inflammation. As I reflect on the beginning of my journey, I recognize how my symptoms were addressed in isolation rather than through an integrative approach. At last my primary care doctor connected the dots and referred me to a rheumatologist. After my first examination by the rheumatologist and subsequent bloodwork, I was diagnosed with rheumatoid arthritis. Despite the diagnosis, I felt a huge sense of relief to know that my symptoms were occurring for a reason and there was treatment. I knew very little about this disease that ailed me. My first appointment to discuss treatment options was a blur of information. The me I used to know had two children through natural childbirth and rarely took medication. Suddenly I held prescriptions for expensive medicines with pages of possible side effects in a size two font. I wondered if my doctor's recommendation for taking an aggressive approach in treating my disease would result in cancer or organ failure. I had more questions than I had answers. Whenever I had been ill in the past, I took the necessary antibiotic or let the flu run its course. Having an autoimmune disease was a whole new ballgame. I recall asking my rheumatologist which medicine I should take to make this go away and I will never forget when he told me there is no cure at this time but we will attack this in its early stages to prevent joint damage as much as possible and manage symptoms. It was odd to feel hopeful yet helpless at the same time.

Filled with fear of my fate, I felt alone. I knew no one with rheumatoid arthritis. Why rheumatoid arthritis and why now? Maybe my younger years of constant illnesses with strep throat and bronchitis or the bacterial infection I had as a child were the root cause. Maybe stresses of adulthood unleashed this dormant disease. I considered what my life would be like if this disease progressed quickly. The thought of not being able to help provide for my family caused stress. No matter how much I tried not to think about having rheumatoid arthritis, it was simply impossible. I became distracted from daily life by needing to research anything and everything related to inflammation and rheumatoid arthritis. I learned about CRP levels, ESR rates, DMARD, NSAID, IL-6 inhibitors and biologics. Numerous acronyms made this time of my life baffling. I read research reports and made lists of questions for my next doctor's appointment.

My inner pain was all too real, yet to others my struggle was invisible. I remember wondering if people thought I was being a hypochondriac. I shared my diagnosis with those close to me and the response was mixed with thoughts that I was too young to get arthritis and misconceptions that all forms of arthritis were alike and easy to treat. In the first years of the onset of my disease I had trouble letting others jump in to help me. I thought I was supposed to do it all, and if I paused to nap or ask for help, it could be perceived as a sign of weakness. It was very difficult for me to let go. When I realized that I could neither control or predict when I would face a debilitating day, I began to reach out to others with whom I could relate. I joined groups on social media and instantly felt validation by the people I met who had similar questions and by those who had experiences to share to help me pave the road ahead. Soon I figured out that I had a lot to learn from others and my rheumatologist was only one form of information and support. I had mixed emotions about taking pain relief medicine because I did not want to mask my symptoms, I wanted to be certain my prescribed medicines were working as intended. Everything I did to help myself felt like lessons in trial and error. In the beginning, I spent many days in pain all the while hoping my medicine would work better tomorrow. I was unaware how all of these changes to my body and my spirit would impact myself and my family in days to come.

*

BRENDA KLEINSASSER
Brenda was diagnosed with
rheumatoid arthritis in 1991 at age 31

I believe that from a young age my immune system was trashed. I had chicken pox in the first grade and missed two weeks of school. When I returned, I had pink spots all over and ended up with painful boils. I have scars to this day, some of which are quite deep. In the fourth grade I was hospitalized for bronchial pneumonia. I then came down with measles, several bouts of bronchitis, and always seemed to have a headcold. I ended up missing the allotted amount of schoolsdays but was allowed to enter fifth grade because I had miraculously kept up with homework assignments. I never seemed to bounce back from colds as fast as others, and I had a lot of sinus infections. Over the year, I had bouts of pharyngitis, laryngitis, and was even on voice rest. I also had bouts of tonsillitis when younger, but not so much as an adult.

In my late twenties I started experiencing painful costochondritis, a condition caused by inflammation of the costochondral junction in the chest wall. In September 1988, I was seen at the famous Mayo Clinic in Rochester, Minnesota. They injected me with cortisone and it felt better—until it wore off. When I came home, the vascular surgeon I worked for went to the ends of earth to find a surgeon who could help. In November 1988, a heart surgeon removed cartilage from the costochondral junction, leaving me with a five-inch scar. It seemed to relieve the pressure, and the surgeon was sure that this would be my answer. For a time, it seemed that way.

Three years later, things started cooking up again. In early 1991, I started experiencing pain in my ankles and fingers, and had a bad bout of bursitis in my left shoulder. My primary physician wasn't available so I saw another doctor who suspected lupus. He sent me for an ANA test and also a rheumatoid factor which was high, though I still wasn't diagnosed with rheumatoid arthritis. Several days later I received word that the lupus test was negative.

Symptoms progressed. I now had trigger finger in the left pinky which required bending back into position. I was in a lot of pain and started using a cane so I could walk to work. I had no idea what was going on, but something was—and it was worsening by the day.

In May 1991, I saw my rheumatologist again, as I was not getting better. He said, "I'm afraid that this is going to take a little longer than we thought." His nurse handed me fifteen to sixteen pamphlets for how I was going to live with this for the rest of my life. I had my answer, though the words were never actually conveyed to me. I had rheumatoid arthritis. I thought my life was over. I was thirty-one years old. How was I going to cope with this? Would I be able to continue working? That first month was a dark time.

*

CHANTELLE MARCIAL
Chantelle was diagnosed with
rheumatoid arthritis in 1999 at age 19

As a teen I was tapped by local photographers and shop owners to become a model. Through that I entered into the field of makeup artistry and was booked quite regularly for photoshoots and fashion shows. In addition to working full time, I had a very vibrant and colorful social life. Restaurants, nightclubs, dancing and traveling was incredible. It was a charmed life until one night when it all came to a screeching halt.

I had been out dancing with friends and came home pretty late. Taking off my nine-inch platform heels, I thought little of the fact that my ankle was a bit sore (did I twist it while dancing in the DJ booth?). I fell asleep but woke in pain. Not just a little dull pain; it was a fierce, crazy, sharp and intense pain. Then I looked—my ankle was the size of a softball! Luckily, I had stayed at my parents' apartment in the city that night. My mom, a nurse and longtime patient herself, said I had to get myself to the hospital ASAP. This was way out of the ordinary.

Hours in the emergency room resulted in x-rays, a few different specialists stopping by, and doctors taking a huge needle to my ankle to pull out some fluid. I was sent home with pain meds and instructions to call for lab results on the fluid and bloodwork. When I did get the results, I was immediately referred to rheumatology. Now, since my mom had been diagnosed with lupus, she suggested that I go to her rheumatologist. Okay, I'll give her a shot. Well, this doctor was

14

not my match. I never spent more than five minutes with her at an appointment. She diagnosed me quickly with lupus and put me on Plaquenil. Later we added prednisone, methotrexate and there was a failed experiment with Depo-Provera. The thought was that if I didn't have a menstrual cycle, I could avoid flares. Fail!

One evening I was introduced to a fella at a bar. He had lupus, too. I told him the name of my doctor and he immediately said I had to stop seeing her and he would get me in with his doctor. So, I went. This doctor was a total aboutface from my first. His first order was to take me off everything. Everything. I gained fifty pounds from prednisone and was losing my hair from stress. So, I was willing to try anything, even tapering off all the meds. Over the next few weeks I was in pain like I had never before experienced. By the time I had my follow-up appointment, I was kind of nervous. He was calm and measured, but I was a wreck! He very quickly said my diagnosis was incorrect, and I did not have lupus. But I did have rheumatoid arthritis, and he would make a plan to get me well. He asked me what my goal was and I said right away, "Get me back into my heels!" By chance there was an upcoming trial that he wanted me to be part of. Really? Okay, I'll try anything! I was to come in for regular injections, and within a couple of weeks my rheumatoid arthritis seemed to disappear. That year-long trial changed my life.

I was totally committed to my doctor, and am to this day, but when the trial ended reality hit. We had to find something that worked in the interim. Things got tough. I tried biologic after biologic, all with moderate success fading into barely any relief. This was especially tough as I was gaining weight, miserable, and fighting my insurer for medication coverage.

Thankfully, the FDA-approved the trial medication and I was prescribed the drug. It took a few rounds of fighting to get the coverage approved since it was a new—and very expensive—drug. I have to credit my doctor and his staff for helping me, though I'm sure my tenacity helped. To this day I remain on that same medication with pretty good results. Sure, there are bad days and flares. But compared to the past, this is a cake walk! Heck, I can walk!

Learning how to navigate insurance and having a great team of doctors and nurses has changed my life immeasurably. A lot of things I never thought possible for me are now possible. Every time I want to give up, I remember that I am worth fighting for. I am all that.

*

LAYNE MARTIN
Layne was diagnosed with
psoriatic arthritis in 2007 at age 47

Having worked as a nurse most of my life, when my symptoms of psoriatic arthritis started I just chalked it up to long days and being on my feet for twelve-hour shifts. As my disease progressed it started a series of misdiagnosis by multiple doctors which delayed proper treatment and further damage to my joints.

Now that I look back, I know that my disease may have been dormant in my body for many years and was triggered by a life-altering event in 1999. One day my husband came home and said he had quit his job as a teacher. Not only was I shocked, but our life as we knew it for the past fifteen years was turned upside down. For the sake of our children I put on a happy face and held strong as my husband uprooted us across state to his new teaching job. I got the kids settled in their new schools and then started hunting for employment. I soon landed a job as the emergency department manager at a hospital in the greater Seattle area. It was a much larger hospital than I was used to, and I managed over one hundred employees.

My first symptom of psoriatic arthritis started soon after. It began with intense itching and flaking of my scalp and became so bad that I started wearing only cream colored or pastel blouses and tops. My hairdresser put blonde highlights in my brunette hair to camouflage the flakes. After trying different shampoos, I went to the doctor who said it was just a bad case of dandruff and prescribed a steroid lotion.

Next, my feet started to bother me. As a nurse manager, I had to wear business attire each day. Walking around the large hospital in dress shoes was excruciating. After an endless variety of shoes and inserts, I went to see a podiatrist who diagnosed my swollen sausage toes—a classic sign of psoriatic arthritis—as Morton's neuroma. I was also having a terrible time with my right hip. I was born with bilateral congenital hip dysplasia and spent the first year of life in a body cast. My primary doctor determined from x-rays that I had hip bursitis likely caused from long hours on my feet. That was the point when I began a series of cortisone hip injections every three to four months.

As my disease progressed I started having joint stiffness and low back pain. I went to my doctor and after some lab testing he said it was probably polymyalgia rheumatic and placed me on daily low-dose cortisone. I felt fairly well on the cortisone and continued working and raising my two busy active teenagers for the next eight years. But then my hip stopped responding to the cortisone injections, and an MRI revealed that I needed a total hip replacement at the age of forty-seven.

We then moved back to the small town we had originally raised our children, and my husband started a new job as a school principal. I was now the nurse manager of not only an emergency department but also the medical-surgical unit, so I worked right up until the day before surgery. It wasn't until after the surgery and the pathology came back on my hip that the doctors considered an autoimmune disease. I was finally referred to a rheumatologist where I was diagnosed with psoriatic arthritis.

I returned to work after eight weeks of rehabilitation. However, many years of cortisone therapy had taken a toll and I developed two compression fractures in my thoracic spine that cause excruciating pain. I struggled and fought the inevitable but, at age forty-nine, relented to my disease and retired from the profession I dearly loved.

Retirement threw me into a very dark place. I struggled with my identity and sense of self-worth and found comfort in vodka. My affair with vodka started in 1999, when I was uprooted from a place and house I dearly loved. As the years progressed I never once thought it was a problem. After all, everyone had a cocktail or two when they got home from work. I told myself that I worked a stressful job, and it was a nice way to unwind and relax at the end of the day. Besides, I never called in sick and it wasn't affecting my job performance, so who cared? Once I was diagnosed with psoriatic arthritis, then I really had a great excuse. I told my doctors and physical therapist that I used it for medicinal purposes. That opened the door for lots of valid excuses and the drinks became taller and stronger. One doctor told me I should probably cut back a bit, but my alcohol use really didn't seem to be a big concern so I continued to indulge and self-medicate, sending me on a rollercoaster ride that eventually came to a sudden stop.

Finding my sense of purpose and taking control of my health and my life was a long tough battle. I still battle every day, but without the use of vodka. A lot of what I've learned has been trial and error, but I love sharing my story and I hope I can reach out and help others by sharing what I've learned.

*

KATHLEEN MEKAILEK
Kathleen was diagnosed with chronic regional pain
syndrome in 2005 at age 38, rheumatoid arthritis in
2014 at age 46, and ulcerative colitis in 2016 at age 49

September 2013, I opened the refrigerator door to get a pitcher of tea. I picked it up with my left hand and felt a pop sensation along with pain running up and down my arm. My ulna shifted to the top of my arm from the side. I went to the emergency room and when the registration nurse asked me why I was there, I showed her my wrist and said,"I don't think it's supposed to look like this." It was the first time I never had to wait, she took one look at it and buzzed me back. X-rays were taken. A couple of doctors came in and said they couldn't find anything broken, but I had what looked like cysts on my wrist and should follow up with my primary care doctor for further treatment. I was discharged home with a brace to stabilize the arm.

I saw my primary care physician and he recommended I see a hand surgeon along with a rheumatologist. I made the appointments and saw the hand surgeon first. He sent me for an MRI which showed that the triangular fibrocartilage had snapped and my carpal bones didn't have space between them. He thought that a partial fusion with removal of three carpal bones would remedy the situation, but he wanted a second opinion, so off I went to see another hand surgeon.

In the meantime, I saw the rheumatologist. After reviewing my medical history and family history (at the time, I didn't know of any direct familial connection to rheumatoid arthritis even though I had asked my parents), she was hesitant to call it rheumatoid arthritis, but said it was a possibility. All my lab work came back in normal range. She suggested I see a neurologist to rule out other diseases such as multiple sclerosis.

Now it was time to see the second hand surgeon, who went over the same things I had gone over with the first hand surgeon and the rheumatologist. He agreed a partial fusion was the best course of action. Back I went to the first hand surgeon and a date was set, February 14, 2014, Valentine's Day, and the beginning of a hard three years.

Surgery went fine. I was in a couple different casts for about six weeks followed by physical therapy and wearing a brace for four months. I should also mention that somewhere along the chain of custody in this surgery, the bones removed where lost, so no biopsy could be performed.

It's now May 2014, and I was in the neurologist's office for a series of tests. He wanted a brain MRI to rule out multiple sclerosis, but I have to get preauthorized by my insurance company. The next day I was at my daughter's high school graduation when my cellphone rang. My insurance company had scheduled my appointment within twenty-four hours. I started thinking that it must be bad if they move this fast. I start to feel tears well up, so I ran to the restroom to cry. I composed myself and returned to my seat and continued through the ceremony and the party afterward like nothing has happened.

The MRI was done and I was cleared of multiple sclerosis. The rheumatologist put me on prednisone to help with swelling. The hand surgeon injected my wrist and fingers with steroids which helps keep them moving when I feel like they are locked in place. I then went for my yearly well-woman exam, and was immediately sent for a sonogram. The doctor tells me the results: I have large fibroids and need a hysterectomy. He wants to do it next week, but my daughter is leaving for military college and I have to see her off. The surgery is scheduled for the beginning of September.

Following surgery, the surgeon told me that the fibroids were too big to be removed laparoscopically. Even though they had made the incisions, they ended up having to finish vaginally and it was a complete hysterectomy because my ovaries had been pushed so far back, they were damaged. I also had to have my bladder repaired because it was smashed.

I started to feel better, but then my right elbow wouldn't straighten. I went to an orthopedic surgeon. He tried a steroid shot, but it didn't work. The MRI showed lots of fluid so surgery was scheduled for November so he could scope my elbow. During the procedure biopsies were taken from my synovial tissue, fluid, and muscle. The results come back showing signs but it wasn't the typical repeating pattern of rheumatoid arthritis. Labs were still negative. A diagnosis was finally given: seronegative rheumatoid arthritis.

Now my left wrist was really hurting—the fusion was failing. Distal ulnar head replacement was scheduled for January 2015. I got through the holidays and then had the titanium wrist replacement. I was amazed that five days after surgery I was in the hand surgeon's office doing physical therapy, and it didn't hurt, at least not like before. I started to see a light at the end of the tunnel.

I got through spring and summer with regular visits to the hand surgeon, some for checkups and some for steroid shots. I saw the rheumatologist regularly and began methotrexate, starting with two pills, then four, and now six. Although I was willing to try anything, I hated them. I took them on Sunday and they made me feel awful. I slept all day and felt like crap on Monday and half of Tuesday. I started to wonder whether my whole life would be like this.

By September, both hands are tingling and hurting. An EMG showed cubital tunnel syndrome in both elbows requiring surgery. In early October my left elbow was done and two weeks later my right elbow was fixed. So far so good. But the pain was now in my right wrist. The hand surgeon thought he could save it by shortening the ulna. Surgery was scheduled a few days before Thanksgiving 2015. An inch of bone was removed and a six-inch steel rod inserted along with seven screws. The tears in my triangular fibrocartilage were fixed along with a total wrist debridement. But my right shoulder wasn't better. The orthopedic surgeon thinks shortening the clavicle should fix it. But since I had a bone broken, I had to wait six weeks for surgery.

On December 23, my clavicle was shortened about an inch, my acromioclavicular joint was shortened, and all the arthitic damage was removed from the shoulder. I now have divets in my shoulder. For the first time, I tested positive for RA.

I went into 2016 thinking it would be a good year; no surgeries were scheduled, and I was in remission. Then came August. I had excruciating abdominal pain. A visit to the emergency room showed that a one-centimeter stone was blocking my gallbladder duct. Upon removal, it was inspected and found to be filled with stones measuring up to an inch in diameter.

The pain didn't stop. I was sent for a colonoscopy, and woke up crying in pain. The gastroenterologist suspected abdominal bowel disorder and sent me back to the general surgeon. In the meantime, the pathology results showed I had developed ulcerative colitis. I underwent another scope of my abdomen to look for scar tissue. None was found, and I was diagnosed with acute costochondritis.

I started to look like I was dying. I went from size ten to size two in four months. My husband asked me if I had given up. I told him that I was fighting, but it was hard. I researched what might help and eliminated sugar, gluten, soy, dairy, and caffeine. I stopped taking the methotrexate but continued Plaquenil and etodolac, and all the trauma done to my body started to heal. I don't look dead any more.

The rheumatologist was not happy with my decision but I told him I was choosing quality over quantity. He agreed to monitor me and if anything changes, we will discuss the use of biologics. It has only been three and a half years. I wonder what the next three have in store.

*

RICK PHILLIPS
Rick was diagnosed with type 1 diabetes in 1974 at
age 17 and rheumatoid arthritis in 1999 at age 42

Despite having diabetes for twenty-four years, come fall of 1998, I was in relatively good health and had had a good summer. Labor negotiations at the school district had concluded. I was in charge of two building projects, and both were progressing well. The new elementary school, Oak Trace Elementary, had begun construction while a new wing of Westfield Washington High School was set to open on time. With two multimillion-dollar building projects going on, I wasn't worried about my health. And I certainly wasn't worried about a new health issue. That was when I noticed something wrong.

It happened when my son brought home a brand new car, which he loved. It was a great car. It looked wonderful, and it went fast. My wife nicknamed the car, a 1999 Pontiac Trans Am WS6, "The Beast." It was sleek and fast and everything a young man would want times two. But I could not sit in the car. Our son asked me to go for a ride around the neighborhood, and I simply could not get in the car. As the car roared off, my son angry at the terrible snub given by his father, he took my refusal as a rejection of his accomplishment as a young man who could afford such a car. He could not have been more wrong.

I knew I had hurt his feelings, and there was nothing I wanted more than to ride in that car, if only to show how much I admired him and what he was doing with his life. He and my wife were very disappointed in me, but no more than I was disappointed in myself. I cried as I heard the car leave the cul-de-sac. For me, there was something new to fear. What would keep me out of that car? It had to be something very powerful, yet unnamed.

In 2000, I was busy at work—very busy. I was hitting my stride. Our youngest son was completing his senior year of high school and preparing for the next phase of life. First, however, came the college visits. Our son hadn't yet selected his school, or even expressed much interest in college. When he suggested we tour my alma mater, Indiana University, I was thrilled.

On the day of the visit, I awoke to a cold, rainy morning—and a terrible backache. Snow was still on the ground and remnants of winter hung in the air. I attributed my backache to the weather.

Once we arrived in Bloomington, it was impossible for me to take the tour. I made an excuse about how busy I was and how I needed to answer email. So I sent my son off on what was for me the one place I wanted more than anywhere for him to attend. Sitting in the visitor's center waiting for the group to return, a counselor sat down beside me. She said it was difficult for many parents to let children go to school, and I should reconcile myself to the inevitable. She also took the opportunity to tell me how much my son would like Indiana University. I assured her I needed no such persuasion. I was sold on IU as the place for my son and was hoping he would select IU for his college career. Looking puzzled, she said I looked like an anxious patient. No, I replied. It's the weather, my back hurt.

On the way home I could not help but acknowledge that I was very tired. But I assured my son it was merely the weather that was making me so stiff. I had to stop again coming home so I could get out of the car. On the way home he told me he had made his college choice. It would be IU. I was thrilled but also a little scared. I knew how out of shape I was and that it would be necessary for me to get in better shape if he were to attend the big university. I resolved to do that regardless of how I might feel. I had a complete summer to get ready for his freshman move-in day. I was so proud he had chosen my beloved university despite my inability to walk with the group of parents that day as they heard the story about the beautiful campus.

My son assured me I had not disappointed him by staying behind and not taking the tour. Maybe not, but I had disappointed myself. I had to acknowledge to myself that I had disappointed both sons in less than six months. That day I resolved to do something about this if I could. Surely there had to be some answer, but what? I simply could not think of a legitimate reason for this stiffness I was feeling. Where to begin and whom to ask was the question.

By late spring 2000, I was scheduled to see my endocrinologist for a regular appointment. At the end of the appointment, I told him about how badly I felt and about my joints hurting. I thought he might refer me to physical therapy or do an X-ray. He listened without acknowledging that the symptoms might actually be something more important. Instead he said he would like to do some bloodwork and check a few things out. Bloodwork for aching joints? Was he kidding? I didn't need bloodwork; I needed my joints to stop hurting. But he insisted, so I took the order and went to the lab for the blood draw.

I was not concerned that the bloodwork would reveal anything so I let it pass once I got the test completed. No need to call, it must be nothing. My job was to complete another set of contract negotiations that summer and oversee the ever expanding building program at the school district I worked at. My job was to get my son off to college and help my older son in his junior year in any way I could. I never called for the results.

Three months later I again had a quarterly appointment with my endocrinologist and my joints still hurt so I asked him about the bloodwork. He replied yes he had the result and he wanted me to see a rheumatologist. A Rreumatologist, for what? Well he said he just wanted someone else's opinion. He gave me a name and suggested I have my wife accompany me when I saw this new doctor.

The rheumatologist asked why I had come to see him. I told him I was having difficulty walking or bending, and my fingers hurt. He asked if I felt better or worse since the bloodwork. I told him worse, or the same. He nodded and did a brief joint exam. He asked questions about when I felt better and worse. Then he asked again what my main issue was at that moment. I told him I was having difficulty walking. He looked a second time at the lab results and said "I am surprised you can walk at all." What? Walk at all? What are we discussing? He said the blood test my endocrinologist had done showed a rheumatoid factor that was off the chart. He then laid out a strategy for how we would proceed. He said he would put me on methotrexate immediately, and start the process of proving I needed to be on a new biologic treatment. He said that would take about six months and in the meantime he hoped the methotrexate would give some relief.

Leaving his office, I was amazed at how things had gone. My wife and I sat in the car and discussed what we had heard. It seemed like there were medications available and that we could expect help sooner rather than later. Our doctor seemed to have a good plan, what else was there to say? That evening I started methotrexate and as promised within six months I was taking Remicade.

Remicade was like insulin for me. It took a bit longer, but within two weeks I was feeling almost normal (whatever that is). I started to be more active, taking walks and enjoying life again.

My young son did attend, love and graduate from Indiana University. Apparently my not walking with him had no ill effect on his college experience. He works as a data manager at the Indiana University School of Medicine and is completing his master's degree at IU. My older son finished his college career and is a mechanical engineer.

*

LESLIE ROTT
Leslie was diagnosed with lupus and
rheumatoid arthritis in 2008 at age 22

My first year of graduate school started off uneventful. Then, about a month into it, I started having joint pain and muscle aches for a few days after I worked out. About a month after that, I realized that the pain came, but never went away. Thus began a journey into finding out what was wrong with me. After many doctors and many tests, I was diagnosed with lupus and rheumatoid arthritis. I was twenty-two years old.

As I started to think back over the years, it was clear I had been sick for a while but no one realized it. Several years earlier, I had a bad episode of vertigo that landed me in the hospital. No one could figure it out, and while I had several more episodes, their severity lessened each time, and eventually, they stopped. As I would later discover, autoimmune inner ear disease, which I now know is what I was experiencing, is a precursor symptom in one percent of lupus patients.

During my senior year of college, I had strept throat and pink eye several times. But I, along with the doctors I saw for those ailments, attributed them to the stress of writing an honor's thesis and applying to graduate school. The summer before graduate school, I started having intense pain under my right rib. I went to the doctor several times and told I was just constipated. It wasn't until everything hit all at once that it became clear there was a problem. And it wasn't just stress or constipation.

When I went to the rheumatologist for the first time, I felt like a deer in headlights. He was lobbing questions at me faster than I could answer. The above events seemed seminal to him, like they were red flags that should have been caught. But before I knew I was truly sick, I didn't really question what doctors told me. I didn't really wonder if it was normal for someone my age with a functioning immune system to be getting sick as often as I was.

It took me about six months to get diagnosed from the time that I truly felt sick. But it was really several years from the time that I first began experiencing symptoms, even though at the time, I didn't realize what was happening.

When I first got sick, everything hurt. It seemed I was having new symptoms daily, many of which were unexplainable and sounded strange, even to me. I had numbness in my cheeks and it felt like someone was pulling off my fingernails. Some doctors took these things seriously, but many did not. I couldn't sleep because my organs and bones felt like they were crushing in on each other when I laid down. But just as I struggled to sleep, I was overcome with a sense of fatigue that would stop me in my tracks and knock me down.

My body was in overdrive, and I felt powerless to stop it. My body was at war with itself. As much as I hate that expression, it was true. I imagined little men chiseling away at my kneecaps. Piece by piece, parts of me felt like they were being chiseled away.

When I was diagnosed, I didn't know what lupus was. And I thought arthritis was something that only happened to old people. So, needless to say, these diagnoses threw me for a loop. When I first got sick, the possibilities ranged the spectrum. I was told it could be nothing; I was told I could be dying. When you find out you're not dying, that's definitely a relief. But when you find out that you've been diagnosed with something that is never going to leave, and that you don't fully understand, it rocks you to the core. It made me question what I had done in my life to deserve what was happening to me.

I was lucky in that being a graduate student allowed me the time to navigate multiple doctor appointments per week. Had I been working full time, I'm not sure what I would have done.

Since I was diagnosed, I've experienced several hospitalizations, countless tests and procedures, and like many with autoimmune diseases, have acquired several secondary diagnoses along the way.

*

TIEN SYDNOR-CAMPBELL
Tien was diagnosed with autoimmune
rheumatoid disease in 2010 at age 40

I should have known that I would get rheumatoid arthritis when my dad started to develop nodules on his elbows, wrists and shoulders

31

in his early fifties. I think that this was my state of denial, because I knew my knees were osteoarthritic in the seventh grade. The x-rays I had to get after trying out for the basketball team showed swollen knees. I was already a swimmer, so it appeared that this would be my only sport moving forward. That and riding my bike. Like most kids in the 1980s, that was primary transportation to everything until one got a driver's license and a car to get anywhere.

I continued to be somewhat athletic well into adulthood, slowing down to take yoga and try Tai Chi. Eventually I decided to train for a triathlon two years before turning forty. Hampered by what I considered training-related injuries, I didn't make it all the way to completing the triathlon until I turned forty. So in August 2010 my determination, in spite of nagging, well-known knee pain in addition to a new wrist pain that required a wristband filled with ice to hold the handlebars of my bike on race day, I did it. After crossing the finishline, I cried tears of joy and pain simultaneously. It was the beginning of the end of my life as I thought I was living it.

I was at work training new employees when I finally had so much pain that I drove myself one-handed in my dream car I named L'il Red Riding in the Hood, a stickshift Jeep Wrangler, to the emergency room up the street. I was literally in tears and could not find a position for my hand and wrist to relax. The emergency room doctor decided that it was likely no more than tendonitis, gave me a shot of prednisone (steroid), discharged me with instructions to see my primary physician.

I scheduled an appointment and the ten days following my emergency room visit were a blur of increased pain that I had never experienced before. Each day seemed to bring up new mystery pains; four days of excruciating jaw pain, three days of right knee pain, two days of left knee pain, one day of back pain that kept me in bed, every other day the wrist pain jumped from left to right and right to left, ten days of nagging neck pain that had been evident for several years while increasing dramatically with each passing day. I knew it was severe, and with my background as a medical massage therapist, I had an idea, but I really had no idea what was happening to me. All I was trying to do was wait it out and return to the gym.

While waiting for lab results and my follow-up appointment the next week, after taking meloxicam and the prednisone, one day I felt good enough to go to the gym. I have never felt as deflated an athlete as I did that day. I got there and couldn't push ten pounds. I tried to swim and after taking a full twenty minutes to put the swimsuit on, got into the water but couldn't lift my arms over my head. I sat in the jacuzzi and let the heat work some relaxation into my bruised ego. This was not looking or feeling good at all. Undaunted, I had already signed up for a rowing class on the Schuylkill River in Philadelphia, where I live. I was not going to miss this event, because I had been wanting to try it for several years. I took the one-day introduction class, and while it hurt to do minimal participation on my sculling crew, I enjoyed the peace of being on the water and did more floating than rowing because my wrists hurt too bad.

The day had come for me to get the bloodtest results. My doctor had a very somber look on his face when he came into the room and said, "I think you know what I'm going to say." (Insert a dramatic pause). "You were right. It's positive for rheumatoid arthritis, and your numbers are sky high. I am going to try to treat you here for a while, but if this doesn't get you better, I've got a rheumatologist colleague I will want to send you to."

After a few months of this, my fingers and hands had started to curl into balls and the deformities were obvious. My hands were perpetually swollen and painful, in addition to the wandering pain points all over the rest of my body, I was declining rapidly.

This had become really scary and very serious so quickly. While I understood that I had an autoimmune disease, it was not clear to me how bad it could get until I had my referral appointment with my first rheumatologist in December 2010. This visit was unforgettable. I was admitted to the hospital after my blood was analyzed and revealed a hemoglobin count of 4.1 and an abnormal blood smear. I was sent to a hematologist across the street, returned to my rheumatologist, and then told I would need at least two blood transfusions to live because I was about to die. Too scared to say no when asked if I would accept the transfusion, I said "Absolutely!" Instead of being on my way to work, I was in the hospital for the next five days.

I would visit the hospital two more times that first year due to a compromised immune system. Over the following year, I was in the hospital for having an ear infection that caused another five-day visit.

During this stay, everything was tested including an excruciating spinal tap to rule out spinal meningitis. They discovered bone spurs on my cervical spine, which gave me the additional diagnosis of ankylosing spondylitis. They also discovered that I had both herniated and bulging discs in my lumbar spine. I felt like a hot mess.

I worked for three years after my diagnosis. As a therapist I had a full-time job and two part-time jobs. Some days were entirely too long for me to be able make it to the end without completely collapsing. I had to let one part-time job go. The missing money would be an adjustment, but I was sure that it would be better. One day I couldn't get out of the bed due to excruciating chest flare. I struggled mightily, but I made it. That was the last time I was able to get to the second part-time job. Only one job left and my struggle would continue. I worked up until 2013 when I had to go on medical leave for multiple surgeries. This resulted in my having no income for approximately two and a half years while waiting for Social Security Disability to accept my application. My family really suffered as a result. The only thing that we were able to hold onto was our house. There was no heat last winter and living in the Northeast is not the ideal place to not have heat and be ill. It has been a relative nonstop medical care scenario in my house. Thankfully I have a very loving, compassionate, caring family and friends.

Last year I underwent total bilateral knee replacement surgeries. It was supposed to help me walk, but autoimmune rheumatoid disease had other plans. I got the use of my knees back, only to have my low back go out completely, my neck to further deteriorate, and my wrist flares to return to 2010 levels. This disease is relentless.

As an advocate and community builder, I finally found something to do with all of my information and experience. I joined CreakyJoints® Arthritis Community and became a Patient Partner in Research in 2016 after seeing an ad at my rheumatologist's office. I became a Patient Governor after I started seeing my third, and hopefully final, rheumatologist. I look forward to sharing whatever I can with autoimmune rheumatoid disease patients of all ages, because I am a firm believer that there should be "no decisions for us or about us without us."

*

CHAPTER TWO

A One-Two Punch

I'm having one of those "I don't know which part
of my body to cry about first" days. -ANONYMOUS

A diagnosis of an autoimmune disease can be likened to a one-two
punch—the second punch being the discovery of a second disorder
such as lupus, celiac disease, or fibromyalgia. The disease pairing can
make medical diagnoses and determining prognoses very challenging.
What other diseases do you live with in addition to your autoimmune
disorder?

*

CHRISTINA AMES
Christina was diagnosed with rheumatoid arthritis in 1987
at age 20 and diagnosed with fibromyalgia in 2011 at age 43

I also have fibromyalgia. That came much later, and had I not had
an appointment with a terrible rheumatologist, I might never have
known. In the fall of 2010, I began having a terrible flare, with
symptoms I had never had before, such as muscle issues and soreness.

Most of my previous pain had simply been just that: joint pain. I tried seeing this particular doctor, since he was local and accepted my insurance. However, he took one look at my hands, and insisted I could not possibly have rheumatoid arthritis since my hands looked "too good." I'd been diagnosed by a very competent rheumatologist who never gave me any reason not to doubt him, so this was a complete shock! I've also been fortunate to have very little shifting of my fingers; at that time, I had none. So he decided I must have fibromyalgia instead based just on a cursory glance at my hands! He did, however, check the pressure points known to be associated with the disease, and I was positive in every one.

I ended up not staying with him as he didn't even apologize when all my lab came back positive for RA, as I had told him at our first meeting, but I am glad he checked for other options, as I might never have known.

*

J.G. CHAYKO
J.G. was diagnosed with
rheumatoid arthritis in 2010 at age 38

I was in my thirties when I was faced with the challenge of living with a disease. They called it rheumatoid arthritis, RA for short, and I was astonished. Wasn't arthritis for old people? Surely it was not meant for someone like me, the ultimate fit bit—a dancer, actress and all around fitness enthusiast. But, as it turned out, it was meant for someone like me. In fact, I discovered no one was immune.

Prior to life with rheumatoid arthritis I ran the gamut of traditional illnesses like chicken pox, strep throat, that communal kissing disease unromantically dubbed mononucleosis and, what seemed to me, every headcold under the sun. But these were gentle knolls compared to the mountain of chronic illness I would soon climb. In my pre-disease world, I walked on a highwire balancing a fulfilling (if not always stable) life in the world of theatre, film, dance and the written word. I reveled in my youth and my strength, believing I could achieve anything, go anywhere, and that I possessed all the time in the world to do it, until the day I stepped off a sidewalk and into the path of an oncoming vehicle.

It was one of those perfect summer days, the kind often found in dreams. I awoke early and went for a jog around the park. The neighborhood lingered in a quiet lull between sleep and wakefulness, the balmy air infused with the heady scent of rose and lilac. My hours at the physiotherapy clinic offered a perfect work-life balance. I took my usual route down the hill toward the metro station, passing quaint brownstones lining one side of the street, and the fruit and vegetable market where I often purchased groceries.

The sun was riding high when I took that fateful step off the curb and was hit by a car with such force that it launched me toward the clear blue sky. I have a vague recollection of flapping my arms, a virtual cartoon character trying to manipulate my body in the vacuum of gaseous substance called air before tumbling down onto the concrete. My shoes were knocked off my feet and my glasses lay on the road just beyond reach. A cacophony of voices surrounded me as onlookers gathered around. "Are you okay? Where does it hurt? Can you breathe? Do you want some water? Can I call someone for you? Are you okay? Are you okay?"

I tried to sit up, resisting the kind hands that insisted I lay still. A large purple contusion spread across my knee like red wine on white carpet. I looked down at a long red gash that stretched from my elbow to my wrist—a thin scar that still remains today as a reminder of how lucky I am to be alive. It happened so quickly I didn't comprehend that I had just been hit by a car. The ambulance arrived, and several hours later I walked out of the hospital with nothing more serious than soft tissue injuries.

I struggled with bouts of bursitis over the next few years; getting struck by four thousand pounds of metal will likely leave some impact. Eight years later, rheumatoid arthritis entered my life. There's vague speculation that trauma somehow invited rheumatoid arthritis into my life. I suppose anything is possible, but I'm not entirely convinced. Rheumatoid diseases arrive in their own unique way. For some, it strikes like a bolt of lightning, creating a turbulent storm in the body. For others like me, it rolled in silently like the tide washing over the sand, eroding my energy and reshaping the foundation of my life.

I am fortunate that, at least thus far, I don't live with any other diseases. Dealing with rheumatoid arthritis is challenging enough, but with a little improvisation, I've learned to reinvent my life.

*

JUDITH FLANAGAN
Judith was diagnosed with rheumatoid arthritis in 2012 at age 32
and fibromyalgia and polymyalgia rheumatic in 2014 at age 34

I live with polymyalgia rheumatica, agoraphobia, social anxiety disorder, generalized anxiety disorder, migraines, TMJ disorder, gastroesophical disorder, hypertension, and fibromyalgia along with rheumatoid arthritis.

*

SHELLEY FRITZ
Shelley was diagnosed with
rheumatoid arthritis in 2012 at age 42

Being diagnosed with rheumatoid arthritis was devastating, but this moment was only compounded weeks later by a second diagnosis of celiac disease. It was difficult to comprehend that I had not one, but two autoimmune diseases, wreaking havoc inside my body. I was compelled to determine which disease came first and if one caused the other to emerge. How did I morph from someone seeing only one doctor every few years to someone seeing multiple specialists each month? Neither my rheumatologist or gastroenterologist can say definitively how one disease may have led to another. What was certain though was the necessity for making drastic lifestyle changes to improve my quality of life and begin healing. Making an instant lifestyle change sounds a lot easier than it was to enact. My husband and two kids were impacted instantly too by my sudden dietary restrictions and appointment schedules.

I researched comorbidities and soon learned that most people with one autoimmune disease have at least one other. What will come next? Is there another disease ready to unleash itself tomorrow, next Tuesday, or in two years? I like mysteries but prefer a good James Patterson novel. This is frightening.

In the years since my diagnosis, other symptoms manifested, resulting in referrals to an endocrinologist, ear nose and throat doctor, a physical therapist, and an ophthalmologist. My ENT diagnosed me with laryngeal pharyngeal reflux disease (LPR), which is when stomach acid comes up into the throat and causes pain, hoarseness, and cough. Without modifying my diet even more to eliminate trigger foods, chronic LPR can lead to cancer. The jury is still out on whether or not I have the beginning of Hashimoto's syndrome. My endocrinologist sees me every six months to do an ultrasound of a growth on my thyroid and discuss my symptoms of hairloss, weight gain, fatigue, and sensitivity to cold. Pondering how all these connected diseases feed off each other makes my head spin. It can be overwhelming, considering how uncertain my future seems and how powerless it makes me feel not to be able to control my own body.

*

BRENDA KLEINSASSER
Brenda was diagnosed with
rheumatoid arthritis in 1991 at age 31

I was diagnosed with endometriosis several years before the rheumatoid arthritis. I found out years later there is a strong connection between rheumatoid arthritis and endometriosis, which explained why the contraception prescribed for my endometriosis actually quieted down my rheumatoid symptoms. However, this very same pill could have been the culprit that caused my brain tumor, a meningioma, as they can be progesterone or estrogen related.

Prior to the meningioma, I was diagnosed with hypothyroidism which had been borderline for years. It is a familial disease, and several family members had also been diagnosed with it. I have an underactive thyroid, and in my case I believe there is a strong connection between endometriosis, the meningioma, and the rheumatoid arthritis.

When the meningioma was finally discovered, it was believed to have been slowly growing for at least twenty years. That was about the same timeframe the endometriosis was diagnosed. As mentioned previously, the medication prescribed for the endometriosis could very well have caused the brain tumor.

If another disease pops up, it's always in the back of our minds as to whether it is a result of rheumatoid disease. I try not to live with that fear, though, as you never know from one day to the next what RA will bring. I cannot allow myself to live in that constant fear.

*

CHANTELLE MARCIAL
Chantelle was diagnosed with
rheumatoid arthritis in 1999 at age 19

I have no other diagnoses other than osteoarthritis in my spine but that's par for the course. I'm not particularly nervous about other diseases creeping in. I'm pretty well adapt at dealing with what I have

43

and can roll with the punches. I think it helps that I have a family with a very strong history of AI diseases and we all can pool information as needed. Having a great support system helps east any fears.

*

LAYNE MARTIN
Layne was diagnosed with
psoriatic arthritis in 2007 at age 47

I do have other diseases that have popped up over the past few years. It seems like when you live with any disease it starts to become kind of a viscous circle and the next thing you know, you're labeled with other diseases too. I have had three different doctors try to label me with fibromyalgia but, I've done my own research, and my symptoms can also be attributed to psoriatic arthritis. With the diagnosis of fibromyalgia they automatically want to put me on medications that are not indicated for psoriatic arthritis and in my opinion the side effects far outweigh the benefits. So, I have chosen to keep that one on the backburner and treat it with diet, exercise (when able) and alternative therapies such as acupuncture.

In addition, I have Raynaud's disease. Living in Texas you would think that it wouldn't be much of a problem but with air conditioning I find it miserable and scary at times. Whenever I get chilled, especially getting out of the shower in the morning, my hands and feet turn ghostly white. They actually look like they are dead. I try to keep my core body temperature warm, double-layer in the winter, wear long sleeves, etc. But, I finally relented to medication and take low-dose blood pressure medication which keeps my blood vessels from narrowing and improves blood flow. It really has helped with the symptoms and I haven't had any side effects from it.

I also have interstitial cystitis, an uncomfortable condition that can cause bladder pain, bladder pressure, and sometimes pelvic pain. When it flares it feels like a bladder infection. It can be associated with irritable bowel, fibromyalgia or autoimmune reactions. I am able to control it most of the time with diet by staying away from citrus. When it flares I just make sure I'm close to a bathroom.

As if that wasn't all enough, I have irritable bowel syndrome and ride the wave between diarrhea and constipation. Again, I have learned to control it with diet. I have found that dairy products and I don't get along at all! If I ingest too much dairy then I might as well live in the bathroom for the day. The urgency to go can be so sudden that I sometimes am not able to make to the bathroom. On the other end of the spectrum is constipation which comes when my psoriatic arthritis flares and I find myself needing pain medications. I that case I take my pain meds and eat six to seven dried prunes to keep my bowels moving. It's a crazy ride!

By far the biggest limitation is the anxiety that comes with living with a chronic disease. The unknown. What will tomorrow bring? Will I have a good day or a bad day? Will I be able to go to an event I've been so looking forward too or will I have to reluctantly cancel again. With that comes sadness and depression. You feel like you no longer have control of your life and the disease is winning. For this, I try to spend some time outdoors each day, spend time with my grandbabies and I read my bible. I also love to garden and look forward to the days when I'm able to get outside and dig in the dirt. I've found that keeps me grounded and gives me a sense of quiet and harmony. It keeps me sane.

*

KATHLEEN MEKAILEK
Kathleen was diagnosed with chronic regional pain
syndrome in 2005 at age 38, rheumatoid arthritis in
2014 at age 46, and ulcerative colitis in 2016 at age 49

I was diagnosed with complex regional pain syndrome in 2005, after a surgery on my rotator cuff, which makes me wonder if that was the beginning of the symptoms and something was missed along the way, even though I have all the classic symptoms of CRPS. In September 2016, I began having abdominal pain and was finally diagnosed with ulcerative colitis, which has been linked to RA. I fear that my rheumatoid diseasewill cause issues with my heart and therefore I will die young because it has been so aggressive in the two and a half years since I was diagnosed. I set my goals six months at a time: my youngest son's high school graduation, my oldest daughter's wedding, my youngest daughter's Citadel ring ceremony, Christmas, her graduation from The Citadel and then....

*

RICK PHILLIPS
Rick was diagnosed with type 1 diabetes in 1974
at age 17 and rheumatoid arthritis in 1999 at age 42

I was diagnosed with type 1 diabetes in 1974. I became ill while at

Disney World, and released from the hospital on my seventeenth birthday, proving that Disney is not always the happiest place on earth. I was diagnosed with ankylosing spondylitis in 2016.

*

LESLIE ROTT
Leslie was diagnosed with lupus and
rheumatoid arthritis in 2008 at age 22

I was diagnosed with lupus and rheumatoid arthritis a few months apart, mainly because while the rheumatoid diagnosis explained some things, it didn't explain everything. I do have symptoms of Raynaud's and Sjorgren's. I have a lot of gastrointestinal issues, but at the current time, I consider everything I deal with part and parcel of lupus and RA.

*

TIEN SYDNOR-CAMPBELL
Tien was diagnosed with autoimmune
rheumatoid disease in 2010 at age 40

I was lucky enough to have been diagnosed with osteoarthritis in my knees as a young adult and had dealt with various aches and pains throughout my body that I attributed to sports-related injury (shoulders from swimming), work-related (wrist pain and cracking). Once I was diagnosed with rheumatoid arthritis at the ripe age of forty, it was coupled immediately with high blood pressure. Somewhere in the first few years I managed to get diagnosed with ankylosing spondylitis due to the formation of multiple bone spurs on my cervical vertebrae, along with a reverse curve. We still don't know

47

what to call the nontraditional chronic low back pain that was finally noted to have herniated discs, but I personally think that's the ankylosing spondylitis. Mentally speaking I was diagnosed with depression related to my medical condition and anxiety related to my fears of having more problems, more complications, and more pain.

Sometimes I wonder if I have fibromyalgia or chronic fatigue, but my biggest fear is that I will end up with cancer because my immune system is compromised and so many of the medications I take include cancer-causing ingredients or formulas.

*

CHAPTER THREE

The Dominoes Effect

Bad things do happen in the world, like disasters, war, and disease. But out of those situations always arise stories of ordinary people doing extraordinary things. -DARYN KAGAN

Our immune system attacking healthy cells puts us at risk of secondary conditions such as eye problems, lung or heart inflammation, brittle bones, vasculitis, and more. This can result from the disease's progression as well as from treatment side effects. No matter the cause, once it gains momentum it can feel like cascading dominoes. Has your disease caused secondary health issues for you?

*

CHRISTINA AMES
Christina was diagnosed with rheumatoid arthritis
in 1987 at age 20 and fibromyalgia in 2011 at age 43

I have elevated blood pressure as a result of this disease. I do take medicine, and my primary care physician does an ECG, or electrocardiogram, every year, just as a baseline for any problems that might pop up. I also tend to have very low levels of vitamin D. I do worry about my blood pressure, but I try not to stress too much since that can be bad for both blood pressure and RA. I try to control it by avoiding sodium, eating well, and exercising as often as I can. I'm on medication for it and it does help, but my ultimate goal is to be off medication if possible.

*

J.G. CHAYKO
J.G. was diagnosed with
rheumatoid arthritis in 2010 at age 38

At first I didn't realize something new was going on. It was simply there one morning, a disagreeable pain consuming my right upper back. It was not the usual pain attributed to RA. I thought maybe I had strained something during a restless night, and the twisted sheets gnarled around my body the next morning seemed to support that theory. Over the next several months the pain ebbed and flowed, some days lost beneath the veil of a busy life, other times sharp and severe like a female grizzly protecting her young. I attempted to alleviate the issue on my own through yoga and a new pillow to provide proper support to my neck. I was more active during the summer months, and the pain seemed to recede. When nights grew chilly and autumn leaves began to turn, the pain resumed with more intensity, radiating into my hip and leg. Yoga and a new pillow weren't the answers. I needed help. I talked to my rheumatologist about physiotherapy to strengthen my core and upper back. I reasoned that a weakening core and poor posture might have been contributing factors.

I missed the energy of my dance classes, and I really wanted to get back into a program to strengthen and increase flexibility without adding extra pressure on joints. The pain and fatigue of rheumatoid arthritis caused me to fall off the exercise wagon more than a few times, and I was determined to climb back and stay on for the ride.

At my first appointment the physiotherapist gave me a set of exercises to try for a few weeks. I went home and diligently performed them, returning four weeks later for her to assess my progress. It was at this second appointment that she noticed something unusual about my posture. The cause of my new pain finally revealed itself—scoliosis.

Scoliosis is a curvature of the spine, and like many rheumatic diseases, there seems to be no definite cause. I could have been born with it, or could have developed it in early adolescence when I broke my hip and was hunched over on crutches for six weeks. It's entirely possible that deteriorating muscle strength and soft tissue weakness caused by rheumatoid arthritis could be a factor. I'll never really know. I was given a new set of exercises to stretch out my compressed right side, strengthen my weakened left side, and advised to get a four millimeter heel lift for a left leg which was a bit shorter than the right.

A few bewildering symptoms have turned up since rheumatoid arthritis made its debut: a roving rash that comes and goes with no definite cause, dry irritated eyes, surprise allergic reactions to medical tape adhesive and also various foods. I try not to worry about the possibility of future issues. I focus on the present, and do the best I can with what I've been given. Rheumatoid arthritis and scoliosis have altered the way I move, but I can still move—and I take advantage every day. There may come a time when I lose my mobility but I'm determined to do everything I can to prevent that. I'm doing my best to take care of myself, to put myself first, so that if anything else should present itself, I am prepared to stand up and fight.

Our bodies change as we age, adapt to environmental exposures and lifestyles, and that change can sometimes bring about new health issues. I have no idea if rheumatoid arthritis invited my latest issues along for the ride, or if they would have appeared at my doorstep on their own time, but I take them in stride. Right now, I am grateful to be healthy enough to live each day the best I can.

*

JUDITH FLANAGAN
Judith was diagnosed with rheumatoid arthritis in 2012 at age 32
and fibromyalgia and polymyalgia rheumatic in 2014 at age 34

I live with hypertension, gastroesophical reflux disease, anemia, fibromyalgia, and dry eyes, all of which only became symptoms after the diagnosis of rheumatoid arthritis in 2012. Living with that diagnosis, along with the chronic pain and extra conditions, were at first quite a shock. It didn't take long for me to realize it was my new normal, and I really had no choice but to adjust my life around that new normal.

I fear the fibromyalgia, rheumatoid arthritis, and migraines the most, as they are the ones I have the least control over. I really couldn't just name one as being the most problematic. Well, maybe migraines, as I have lived with those since I was seven. I turned thirty-seven this year. In reality, though, all of them are problematic at some point, sometimes even all at once.

It's hard to distinguish whether the rheumatoid arthritis or fibromyalgia is causing the most pain bodywise, but I know the migraines cause the most annoyance headwise, causing many other symptoms. Why do I mention migraines? The pain and discomfort from the other conditions can bring on and trigger a migraine.

*

SHELLEY FRITZ
Shelley was diagnosed with
rheumatoid arthritis in 2012 at age 42

It's not clear why I have frequent respiratory infections. My RA itself can cause inflammation of the lungs, and the medicines I take weaken my immune system and make me more susceptible to catching a cold or flu. I have missed work due to respiratory illnesses, and because the medication weakens my immune system, I sometimes need to pause treatment to boost my immune system and recover from illness. Working in a school setting probably contributes to my cycle of respiratory problems.

My body does not absorb vitamins from food very well so for the past two years I have been giving myself monthly B_{12} injections and I have to take other vitamins sublingually for better absorption. One of my medicines, Plaquenil, was originally used to treat malaria but now treats rheumatoid arthritis, can cause blurred vision, so I see an ophthalmologist every six months. Corticosteroids helped treat my uveitis, a form of eye inflammation. I take medicine to control nerve pain, presumably from inflammation that is compressing my nerves, possibly residual pain from having shingles in 2012.

The condition that scares me the most is rheumatoid arthritis. I can control celiac and laryngopharnygeal reflux through diet. I cannot control the rheumatoid arthritis despite my efforts to take the most effective medicines. The medicinal treatments themselves can lead to devastating consequences like lymphoma, but I maintain my focus on the benefits outweighing the rare consequences. If I decide not to treat my RA, this disease could get the better of me through destruction of my joints and continued inflammation of major organs. Worrying about the unknown leads to more stress and stress causes more intense rheumatoid flares.

*

BRENDA KLEINSASSER
Brenda was diagnosed with
rheumatoid arthritis in 1991 at age 31

Over the years, my hair has become more fine and thinner due to the medications I've taken. The skin on my hands has become paper thin with no explaination for it. My fingernails have become brittle and some of them actually break in the middle of the nailbed. My dermatologist recommended biotin, which seemed to help with the hair thinning a bit. My eye problems consist of early onset cataracts which my ophthalmologist is monitoring. Retinal tears and glaucoma could develop down the road. My cataracts are grade II, so it will be years before they'll be extracted. I was told I'll probably see more vision changes and eventually need complete eye exams more than once a year. So far, that hasn't been the case. I do have the cataracts, so I'm checked yearly for retinal tears and glaucoma pressures.

I used to have thick hair, and am now limited in style options. I used to have beautiful nails, but my dermatologist advised me to keep them short to avoid risks of having them tear at the nailbed.

Rheumatoid arthritis can cause so many problems, far more than just with joints. My fingers are deformed, which took place early on and is now irreparable. I have had myriad of problems throughout my body. Some I can blame on rheumatoid arthritis, and some may be just because of a weakened immune system. Anytime I go to a physician with a new problem, it's always at the back of my mind whether rheumatoid disease is responsible.

I have been taking a biologic for over sixteen years, which can weaken the immune system. Three years ago I was diagnosed with basal cell carcinoma, a skin cancer, on the right side of my nose. The dermatologist didn't want to say that my biologic was a bad drug that could have caused this, but we will never know. I would like to think it's the result of years without sunscreen. I now use sunscreen even during the winter months. They were able to remove all of the skin cancer during the first treatment, a MOHS procedure, but they had to dig deep and examine the tissue under a microscope to make sure all margins were clear. I had to have skin grafted from my forehead to my nose. It was almost a complete match, and isn't noticeable. It took almost a year for complete healing. Now I have to have full body skin checks every year.

*

CHANTELLE MARCIAL
Chantelle was diagnosed with
rheumatoid arthritis in 1999 at age 19

The condition that has caused me the most issue is uveitis. I spend a lot of time with my eye dilated, doing drops every hour and lots of time at the uveitis specialist. It's frustrating but I take it as a part of my disease. I can handle it with help from my doctor and a speedy pharmacist.

*

LAYNE MARTIN
Layne was diagnosed with
psoriatic arthritis in 2007 at age 47

The psoriatic arthritis has caused several bouts of uveitis which is an inflammation of the middle layer of the eye. My symptoms are eye pain and redness along with blurred vision. Each time it happened, it came on suddenly without warning and affected both eyes. Without treatment it can cause permanent loss of vision. Fortunately I've been able to get treatment immediately consisting of cortisone eyedrops every two hours around the clock for twenty-four hours followed by another visit to the eye doctor with additional eyedrops, depending on how well I respond to treatment. It's scary to think I could lose my vision permanently, and has given me quite a bit of anxiety.

Another condition resulted from long-term cortisone use. I have osteoporosis and have developed two spontaneous compression fractures in my spine which were painful at the time.

Most recently I'm dealing with mellatosis, metal poisoning that can occur from certain joint replacements done with metal-on-metal implants. I had a total hip replacement nine years ago due to the psoriatic arthritis. Two years after it was replaced, it started to squeak when I walked but wasn't painful. The squeaking only lasted about a day. I went to my orthopedic surgeon, who took x-rays and said the hip looked fine and not to worry. Over the years I've had hearing issues in one ear, cognitive issues off and on, and pain in my hip. I've gone to several doctors about my ear feeling full and plugged, but they all tell me it might have a little fluid in it and to take an antihistamine.

The cognitive issues are all chalked up to the medications I take for the psoriatic arthritis. And the hip pain was actually my sacroiliac joint. I was sent for physical therapy which never did any good. I recently started having increased hip pain and went to a new orthopedic surgeon. He took x-rays, did a bone scan, cat scan, and checked my chromium and cobalt levels. The x-rays and scans all looked fine, but the metal levels came back extremely high. In fact he said my cobalt level was one of the highest he has every seen. Yikes! So, now I am facing a revision surgery of my hip in a few weeks so they can replace the metal parts with ceramic. Everything I've read say my symptoms from the mellatosis should subside in a few months once they get the metal parts out.

*

KATHLEEN MEKAILEK
Kathleen was diagnosed with chronic regional pain
syndrome in 2005 at age 38, rheumatoid arthritis in
2014 at age 46, and ulcerative colitis in 2016 at age 49

My RA has caused issues that I never knew were connected until I started researching. I had a total abdominal hysterectomy to remove fibroids up to five inches, too big to remove laparoscopically. I also had my gallbladder removed, which seems common. I had both my triangular fibrocartilage complexes fixed, both cubital tunnels opened, and both wrists, right elbow, and right shoulder debrided to stop further damage.

Before diagnosis, I had Lasik eye surgery, and now my vision is going blurry. My skin is thinning. I am anemic and have a low white cell count because of the medications. I'm constantly fatigued and need afternoon naps. I have also had bladder stones. I have also had my teeth rot from the inside out. I never had a cavity until a year before my diagnosis, and had I known it was a symptom, I might have been able to do something sooner.

The condition I fear most is losing my vision completely because I love to take photographs—I've sold my photography and been in a lot of shows. Without my eyes, how can I envision a picture? The one that has been most problematic for me is also the blurring of my vision for the same reason. I will be able to find another way to express myself through art, but to lose my ability to see it and appreciate other's works will be the greatest loss to me. But, most of all, crowds scare me. I used to love a good art opening or museum, but now I hear a sneeze or cough and all I can think about is how my counts are low and will I end up in the hospital with IV antibiotics. I can't live in a bubble and won't live in a bubble, so I carry a mask, Lysol wipes and Purell with me. The first cough/sneeze I hear, mask goes on. I don't shake hands, but instead smile and say I have a compromised immune system. My husband wipes tables and chairs down for me and opens doors. I try to keep exposure to a minimum, so I guess this disease has turned me into somewhat of a germaphobe, something I did not realize until right now, writing this down.

*

RICK PHILLIPS
Rick was diagnosed with type 1 diabetes in 1974
at age 17 and rheumatoid arthritis in 1999 at age 42

I was diagnosed with type 1 diabetes in 1974 while at Disney World in Florida. My family and I were on a much anticipated final trip before I was to begin working, leave home and start college. Knowing what was probably wrong (my mother was also a type 1 person with diabetes) we rushed back home to Indiana. The next morning I was admitted to the hospital and diagnosed as a person with type 1 diabetes. I was released from the hospital on my seventeeth birthday. I always say that my experience proves that Disney World is not always the happiest place on earth.

When I was diagnosed, I mistakenly believed my time on this earth would be short. As I left the hospital, I resolved I would do everything I wanted as quickly as I could. Within three years I was married, two years after that I graduated from college and started my first professional job. My wife and I have been married thirty-nine years at the time of this writing, and our two sons are grown with children of their own. My life was lived at such a rapid pace that I often forgot to enjoy it. It took me many years and professional therapy to understand that I could enjoy life. I nearly forgot that when I was diagnosed with RA. Even today, forty-two years after being diagnosed with diabetes, I have yet to master the art of slowing down and appreciating life.

*

LESLIE ROTT
Leslie was diagnosed with lupus and
rheumatoid arthritis in 2008 at age 22

At this point, I consider everything I deal with completely tied to lupus and RA. Let's be honest, it is literally the cause of everything.

At the end of 2016, I had gum grafting surgery. I had pretty significant gum recession. My dentist originally pointed it out to me about a year and half before I really noticed it. But one morning I woke up and couldn't believe what I saw. It was like my gums had decided to vacate my mouth. My dentist said that my issue was significant and I would need to see a periodontist. Because my gums not only looked bad, but I was having significant pain as a result of the gums receding far enough to begin to expose root. The periodontist felt that surgery was my best option.

Surgery. Basically my first since I got sick. While the idea of this did not thrill me, and I had no idea how my body would react to the stress, I didn't have much choice. Honestly, the hardest part of surgery was having to be off my lupus and rheumatoid medication for one week prior surgery and one week after, so three weeks total without medication. When I first got sick, I had nightmares about my teeth falling out. Sometimes I'm afraid to look in the mirror for fear that I will see a toothless grin staring back, so this whole gum thing confirmed one of my worst fears, rational or not.

I've always had good oral hygiene. I had a lot of teeth pulled when I was younger because my mouth was too small to hold them all. And I had braces. But other than that, I didn't get my first (and only!) cavity until I was twenty-five years old. I blame that on the prednisone.

It's interesting that as a result of my illnesses, my body is attacking my organs and joints, and yet I had tissue from one part of my mouth moved to another part of my mouth, and it worked beautifully. Just call me the bionic woman.

*

TIEN SYDNOR-CAMPBELL
Tien was diagnosed with autoimmune
rheumatoid disease in 2010 at age 40

The most shocking diagnosis I received in the first few years was pleurisy. I was under the impression that condition had disappeared a long time ago, but my lungs and breathing were so compromised that if it wasn't pleurisy, then I was convinced it was a heart attack. My friends and family were just as shocked, well, at least the ones who don't have RA. I felt somewhat more prepared for the DEXA scan to reveal that I had osteopenia, a precursor to osteoporosis, because I had been taking steroids like they were candy for extended periods of time.

The condition that confused me the most were the eye problems. Periods of disappearing vision were striking with a frequency that was concerning because prior to my diagnosis I scored a perfect ten on a vision exam. That's what they call sharp-shooter vision, and I was so proud of that. Unfortunately within the first few years of diagnosis, I went from that to bifocals nearly overnight. It was certainly a blow to my self-esteem to lose perfect vision. I've learned to live with the new look of glasses, but when I have to put them on to see something, it's another reminder of what this disease has taken from me.

Another thing that really and truly dented my self-esteem was the disappearance of my big toenails. It started with a weird deadening of my nail and a new one starting, that one growing for a month or two and then it would die and fall off. Now, anyone who knows me knows I have extreme vanity about my pretty feet. Summertime was my favorite because I could get designs painted on them and feel fabulous literally from head to toe. This issue was only accepted after I had an entire year of no new growth of nails on either of my toes. I had to resort to fake nails on my toes in order to keep up appearances and, like I said, this was absolutely devastating.

Emotionally speaking, I have so many thoughts and my most immediate thought is anger and feeling betrayed. Anger because it is the most insidious disease that too many people don't know about and should. I had no idea, until I was in the middle of the storm trying to just stay able to walk upright. Anger because it is incredibly unfair that I have to have this condition. Why? I am a body-centered psychotherapist and I help others to deal with chronic conditions like pain and as an expert. I couldn't even help myself. Betrayal is the other emotion that can be even more disabling than the depression. I was a very active adult when my health plummeted. I had completed a minitriathlon a few months before my diagnosis. I eat right, I exercise, I stayed active, did my job helping people, and this is was I got in return: betrayal.

I have a host of other feelings and emotions, but the most concerning is fear. Not only fear for my future, but what I fear most is completely losing my eyesight. I have a close friend who was blinded as an adult from an allergic reaction to a vaccine. I see how much she is able to do for herself and maintain a level of independence, but not being able to take myself where I want to go is terrifying. I got a tiny taste of that while I was recovering from bilateral knee replacement and that was a very difficult time for me. My fierce independence is hardwired. Luckily I married a man who understands that.

*

People who need help sometimes look
a lot like people who don't need help.

GLENNON MELTON

*

CHAPTER FOUR

Describing the Pain

"Yes, hello, I'd like a refund on my body. It's kinda defective and really expensive." -ANONYMOUS

Living with autoimmune disease means pain. Some days are better, some are worse, and some require medical attention to manage. Because pain is an invisible symptom, it can be difficult to define. How would you describe your daily pain?

*

CHRISTINA AMES
Christina was diagnosed with rheumatoid arthritis in 1987 at age 20 and diagnosed with fibromyalgia in 2011 at age 43

My daily pain level is around four to five. There is never a day when I'm completely pain-free; I just have varying levels. What can be frustrating for a rheumatic disease patient, or any chronic disease patient, is that we never know how we'll feel any given day. It can also vary during the day. I might feel well in the morning and go to the gym but if I overdo it, I might not have enough energy left over to make dinner or attend one of my daughter's activities.

I personally try to leave pain medication as my absolute last choice. That is my choice, and it doesn't work for everyone. I am a very tough person who has lived with pain my entire life, so I'm comfortable with that decision. I have found that heat therapy works well for me: heating pads, hot showers, hot tubs; all of these are very soothing, and help when I have a flare. I also use creams such as Epsom salt lotion and muscle rubs that add a bit of heat on the skin.

Although my daily pain levels are usually low, I can get very strong flares. Weather changes and cold weather affect me the most. The first sign of cooler temperatures have me cringing, since I know what will be coming. During the fall and winter months, there is not a day when I don't have pain. Another of my triggers is hormone spikes, which are harder to avoid.

I try to stay as warm as possible, dressing in layers, and using blankets. Since I'm at the age of going through menopause, it's a bit more challenging. I can have a hot flash, and be cold five minutes later. I'm hopeful that particular trigger will go away very soon. My husband and I are also planning to move south when he is eligible for retirement in six years. I am hopeful that having a climate that doesn't have such a definite winter will be easier on me.

*

J.G. CHAYKO
J.G. was diagnosed with
rheumatoid arthritis in 2010 at age 38

Rheumatoid arthritis has its own modus operandi when it comes to pain. For me, the pain is best described as a hot burning pulse that infiltrates my joints, puffing them up like a blowfish. The first influx comes on like a tidal wave swamping everything in its path. Once the waters recede, I'm left with the dull aching ruins of what transpired. The pain is always there, rising and falling with the rhythm of my life.

My daily pain is a solid four on a ten-point scale. There are days when it is definitely worse, but four is what I've grown used to and is my normal (if anything about this wily disease can be called normal), and the scale I use to gage any increase in pain. It's not unlivable pain, at least not for this former dancer who has lived through sprains, strains, bruises and falls. It just lingers like white noise in the background. When the flares come, they erupt like tiny volcanoes flooding my joints with angry red lava, coloring them with the blistering heat of inflammation.

Stress, excessive exercise and the erratic climate of the west coast are typical triggers for flares. Our climate can experience up to three different types of weather in one day, causing my body to become a walking barometer. The winters are chilly and damp, the summers mild with a touch of humidity. Warm dry days offer me a reprieve from gray days thick with rain-swollen clouds that breed perfect conditions for a tempestuous storm in my joints. Rheumatoid arthritis is such a personal disease, never presenting itself the same way. If I overdo activity on any given day, which I am inclined to do, my body will always send me a pointed reminder to take a step back. If on the occasional celebratory evening I overindulge, I run the risk of suffering for it the next morning.

Ice and heat have become my partners in crime. When my joints are hot and puffy, ice cools and reduces the swelling. When feeling sore and raw, I turn to the comfort of a heating blanket or hot bubble bath. The heat soothes my painful joints, and takes me back to a time before RA. I've learned to listen to my body, be kind to myself, slow down and rest when needed. Appreciating the slow and steady can really win the race, even if I'm only racing against myself.

I'm not the same athletic dancer I used to be. My swollen joints are not as flexible or as resilient as they once were, and I don't have the same stamina when it comes to working out. I'm mindful of what can trigger a flare, and aware when that flare is caused by me. But for every day that RA knocks me down, there are rare moments when I forget I have it. Numerous days are filled with distraction, and I participate in things I love like coffee with friends or family, getting lost in a good story with a cup of hot tea and a cozy blanket, losing myself in a role beneath theatre lights, or taking a stroll through the park on a sunny day. I am grateful for all the little joys and in those seemingly insignificant moments, rheumatoid arthritis plays no part in my life.

*

JUDITH FLANAGAN
Judith was diagnosed with rheumatoid arthritis in 2012 at age 32
and fibromyalgia and polymyalgia rheumatic in 2014 at age 34

I would rate my daily pain as an eight or nine. It may go up or down, depending on situations or environmental factors such as weather. I tend to take each day as it comes, and try to prepare for both extremes.

For example, my pain level for all conditions increase during hot weather, or may decrease a little with cool temperatures. Heat is definitely a major trigger. To help manage my pain from flares, I use ice packs, TENS machines, cold cloths, ice bricks, pain gels, medications, massage, gentle low-impact exercise, mindfulness exercises, listening to health webinars. I am always open to other options also. The heat definitely makes my pain worse and is a major trigger for fibromyalgia and rheumatoid arthritis. Rain and chocolate are major triggers for migraines, so I rarely eat chocolate but I have no control over what the weather does.

*

SHELLEY FRITZ
Shelley was diagnosed with
rheumatoid arthritis in 2012 at age 42

To some degree I'm in pain every day. A debilitating day will keep me home from work or cause me to cancel with friends. On a ten-point scale, I'd rate my daily pain at six. In the early morning it is a seven or eight. From mid-morning until late afternoon, it levels out to about five. After an hour-long drive home, the synovial fluid around my joints hardens just enough and I'm unable to get out of the car without difficulty, and walking is painful even at the pace of a turtle. Experience has helped me figure out a few elements that trigger my pain: stress, being too cold, sitting or standing for more than forty minutes at a time, and eating certain foods.

Typically, my pain is managed with minimal medication and by removing myself from toxic people and situations that elevate my stress. Changing jobs was a part of that plan and turned out to be a truly great decision. I work full time to manage my pain. If I were to stay at home, I think I would rest maybe too much. Moving and having lots of short-term goals at work keep me motivated and distract me from pain. Sometimes I don't even think about pain while teaching a lesson. Of course, I'll notice it while walking to the next classroom, but for moments in my day I can enjoy not thinking about pain.

I use medication to manage pain when necessary so I can function and live a somewhat normal life. This past year when I lost my mother to cancer, I felt enormous stress without this amazing woman whom I spoke with every single day and cared for the last few months of her life. The events that followed with the funeral, finances, and legalities compounded my stress. I'm still working through my grieving process and feel I will never get passed missing Mom, but I hope to better control my stress through meditation, counseling, writing, working, and spending time with family, friends, and pets.

*

BRENDA KLEINSASSER
Brenda was diagnosed with
rheumatoid arthritis in 1991 at age 31

I live with pain pretty much every day. Most days I'm probably at midrange, about a five. Some days are better than others. Flares, or attacks as I prefer to call them, can come on with weather changes or stress, so I need to have my life as even keeled as possible.

I use topical ointments, and hot or cold packs. Hot showers can help if I have enough energy to take one. The average healthy person may not realize that something as simple as taking a shower can cause so much fatigue that it might be all I can do in a day. I rest a lot when under a rheumatoid attack. Resting is doing your body a great service. It is not defeat. I find that relaxing or reading a good book can take me to another place and help get my mind off it, if only for a little while.

*

CHANTELLE MARCIAL
Chantelle was diagnosed with
rheumatoid arthritis in 1999 at age 19

My daily pain is actually pretty low since I am well controlled. That could be skewed though since I've been dealing with pain issues my whole life and have a different pain scale than a healthy person would. I do experience flares from time to time and every month when my injection is wearing off I have to be careful about having a uveitis flare that could send me to the hospital. So I keep steroid drops and dilating drops on hand just in case. I also have a direct email line to my doctor so if I need a prescription for prednisone it can be filled asap. He's been great at teaching me how to manage my flares so the length and severity is lessened.

*

LAYNE MARTIN
Layne was diagnosed with
psoriatic arthritis in 2007 at age 47

My pain level varies from day to day. I never know until I wake in the morning what kind of a day it's going to be. It also depends on how well I sleep at night. I'm always stiff and sore when I first get up in the morning. Sometimes I'm out of bed very early because I get stiff and sore just from lying in bed.

On my good days the pain level is about two or three. On bad days it's a five or six. However, I've had this disease and lived with pain for so many years now that my five might be someone else's ten. Chronic pain is something you become so used to—a two is like having no pain at all. Rarely do I take pain medications. Instead, I've found stretching, a short walk, or swimming keeps me mobile and are also good for bone health. On bad days I'll take pain medication but try to resort to an Epsom salt bath if I can get into the tub, or a heating pad and my TENS unit. If I have a joint that's red, swollen and inflamed, an icepack brings the best relief. I also have a variety of splints to wear, which allows the flaring joint to rest as much as possible.

I've also done a variety of elimination diets and found that I'm sensitive to foods in the nightshade family such as tomatoes, potatoes, green peppers, and eggplant. I can eat them in small amounts if cooked, but when eaten fresh, my joints swell and become inflamed for about five days before simmering down.

Several people have advised me to include turmeric and ginger in my diet but both give me terrible heartburn. I have tried pill forms and they all seem to upset my stomach, so I've come to the conclusion that they are not for me.

I've also found that stress is a big factor for me. I used to be a worrier but have learned over the years that it doesn't do me any good to worry about things I can't control. I joined a bible study and community group with my church and that has really helped me to stop worrying so much. I now find peace and comfort from reading a daily devotional each morning to get myself in the right frame of mind. I also enjoy writing; it helps keep my mind off aches and pains, and it's therapeutic for me. In addition, I volunteer with a group called CreakyJoints and write occasional blogs for them and participate in various research projects. It gives me a sense of self-worth.

About four years ago I found my health really deteriorating and I was on a variety of medications for high blood pressure. I decided that I needed to take off some weight and try to at least help myself. It wasn't easy, but I was able to shed seventy-five pounds and get off all of my blood pressure medications. I feel so much better now and, with the exception of my current hip issue, I'm typically able to get out and walk and spend time outdoors, which has been great for my stress and mental health too.

*

KATHLEEN MEKAILEK
Kathleen was diagnosed with chronic regional pain
syndrome in 2005 at age 38, rheumatoid arthritis in
2014 at age 46, and ulcerative colitis in 2016 at age 49

I live in constant pain that travels around my body. As my pain management specialist once told me, "Your body can only feel one great pain at a time, but it can have little pains everywhere." My daily pain level remains pretty steady around five, and flares to ten a few times each week. According to the doctors who performed many procedures on me, my pain tolerance is relatively high, so my five might be someone else's eight or nine. This comes from living with pain for such a long time. I find things that keep me occupied, and it helps me get through the days. I manage my pain by taking my medications as needed, using a lot of biofeedback and a heating pad. If that doesn't work, then I switch to an icepack to the affected areas.

I use a TENS unit on my shoulders, arms and back, and a hot paraffin waxdip bath for my hands and feet. The TENS unit helps to relieve some of the muscle aches and stiffness and the paraffin on my extremities helps to reduce swelling and pain.

Changes in weather can cause flares, so I try to keep my body temperature constant through wearing layers that I can easily put on and take off. Overdoing it triggers flares. I have learned to listen to my body and take breaks as needed, where before I would be stubborn and try to push through the pain. I make sure to get rest, even if that means a four-hour afternoon nap. If my body needs it, it gets it.

I have dramatically changed my diet, not just for the RA, but also for ulcerative colitis. I have gone sugar, soy, gluten, dairy free. It seems to have helped, but it has only been a short while and I am relatively new to all the information, so I don't know what effect it will have in the long term. I avoid alcohol and caffeine, so my drink of choice is water with a lemon in it.

*

RICK PHILLIPS
Rick was diagnosed with type 1 diabetes in 1974 at
age 17 and rheumatoid arthritis in 1999 at age 42

I always say my pain is about six, but that depends on the day of the week and time of year. In the summer when I ride my bicycle more, pain is less than during winter when I hate to go out in the cold. I get a great deal of comfort from exercise and pain medications. I try hard not to use pain medications but especially in the winter months I tend to use them more. I find that being happy, laughing a lot seems to forestall pain. When I laugh I like to say take that RA, nothing can stop me from laughing.

*

LESLIE ROTT
Leslie was diagnosed with lupus and
rheumatoid arthritis in 2008 at age 22

Daily, I would say my pain averages a three. Are there days when I have little to no pain? Rarely. Are there days when the pain is so intense that I cannot function. Yes. There are days when it hurts to breathe and think. But most days, the pain is always there, but I have gotten used to it enough to function. I would say that I have a pretty high pain tolerance at this point, so what is a three for me may not be a three for someone else.

I have pain and illness flares. Stress is definitely a trigger for me. When I first got sick, the smallest emotional upheaval would send my body into a tailspin. Thankfully, that has gotten better, and even more significant events that I have gone through, though they have been difficult emotionally, have not been as difficult physically, as they once would have been. I try to eat healthy, relax as much as possible when I can, and while I try and push through the pain, I know there are times when I have to deal with it rather than ignore it.

*

TIEN SYDNOR-CAMPBELL
Tien was diagnosed with autoimmune
rheumatoid disease in 2010 at age 40

On a scale of one to ten, I hover around six to seven as long as I don't try to do anything like cook, walk for more than half an hour, or any activity that can't be done from a chair. Sometimes it's hard to hold a book, so I've started listening to audiobooks but as a reader, I feel like I'm cheating on my mind. I am a visual learner.

Flares can last anywhere from one hour to two months. When I have an acute flare, they typically are at a level where I would go to the emergency room because they're at an eight. Now that I know what the pain is from, I employ every trick at my disposal. The longer flares tend to take my pain as high as seven and require daily attention to medication, meditation, and mindfulness about what I am able to reasonably accomplish. This is especially true if I have set a goal to clean up around my comfy chair, write or read, as well as the monumental number of medical professionals that I have to see in order to manage this disease.

I have not been able to isolate a trigger to a flare. They have always been very sudden and sharp. I can be sitting in my chair, laying on my bed, or walking. There is no rhyme or reason to their effect on my body and that is yet, another thing that frustrates me incredibly.

My therapist and I have worked out a few things that I can do daily including meditation and doing things to distract my attention. It doesn't work to wish the pain away, or to try not to think about it. When you stub your toe, not thinking about it is impossible. Rheumatoid disease does that times a hundred over, then it robs you of your sleep, which should be restorative but isn't.

I take my meds, stretch, and use heat for areas that need it. I am better at dealing with the pain when I am more distracted, but I can't get too active or I end up flat on the bed for two to three days. The only way that I have been able to avoid it is to take precaution with everything I do. That includes getting out of bed, getting into the car, walking in a store and deciding whether I need the motorcart or I'm feeling good enough to walk around the store. You can't imagine how embarrassing it is to look completely healthy and need to have a cart brought to you in a store. It is not cool. Most times I pick the cart over the walk unless I've had a fairly minimal flare over the past few days.

What may look like a small act of
courage is courage nevertheless.

DAISAKU IKEDA

*

CHAPTER FIVE

work vs Disability

There is a plan and a purpose, a value to every life, no matter what its location, age, gender or disability. -SHARON ANGLE

Rheumatoid diseases are progressive in nature. To some, applying for disability is welcomed because it means more rest and less pain. Others see it as a point of no return and want to stay in the workforce for as long as possible. Where are you on the spectrum?

*

CHRISTINA AMES
Christina was diagnosed with rheumatoid arthritis
in 1987 at age 20 and fibromyalgia in 2011 at age 43

I actually do not work outside the home. When my kids were first born, I made the choice to be home with them, since neither my husband nor myself wanted them to be in daycare. It is a personal choice, and not for everyone, but with my husband's work schedule, we felt comfortable with it.

In 2010, I wanted to go back to work, as my son was starting high school. I had several interviews, but nothing seemed to pan out. I was getting discouraged. In September, I noticed that I could not pull my left leg up into my SUV. It got worse and more noticeable. By October, I couldn't dress myself or tie my shoes. I realized I was in a terrible flare, and spent several months basically unable to do anything as a result. I came to realize that not getting a job was a blessing, since I would have had to quit.

A few years ago, after it was apparent my rheumatoid arthritis was not going into remission, my husband suggested applying for disability. It definitely would have made a difference in our one income family, so I did. I was denied. We decided to consult a lawyer, and he felt that I had zero chance of getting any sort of help because I had stayed home with my children and hadn't received enough work credits to qualify. It was crushing. I feel as though I was punished for doing what I felt was the right choice for our family. But because I cared for them without the benefit of hiring a nanny, I clearly wasn't in need of help. Yes, you can tell that the sarcasm is dripping from my lips, or my keyboard as it were. If I could hire a nanny, I'd certainly be in the position to not need a job or any sort of financial help. Yet, because I simply did what needed to be done, it is counted against me. I don't include my husband in this at all; he's an excellent father. But as the sole provider for our family, he has to work.

At the end of the disastrous meeting at the lawyer's office, he mentioned two things that made me question the entire process. The first was that he said that he wouldn't take my case because he knew he'd have no chance of winning, and therefore would not be paid. However, if we wanted to pay him, he'd go to bat for me, and argue with the judges in the state. Really? The second thing was that he recommended I get a "nothing" job, like working as a ticket taker in a parking garage where I could sit all day until I could be eligible for benefits. What a pompous jerk to imply one job is better than the next!

I will say after several years of being on biologics, I wanted to go into the workforce. I've been applying for jobs, but since I've been away for so long, and even though my long period of not working is easily explained, it seems no employer is willing to take a chance.

I also feel there is no easy answer for those who are on, or need, disability. There is such an abuse of the system; indeed, my husband has dealt with many individuals who are on disability and yet are able to work; they told him they just don't want to. This type of behavior makes it hard for those who legitimately qualify, and yet are repeatedly denied or are forced to wait several years due to hearings and the like. I believe a complete overhaul is in order.

*

J.G. CHAYKO
J.G. was diagnosed with
rheumatoid arthritis in 2010 at age 38

I started my working life at a young age. My first stretch of responsibility came in a small suburban town when I was eleven years old. It began with my younger brother. Both my parents worked in the city, an easy hour away from home, and my afterschool time was spent looking after him. I was reluctant at first, believing I was missing out on afterschool play with kids my own age, but in the end it taught me to be responsible, not only to others but to myself.

Our neighborhood was an emerging community in a cozy cul-de-sac decorated with lush turf-covered yards and the lingering smell of fresh timber being molded into new homes. Our block consisted of many families. As with most small communities, everyone knew each other, and it didn't take long to discover that almost every family on our block were somehow related. There were cousins, aunts, uncles, sisters, brothers, grandmothers, and mother-in-laws. My girlfriend and I became the neighborhood treasures, babysitting two or three times a week, allowing the adults to indulge in happy evenings at the local pub. I earned my first salary during those years, and became addicted to the power of making my own money. It gave me a taste of confidence and helped me recognize my own self-worth.

In my thirteenth year, we moved away from small town life to be closer to the city. I started again in another high school. There weren't many kids to babysit in our new community, but by then I was old enough to get a part-time job. I worked two to three times a week in fastfood and retail outlets, but still managed to maintain a high grade point average. I was driven, motivated, and inspired to succeed in whatever job or activity I undertook.

All that commitment paid off. I graduated with honors from high school and was granted a small college scholarship. I immersed myself into the world of gainful employment, sometimes working two to three jobs to pay rent, buy food, and support my growing creative life. I worked all sorts of jobs, anything from administrative office assistant to serving in restaurants and banquet halls. I always offered the best of myself, earning raises and praise from employers. In the evening, I attended dance class, theatre workshops, rehearsals and performances, collecting awards and accolades along the way. By the end of most days I had spent thirteen to fourteen hours on my feet. That is the gift of the young and healthy—we think we'll never run out of steam.

All that vitality and drive came to a screeching halt one November morning. I opened my eyes to a gray day, feeling thick, swollen, and feverish. I assumed the flu virus that had infected almost everyone I knew had finally caught up to me. I rested, drank fluids, and consumed chicken soup and vitamin C. The mornings were hardest. Getting out of bed felt like I was pulling my limbs out of a sludge of wet cement. I was baffled by this virus. I didn't have stomach symptoms, nasal or chest congestion, yet I felt ill. I always seemed to improve as the day wore on, but I wasn't able to shake off the pall of fatigue that hovered like thick marine fog. It never occurred to me that it could be anything other than the flu, and so for six weeks I continued to struggle through a full-time work schedule and rehearsals before finally visiting my doctor and being sent on the path that led to the diagnosis of early RA.

I continued to work full time after being diagnosed. I was determined to keep up with the life I had built, but found my days more challenging. I was like a balloon with a slow leak, tired and droopy by the end of the day. In the mornings I was exhausted and stiff, feeling years beyond my age, struggling to get out of bed. I was no longer the girl who rose at the light of dawn to exercise before that first cup of coffee. I was sore a great deal of the time. By mid-afternoon, I was completely drained with nothing left for my friends, family, or my activities. I had been able to overcome most obstacles in my life, but I really had no idea what I was up against with RA. I had always worked. I never considered not working as an option, even with the difficulties rheumatoid arthritis presented. I had to make a change, and so I made the decision to switch to part-time work.

I made this choice for two reasons: First, I was finding it more difficult to fight the fatigue and make it through a forty-hour workweek. Second, I decided it was the right time to switch gears and focus on a longtime dream. The concept of all the time in the world to achieve your goals is suddenly condensed when a disease enters the picture. I looked back at the life I had already lived, and with an uncertain future looming, there were no more excuses to reach for the life I wanted to create.

With part-time work I was still able to feel like a valuable contributor. I was still earning my own money and finding satisfaction in achieving tasks within the job. I believe it's important for people to feel valued, and no matter what challenges we have, we all have something to contribute. Switching to part-time work allowed me to focus on taking care of myself. I learned that it was okay to be selfish and focus on ways to gain control of my disease. I didn't worry about pushing myself too hard. I didn't worry that I was letting anyone down. I still had energy left at the end of the day for housework, visiting friends and family, and spending time with my partner, instead of crawling into bed after a rough day. I take better care of myself now and have returned to some of the activities I abandoned. I sacrificed a certain salary and adjusted to a different lifestyle, but found a wonderful balance between my working life, my health and my passions. I am still years ahead of retirement, and can only hope that I will be able to maintain this balance for many years to come.

*

JUDITH FLANAGAN
Judith was diagnosed with rheumatoid arthritis in 2012 at age 32
and fibromyalgia and polymyalgia rheumatic in 2014 at age 34

I am on disability and didn't make the decision to go for it lightly. I weighed the pros and cons of every condition I live with, and decided it was for the best. Luckily, I was granted disability on the first attempt, unlike most people. I feel for those who really need disability but aren't granted it, and my advice is don't give up keep trying. It was a huge relief when I was granted disability; it meant less stress and I could focus on me.

*

SHELLEY FRITZ
Shelley was diagnosed with
rheumatoid arthritis in 2012 at age 42

I've continued to work in the education field since my rheumatoid arthritis diagnosis over five years ago, but not without struggle. Prior to my diagnosis, and at times since, I writhed with some of the physical aspects of my job such as standing or sitting for long periods of time, typing extensively, and moving heavy materials. My work often required driving to multiple locations in a single day, set up heavy workshop materials, then stand on my feet training adults for long stretches. Some days this became so challenging I contemplated finding a way to work from home. Swollen, painful feet and throbbing hands shouted out to me frequently to quit. Stress mounted from working around others who demonstrated lack of compassion or of basic understanding of my condition. I found a new venue and new work family accompanied me on my journey to begin again.

I hope to remain a full-time teacher for years to come but I cannot help wondering what the future holds for me. Dozens of questions swirl around in my head. How rapidly will my disease progress and will I become unable to maneuver around as a teacher needs to throughout the day? At what point will I become more reliant upon handicap accessories? One day if I require the use of a wheelchair, will my current place of employment be able to accommodate me or will I need to seek another location or possibly another career? At home I have lots of gadgets in place to help me open doors, open containers, etc. but I have never asked to have these installed at work as they have been unnecessary.

*

BRENDA KLEINSASSER
Brenda was diagnosed with
rheumatoid arthritis in 1991 at age 31

Even after having lived with rheumatoid arthritis for over twenty-six years, I am still able to work full-time. Over the years, the disease has progressed but my human resources department has been very helpful in that aspect. I was instructed to concentrate on things I could do, and not lament on the tasks I could no longer handle. I am grateful to still be working. In the beginning, after the diagnosis of rheumatoid arthritis, I wasn't sure how long I would be able to work.

At the time, my rheumatologist suggested I go on disability and let my husband take care of things. He really didn't know me—I was not married, and the sole breadwinner. My response was, "I am going to keep working until I am no longer able to." He seemed to think that giving up and climbing into bed for the rest of my life would be the answer. This made me dislike him even more. His attitude was that I was going to get worse, something I was already thinking about. I did not need to have that reinforced at every visit. I finally stopped seeing him and had all my workups done through my primary care physician.

I pretty much cried through that first month of trying to adjust to this disease, and sought out a friend who had been diagnosed with a rare disease several years before. I wanted to get her perspective on how she dealt with the shock and everything else that encompassed it. What I gleaned from her was very helpful. As a single thirty-one-year-old, I felt pretty much alone in this battle.

In the beginning, I used a cane to get around but even that was hard because my fingers quickly became deformed, making it hard to hold the cane. I worked hard at keeping my job, but the administration at the time had different things in mind. That is when my fighting spirit came in. I never gave up.

*

CHANTELLE MARCIAL
Chantelle was diagnosed with
rheumatoid arthritis in 1999 at age 19

I work a forty-hour-plus workweek. If I needed accommodations within the workplace, that wouldn't be a problem. I work in academia, so inclusiveness is mantra here. In the past, I have had issues with jobs where if I needed time away from the office to deal with a flare, it was a problem. Luckily, here I have a great boss who allows me to work both at the office and from home as needed. Not having a set schedule helps too. I don't have to clock in and out; we use flextime here so as long as the hours are worked within a week its all good.

*

LAYNE MARTIN
Layne was diagnosed with
psoriatic arthritis in 2007 at age 47

Unfortunately, I have been classified as permanently disabled. At the time I was diagnosed with psoriatic arthritis, I was working full-time as an emergency room nurse and just had a total hip replacement about six months prior.

I had been living with psoriatic arthritis for years but had been misdiagnosed over the years, always thinking that the bursitis in my hip, the low back pain or my aching feet were just from working long twelve-hour shifts, lifting patients, pushing and pulling stretchers, running down a long hallway to meet an ambulance with a critical patient. It wasn't until I had to have a hip replacement that I was finally referred to a rheumatologist. He put me on a biological the very first time I saw him and he classified me with severe psoriatic arthritis. However, the biological medication compromised my immune system and my white counts dropped fairly low. I wasn't able to fight off even a simple cold. I kept getting sick and basically ended up with every aliment that plagued my patients in the emergency room.

My employer was great and I was able to move into more of a desk job doing staff scheduling, entering trauma data for the state, teaching CPR classes, etc. However, about a year later I suffered two spontaneous compression fractures in my thoracic spine due to long term steroid use. It was at that point that I decided it was time to retire after thirty years of nursing.

I loved my job and it was a really tough decision. Besides the physical pain, I also suffered from fatigue and found it difficult to do my job as meticulously as I once had. I knew it was time to hang up my hat, and I wanted to go out with my peers respecting and valuing me. In the past, some nurses who needed to retire but hung on too long, by the time they retired everyone was glad to see them go. I didn't want to be one of those nurses.

Retiring at the age of forty-nine was an agonizing decision, and one that caused me a lot of grief and emotional pain. I had always wanted to be a nurse and I loved my job as much as I loved my family. I had excelled as a nurse and was well respected by the physicians and my peers. It gave me a great sense of self-worth and satisfaction. I'm a very social person, I loved my patients and enjoyed visiting with people on a daily basis. Retirement seemed like a death sentence to me, you might as well throw me in a prison cell.

However, once I retired I started to do volunteer work at a local thrift shop. And, I joined a stay fit class for people with arthritis. Once I realized that I wouldn't be isolated from people and could still socialize then it was easier. But, I still miss nursing! I will always miss it, I absolutely loved my job and am so thankful that I had the opportunity to do it for thirty years.

*

KATHLEEN MEKAILEK
Kathleen was diagnosed with chronic regional pain
syndrome in 2005 at age 38, rheumatoid arthritis in
2014 at age 46, and ulcerative colitis in 2016 at age 49

I am classified as disabled and after my last visit with Social Security when they ask you to list if you had any surgeries since the previous date, I ran out of room listing nine surgeries (I'm up to eleven now) in three years. They put me on a seven-year review.

It took me a long time to come to terms with my disability. I know other people who have rheumatoid arthritis and they can work. Why is mine so extreme and aggressive? It's not fair to my husband who can't cuddle with me because it hurts. I can't hug my friends and family and, most importantly, my children because it feels like they've squeezing the life out of me. I struggle with the question, why me? People tell me that I'm a good person with a shiny heart, so why did this happen to me?

The biggest emotion that hits me is fear. When grandkids have a cold, I wear a mask and they are afraid of me. It's hard to be shunned by people who don't want to see you weak. So I try to be strong, smile, and say, "I'm good," even though it's a lie. I become sad, remembering how I used to have fun and laugh all the time. Now I'm an actress putting on a front because people don't want to see reality. Even I don't want this reality. So I wait until I'm alone or everyone is in beds and then I cry and long for how it used to be.

*

RICK PHILLIPS
Rick was diagnosed with type 1 diabetes in 1974 at
age 17 and rheumatoid arthritis in 1999 at age 42

I am classified as disabled and I hate it. I loved working and still would if I could do so. I think the hardest thing is when someone asks me what I do. I am a nearly sixty-year-old male, and sixty-year-old males work. It is part of who and what I am. I lost my identity when I became disabled.

When asked about my work, I say I do nothing. And saying that makes me feel like nothing. At least that was the soundtrack in my mind. So it was incumbent on me to find something to do. I first went back to school to earn a doctorate in education. I knew I could not work, so I still needed something else.

In 2012, I started to advocate in the rheumatoid and diabetes communities. I write and work to support and help others. It gives me new meaning and purpose. I am not paid for my work, but I find it very satisfying. Today when people ask what I do for a living, I say nothing. Then I explain: nothing that I am paid for. Rather, now I work for the future of my grandchildren and their children. What could be more satisfying than that?

*

LESLIE ROTT
Leslie was diagnosed with lupus and
rheumatoid arthritis in 2008 at age 22

I am able to work, and grateful for this. It has been a challenge, though. I recently began my first full-time job after eight years in graduate school. I work for a healthcare company, so I am lucky in that respect. However, I used up all my of paid time off going to doctors appointments. I will be applying for Family Medical Leave Act. That way, maybe I will be able to use my time off for "fun" things. Although let's be honest, there is never a day off from lupus and RA. My fatigue also continues to be a big problem, which is hard to manage working full-time.

*

TIEN SYDNOR-CAMPBELL
Tien was diagnosed with autoimmune
rheumatoid disease in 2010 at age 40

While I am currently unable to work, I think that the process of being classified as disabled takes an enormous toll on the mental and emotional health of chronically ill people. For me, I kept working for about three years after my diagnosis, and it was brutal. I was unable to hold thick patient files. I couldn't stay awake during treatment sessions with clients, or remember what had been discussed during the session when writing notes. Ultimately, I fell so far behind in my notes that my assistant had to help me get everything done. She did much more than was required, and I was very grateful. My supervisors made as many accommodations as they were able, such as having files delivered to my office and giving me extra time to turn in session notes. Budgetary constraints made it impossible for them to make any physical adjustments such as moving my office to the ground floor so I wouldn't have to go up three flights of stairs when the elevator was inoperable, or purchasing software so I would be able to record my notes when my hands hurt too much to hold a pen.

I was spending more time in doctor appointments and needing multiple surgeries than I was in the office at the end. I finally gave in to the pain, exhaustion, and inability to do the very simple job of listening to the troubles of others and went on short-term disability. Unfortunately for me, my company had not paid their portion of the disability premiums and I was ultimately denied coverage due to my condition being pre-existing. Ultimately, I needed to remain out on long-term and eventually permanent disability. This was an extremely painful multiyear experience, and I believe the events pushed me into a clinical depression. Being a therapist, I had diagnosed myself and knew I needed help. Therapy has been critical in my self-care practice.

Emotionally, being classified as disabled is a double-edged sword. On one side it has helped me to get continuous healthcare. On the other, I have had to come to terms with what that means. The days when I feel normal and try to do things, like clean or cook, I am quickly reminded by my body that I am not normal. I want to be able to do some of the things that I enjoyed such as dancing and skiing. I am still enough of a rebel to occasionally try, but I have yet to be successful at walking for more than thirty minutes straight, let alone "get funky and loose."

*

CHAPTER SIX

Public Mobility Devices

Your pain is the breaking of the shell that encloses
your understanding. -KHALIL GIBRAN

How many of us have judged someone riding a scooter in the grocery store? Or questioned one's use of a disability parking spot? Living with an autoimmune disease means living with struggles that are invisible to the rest of the world—and at risk of being judged and scrutinized when extra assistance is needed to enjoy the little things in life. Do you use disability parking or motorized scooters when in public?

*

CHRISTINA AMES
Christina was diagnosed with rheumatoid arthritis in 1987
at age 20 and diagnosed with fibromyalgia in 2011 at age 43

I have discussed getting a parking pass with my rheumatologist. According to him, in the state of Maryland where I currently live, there has been such an abuse of people getting parking placards or tags, that the state will now only issue them to people who are on oxygen or those who have prosthesis. He agreed I would be a good candidate, but his hands were tied. I do not know if this is the case, as I did not pursue it further. If it is true, it needs to be addressed and fixed; there are those of us who would not mind being able to park closer to a store or even a doctors office on certain days when movement is difficult.

I have had to use a wheelchair once. It was after I'd had pneumonia, and I went to a big box store to find a gift for someone. I knew I couldn't walk, as I was still weak, so we asked about a wheelchair. We were able to use one the store had, and my husband pushed me around the store.

I also have used canes and walking sticks. I try very hard to lead what would be considered a normal life, by doing various activities. I often have my husband for help walking as a steady arm, but on the times he can't be with me, I have used a cane when I knew I would be walking for an extended period of time. I also walked a 10K last year, and used walking sticks for balance. They were helpful, and I was glad to use them.

I can understand the stigma or disappointment about using these items. It seems to indicate a loss of movement and independence. However, if I want to go out and keep my life as normal as possible, and be as involved as possible, I do not mind using them.

*

J.G. CHAYKO
J.G. was diagnosed with
rheumatoid arthritis in 2010 at age 38

I am fortunate in that I am still mobile enough not to require the use of scooters or disability parking. I may not move as well as I once did. My hummingbird speed has slowed to the leisurely pace of a long-legged heron. But I'm still active enough to get up every day, exercise, run errands, do housework, go to work, and indulge in an occasional diversion. I'm optimistic that I will remain mobile for many years but I know it won't be without its challenges. There are days when angry flares make it difficult for me to navigate without the help of my partner. His arm is always there to help me in and out of the car, support me on uneven ground, and encourage me to take it slow when I need to. I guess one could say that my partner is my mobility aid.

I don't dwell on whether or not I'll need the use of these aids in the future. I can't worry about what I can't control. What I can do is take each day as it comes and do my best to remain strong and active. If I ever have a need for a mobility device in the future, I'll be grateful to have them. The wonderful thing about today is that we have these brilliant devices to help keep us moving forward in the world.

*

JUDITH FLANAGAN
Judith was diagnosed with rheumatoid arthritis in 2012 at age 32
and fibromyalgia and polymyalgia rheumatic in 2014 at age 34

I don't use disability parking because I don't drive. I decided against it because it's not safe for me. I have also come to realize the difficulties people face who live with rheumatic diseases. I feel for those who face criticism when they do use disability parking because the symptoms are invisible. You can't see pain, but it's there.

*

SHELLEY FRITZ
Shelley was diagnosed with
rheumatoid arthritis in 2012 at age 42

I faced an annoying, humiliating moment at the movies a few years ago. After sitting for almost three hours, I hobbled down the stairs grasping the theater railing, and slowly made my way to the restroom. I'm not usually one to use the handicapped bathroom, as someone could come along in a wheelchair needing it more than I do. At that moment, however, I felt entitled. I could barely hold myself up and I knew I needed the handrails inside the stall. Able to balance a bit better, I left the stall to find two women glaring at me and shaking their heads. I just looked at them puzzled and limped out. The umpires of the ladies' restroom had spoken and I was awarded a penalty.

I was in pain and justified in my use of the handicapped restroom and yet I felt guilty. I wanted to say something but my thoughts would have been fragments of unorganized rants better left unsaid. Out the door I went, slowly. It was a very awkward half-minute and it made me angry that this disease is so misunderstood. If I could have that moment over again, and chances are I will the next time I venture to the movies, I shall take a stand and speak my peace. How else will others begin to understand the world of chronic pain?

I have not applied for a disabled parking decal as it is not necessary at this time. If I am having a particularly debilitating pain day and am unable to walk well, I have relied on others to run errands or else opted out of participating in whatever event was planned. This is not to say I will not use a motorized scooter though. I have a new set of eyes for people I see on scooters.

Before my diagnosis, I might have been more inclined to pass judgment on someone who hops out of a car from a handicapped spot. I did not understand the world of rheumatoid arthritis and other diseases that are invisible to others most of the time. This disease is unpredictable and unrelenting. If one with a handicapped placard were to feel well upon arriving at the shopping mall and park in a spot far away from the entrance, there is a good chance he or she will be limping or maybe even unable to get back to the car after shopping. For them, that handicapped parking spot is a necessity.

I overdo it, a lot. I am the one who parks far away and limps back or waits until my legs allow me to move again. I rarely go shopping by myself in case I cannot complete the journey—and it does feel like a journey back to the car. Online shopping is a great way to meet my needs.

One day I may need that handicapped placard and that scooter on a regular basis. I wish others would not judge those using handicapped placards. We don't know what seemingly invisible illness they are living with and causing them chronic pain.

*

BRENDA KLEINSASSER
Brenda was diagnosed with
rheumatoid arthritis in 1991 at age 31

I was assigned a handicapped hanging tag to place in the car. It was decided at the time that it would be for life, as my disease was rapidly progressing and walking was becoming difficult. I do not own a vehicle, so I carry the tag and only use it when I need it. The only criticism that I have received was from a former coworker, who said that my mother should have had one instead of me. We encounter a lot of ignorance when it comes to others understanding what it's like to live with a chronic disease such as rheumatoid arthritis.

*

CHANTELLE MARCIAL
Chantelle was diagnosed with
rheumatoid arthritis in 1999 at age 19

I do have a handicapped placard but I've never learned to drive, so I'm the passenger when it is used. Occasionally I'll get a look if I get out of the car wearing heels or am dressed up. I will attribute that to, in part, the fact that I'm six feet tall with huge hair and folks don't realize I'll be walking only a few feet to the restaurant, so it's not like I'm spending a whole night teetering on heels.

100

*

LAYNE MARTIN
Layne was diagnosed with
psoriatic arthritis in 2007 at age 47

The majority of the time I do not use my disability parking permit. I prefer to walk as much as possible to keep my joints mobile, plus walking is good for bone health. I like to save the disability spots for those who are having a flare or really need them. I feel really guilty using the disability spots when I know there is someone else who may be worse off that day and could use it more than me.

However, currently my artificial hip has failed and I am scheduled for a revision surgery. So, lately the only way I can shop is either online or by using a mobility cart at the store. But, the last two times I've tried to go shopping I could not find a disability parking spot or a mobility cart. So, I've just had to sit in the car while my daughter does my shopping for me. It's really frustrating! I would love to get out and go into a store and do my own shopping!

I try really hard not to judge other people as a lot of us have invisible illnesses. A person may be really fatigued but needs to stop by the store for something. They may use the disability parking and look perfectly healthy on the outside but are struggling with every step. In my current state of needing to use the disability parking in order to go shopping I get really irritated when I see someone using a spot that I desperately need and they are walking perfectly normal. I have to remind myself not to judge and what they are going through may be way worse that my temporarily disabled hip. Once my hip is fixed and I'm able to walk without a walker then I will rarely use the handicap spots. I'd rather save them for someone who is in really struggling and having a bad day.

*

KATHLEEN MEKAILEK
Kathleen was diagnosed with chronic regional pain
syndrome in 2005 at age 38, rheumatoid arthritis in
2014 at age 46, and ulcerative colitis in 2016 at age 49

I had avoided using mobility devices until this month when I finally gave in and asked my doctor about getting a handicapped placard for disability parking. I have a temporary one now and only use it on bad days when flares are out of control and I must leave the house. I don't drive anymore, so a placard was the best choice because it can go in any vehicle I ride in. However, I am just starting to have issues with my feet and hips, so I suspect it won't be long before I will need a permanent one.

We made some changes to our house to accommodate my needs. All the doorknobs have been replaced with lever handles, making it easier for me to open and close doors. With wrists in splints or casts a lot, turning a doorknob or faucet was difficult, so we did the same with the sinks—knobs were exchanged for levers to push and pull. We also installed handles on the kitchen cabinets and drawers, which makes them easier to open and close. Little things like that make a huge difference toward keeping some of my independence. Some people don't believe I'm disabled because I don't utilize them, but then I show them the scars on my arms and they apologize and walk away.

I think people who need them should use them, but at the same time I think they are often misused by people who don't actually need them. There are too many people who work the system and make it look bad for the ones who are actually suffering. I know rheumatoid and many other autoimmune diseases are invisible and have no outward signs, so I don't judge because one day that will be me.

*

RICK PHILLIPS
Rick was diagnosed with type 1 diabetes in 1974
at age 17 and rheumatoid arthritis in 1999 at age 42

I have a handicap license plate and we do park in handicapped spaces. It is not something I like doing. I know in my heart I can get along without it most days. But wow, when I need it, I need it. Despite needing it, I still cannot accept that I park there. I feel like I've cheated the system in some odd way. Once, between biologics, I had to use a motorized cart in the grocery store. It was the most embarrassing thing I've ever done. Men in their fifties walk—they don't use carts. I felt hopeless as I rode around in that thing.

*

LESLIE ROTT
Leslie was diagnosed with lupus and
rheumatoid arthritis in 2008 at age 22

I do not use a disability parking or a motorized scooter. I do get upset, though, when I see my fellow rheumatic sufferers post on social media that they have been criticized by others for using such things because they don't "look" disabled. This is an affront to all of us. Just

103

because I do not use those things now doesn't mean that I won't need them in the future, and I would like to have access to them, should I require them.

*

TIEN SYDNOR-CAMPBELL
Tien was diagnosed with autoimmune
rheumatoid disease in 2010 at age 40

I have been using disability parking for almost two years now, and there are times when I think I have enough energy and ability to walk around a store. Unfortunately, I have needed someone to get me a motorized scooter while in the midst of shopping, so I'm less likely to do that now. I am more likely to go in, get a scooter, and not care what people think these days.

It has taken my having a bilateral knee replacement to help me see that help is not a bad thing. I have not yet encountered criticism for it, although I have caught a few eyes wondering why someone who looks so healthy like me would need that kind of help. I've worked on having some replies ready with my therapist and feel confident that they will be less likely to question others after having encountered me. I will say that I probably used to look at people and wonder why they were in a scooter if I couldn't tell. Now I wonder why some people who are obviously struggling don't get a scooter.

*

CHAPTER SEVEN

Braving Social Advice

I'll do my best to not judge you after the ignorant comment you just made about a health condition you know nothing about. -ANONYMOUS

As a group of invisible diseases, a common problem among auto-immune disorder patients is how to explain to others who don't understand. Some well-meaning people suggest remedies in an effort to help. Others make comments that only inflame the conversation. How do you handle comments from those who don't understand?

*

CHRISTINA AMES
Christina was diagnosed with rheumatoid arthritis in 1987 at age 20 and diagnosed with fibromyalgia in 2011 at age 43

I try to take any advice with a grain of salt. It was meant by the person as well-meaning, and even if I don't agree with it, I usually say that I'll take it under advisement. That way, they are happy to have "helped," and nobody needs to feel badly.

I do become angry when I hear things like, "If only you'd just exercise," or "If you just lost some weight, I'm sure you'd feel so much better." I've struggled with weight my whole life, yet in 1987, when I first developed symptoms, I was at the lowest weight I had ever been. Several of the medications I've taken over the years list weight gain as a side effect. And it's true that on days when I'm able to move a bit more, I do feel better, like I've accomplished something. But going for a walk will never cure me. Losing fifty pounds won't cure me. So don't say it. I'm not a lazy, do-nothing person, even if you might think so by looking at me. That's your problem, not mine. I know I'm just a warrior, struggling to get through my day, just like all other chronic disease warriors.

If you wish to say something truly kind, tell me you're thinking about me. Just letting someone know you are keeping them in your thoughts is a wonderfully considerate gesture. They've taken the time out of their day to wonder how you are faring, and there can be nothing more genuine than that.

I've often thought it would be nice to have someone walk in my shoes just for a day, especially those who doubt the levels of my pain. I would pick the worst day I've ever had, the worst day of the flare I call my Big Flare. It went something like this: I was laying on my bed, with tears leaking out of my eyes, but I wasn't crying on purpose. It was just so painful, it was the only way my body could react. I had to wait for help to use the bathroom. I hurt so terribly that I couldn't hold my cellphone to text my husband for help. My shoulders were so painful, I wasn't able to lift my arms to hold his neck. My feet and ankles were dreadfully sore. I could only drag them as I hitched my way to the bathroom with Doug supporting me so I wouldn't fall. It's only seven steps from my bed, but on that day it might as well have been seven million. When we finally got there, I had to clutch him while he undressed me so I could use the toilet. He had to guide me down so I wouldn't fall, and then had to help me stand after I was done. Now I sobbed for real, since it is terrible to not be in control of yourself, and you have to ask for help with personal hygiene. But I simply didn't have the ability to clean myself. My hands wouldn't bend, and I wept in frustration. He took care of it while he reassured me, and told me it was all right. He helped me back to bed, and I hitched along in the same manner in which I got to the bathroom. Grand total of time? It took about twenty-five minutes.

Rest was nearly impossible, even though I was exhausted. I catnapped throughout the day, my body shrieking awake with each small movement. We did the bathroom routine several times, each more difficult than the last, since I had already used up my nonexistent energy. Dinner was served, and of course I needed help since I was not able to manipulate a spoon. It was a simple dinner of boxed mac and cheese, but I could have used a bib.

After dinner I had to rest up for another difficult activity: showering. Because it was so hard, I only did it every other day. I had to have help shuffling to the bathroom again, and when I got there, I needed help turning the knobs and getting in the stall itself. I had to be physically undressed, and I couldn't shampoo my own hair. Soaping was not as bad, and I was able to do my front. The two-inch shower lip felt higher than a fence, so I needed help getting out again, and then drying off. We figured out that pants are easier to put on if they are on the floor, and I tried to hit the leg openings. Shirts were more difficult because they went over my head and shoulders, and led to more insane agony. Of course, everything was made of easy on and off materials like elastic waistbands and open necklines; no high fashion here! Eventually, we made it back to bed and my day was complete. I did not: make a meal, do any housework, read a book, talk on the phone, or simply played a game of Scrabble with my kids. What I did do: survive a day of excruciating chronic pain.

That's the day I wish my naysayers could experience—the people who think we are faking it or lying about the extent of our disease. Yes, that was my worst day, but I've had dozens that were nearly as bad. I'd simply prefer that nobody judge me, and feel the old adage is completely appropriate: If you can't say anything nice, don't say anything at all.

*

J.G. CHAYKO
J.G. was diagnosed with
rheumatoid arthritis in 2010 at age 38

Until I became an advocate and began sharing my experience with the world, I never realized how many people knew so much more about my disease and how to cope with it than I did. It's such a strange thing to imagine that a complete stranger knows the best way for you to treat your own disease.

We are subjected to all kinds of advice once our disease is known. There are people who want to be helpful, having no knowledge of our particular circumstance, offering up suggestions such as heating pads, anti-inflammatory creams, and the old standby: take an aspirin. There are those who declare they have found the cure for our ailment, and usually it involves some sort of herbal concoction, a remarkable oil, the consumption of a particular food, the way that food is prepared, or that popular phenomenon that continues to plague every disease— the one and only miracle water. In the beginning we voraciously read these amazing declarations, hoping one of them will restore us to our former self. Unfortunately it doesn't take long to learn that most remedies are too good to be true. I don't doubt there are some who find relief in one or more of these treatments. After all, rheumatic disease is not all one color and not all medications or therapies generate the same result. The way our disease works in our body is as individual as the snowflake.

It's easy to disregard a stranger's advice, but when friends and family offer suggestions it requires more diplomacy. After all, they're just trying to help. They can't possibly know the remedy they read about on a friend's post will have no effect on our condition. They may not know enough about our illness, so I've learned to take that insufferable phrase, "Why don't you take an aspirin?" with a grain of salt because as absurd as that suggestion is to those with chronic illness, our friend or family member making the suggestion is absolutely sincere. So we need to respond in kind. I usually say "Thank you for thinking of me," or "I haven't heard about that, I'll look into it," and politely shift into another topic of conversation. The truth remains that there is no cure for most of these diseases. Autoimmune disease is difficult to explain because of its capricious nature. I sometimes think the only way to understand it is to live with it.

I don't disregard every suggestion. I've learned to be discerning on the advice I receive. If something catches my attention, I may very well research it further. There's always the possibility of finding that hidden jewel in a bag of stones.

*

JUDITH FLANAGAN
Judith was diagnosed with rheumatoid arthritis in 2012 at age 32
and fibromyalgia and polymyalgia rheumatic in 2014 at age 34

I raise awareness and volunteer with various organizations. I also create my own graphics using a variety of apps. I might feel a little defensive or maybe even angry when people say I don't look sick, or that I'm too young to have this disease. I especially dislike, "You shouldn't be on that," or "You should be doing this _____[insert treatment], or eat this or try that." Well, I say to some of those comments that each and every person has their own healthcare team, and we are open to different options but we know there is no cure.

Certain things may make our life easier to live when it comes to pain, but there is no such thing as one fix for every person who lives with this. What matters is that we work together with each other to support and offer help when needed. That can make a huge difference for those of us who live with rheumatoid diseases.

People being nice and understanding of the struggles we live with brings me comfort because it means they understand; having that support is massive, believe me. People should know that living with rheumatic diseases can be quite difficult at times, and confusing regarding many aspects including food, medications, balancing home duties, knowing when you have done too much, etc. Fatigue is a constant symptom, and the struggle can be very real. Not even a nap can fix it—that's the major difference from general tiredness.

People need to make #CompassionTheNewFashion. We need less judgment and more understanding for one another, because that's very important.

*

SHELLEY FRITZ
Shelley was diagnosed with
rheumatoid arthritis in 2012 at age 42

Quite a bit of unsolicited advice has been shared with me over the years. Occasionally I hear something helpful but that's almost always from someone who has rheumatoid arthritis and truly understands. I have oils, creams, magic powders and herbs, with each one advertising promises to make my pain disappear. What I would give to use these and feel long-lasting relief! In the first year of being diagnosed, I found it frustrating talking with others about my condition because of the misnomer that every form of arthritis must be osteoarthritis. Over the years, I found my voice and began sharing information with family, friends, and strangers about the difference between rheumatoid and osteoarthritis. It's unlikely that conversation will ever stop. I wish others would actively listen and not be so quick to share that my symptoms sound like their own or that of their grandmother. I get defensive when I feel I am being challenged to try something that I know will not cure me. Gin-soaked raisins will not cure me, and I don't need to try snake venom to know it will not fix my problem. No one will really ever know what it feels like to be me, and if I were to describe the daily ups and downs along with the struggles to find the right cocktail of medicine, diet, and homeopathic treatments, I fear others will think I am feeling sorry for myself. I have tried explaining that I have an autoimmune disease and how the biologic I take is supposed to be communicating with cells in my body, yet I have been met with uncomfortable looks and comments like, "You lost me at biologic."

Sometimes I just get tired of the battle to dispel the myths, but I try to remember that there was a time not too long ago when I did not know much about arthritis and about rheumatoid arthritis. For nearly forty years I had the privilege to live without rheumatoid arthritis and without chronic pain. I am forever grateful for the days I could jump out of bed and move about comfortably, running if I wanted. Of course, I wasn't thankful for abilities like that until I lost them. I try to speak to others with the mindset that if we want to break down barriers and help others to see the need to continue research to find a cure for rheumatoid arthritis, we need to let them know that there is currently no cure and that the treatments and symptom management for diseases are different. Every now and then, someone asks me questions about how I feel, what treatments I use, or if certain situations or climates impact my joints more than others, and when that happens, I feel elated. It brings a sense of validation, of hope that I have communicated with someone and that they might then have an open mind and compassion for strangers on the street.

*

BRENDA KLEINSASSER
Brenda was diagnosed with
rheumatoid arthritis in 1991 at age 31

My father was probably the worst offender in all of this. He would say, "If only you would move a little more." I was walking and doing full range of motion exercises twice a day. I would stiffen up so bad after sitting in a chair for too long that I dreaded getting up. I hurt so bad and would have to stand for a few minutes before I could begin to move about.

My mother was truly the only one who understood. She would tell the doctor how hard I was trying, and he agreed. I got really sick and tired of hearing things like, "If you took this supplement, you will start to feel better." I was trying to participate in things outside of work, but at times being constantly barraged by others giving unsolicited advice was more than I could take.

The real kicker was hearing, "If only you had enough faith, then you would be healed." People can be so clueless when they encounter someone battling and dealing with a daily chronic illness. To insult my intelligence by telling me to possess more faith was equal to scolding a child. It made me angry and caused me to become less social in the outside world. I got tired of having to explain to those who thought that a simple magic wand or bunch of pills would solve everything.

I am being facetious here, but there were times when I wanted to escape all the madness. I have fought every day to live, even if that means spending the day resting in bed. I no longer feel the need to explain. It's my life and I am doing the best I can. I realize that keeping my joints mobile and moving is important. I don't appreciate or need anyone to remind me of that. If I could wave a magic wand so others could experience my life just for one day...well, I would not wish that on anyone.

*

CHANTELLE MARCIAL
Chantelle was diagnosed with
rheumatoid arthritis in 1999 at age 19

It's okay by me for folks to chime in with positivity. "Have you tried?" "Do you take vitamin xyz?" Things like that don't bother me. They mean well. But I don't like when I'm basically blamed for this condition, as if I could have done something to prevent it. But instead of anger I choose to educate. Even if it doesn't sink in right then, I've given them a seed. They can choose to toss it or help it grow into understanding. I'm fine either way.

*

LAYNE MARTIN
Layne was diagnosed with
psoriatic arthritis in 2007 at age 47

When people try to give me well-meaning advice I just smile and thank them. I've learned that it takes too much energy to try to explain to them what psoriatic arthritis is and how it's treated. Besides, I've probably already tried their well-meaning advice!

I've done every elimination diet known to mankind. I've spent months without gluten, dairy, and red meat. I tried eating tart cherries, ginger and turmeric which gave me terrible heartburn. I tried yoga, Tia Chi, and pilates. I've researched and tried being vegan. I've done the paleo. I bought an expensive juicer and tried that, and the list goes on.

Basically, I've been living with this disease for well over twenty years now and I know what works for my body and what doesn't. I know stress is a trigger and when I get well-meaning advice it's not worth me getting defensive about it or trying to explain why I don't think it will work for me. It's just much easier to graciously accept the advice and thank them for their concerns and go about my day.

I know they can't possibly understand what it's like unless they have the same condition or have a chronic illness that causes daily pain and fatigue. It's not something you can explain to a person. And, I certainly wouldn't wish any of these diseases on anyone. In the meantime I will continue to weed through the well-meaning advice and you never know, I might just try one or two.

*

KATHLEEN MEKAILEK
Kathleen was diagnosed with chronic regional pain
syndrome in 2005 at age 38, rheumatoid arthritis in
2014 at age 46, and ulcerative colitis in 2016 at age 49

The one thing I can't stand is when someone tells me about their eighty-year-old grandmother and tries to compare what I live with against her osteoporosis. It is like talking to a brick wall. People think it is my joints. I go into details about how the disease attacks my soft tissues, basically eating me alive, and how the medications make me sick, sleepy, and causes my hair to fall out, and they still don't get it.

Another thing I can't stand are all these miracle shakes, powders, and diets that people try to push on me to clean my body of toxins and cure me. It's genetic—traced back on the paternal side of my family! Unless they do a complete DNA swap on me, which I don't think is possible, I drew the unlucky gene! Out of all my cousins, I have it and if it dies with me, I am willing to take it on as long as none of my children, grandchildren or any of my cousins' kids and grandkids inherit the gene. Just let it die with me.

The only comments that bring me comfort are by those who experience what I am going through, and let me complain to them. They then tell me to put on my big girl panties, stop feeling sorry for myself, and get on with living. Also, when my husband cracks jokes about changing my diapers, if it gets to that, or if I need a wheelchair, he'll dragrace me down the street, that he will always be there for me and is not afraid to face the uncertain future with me.

I wish people knew how hard it is for me to get up everyday when I hurt. How hard it is to wear a facade with a bright sunny smile, to watch them munch down on all sorts of food in front of me while I carry on a normal conversation like nothing is happening. I feel like I am on the outside looking in.

I get exhausted easily. Parties that last for hours, I look for excuses not to go otherwise I'll just be miserable with all the talking, smiling, and all that eating and snacking again. I keep my hands busy holding a glass of water. Then there are the people who assume I am an alcoholic because I don't drink. When I explain it's because of the medications I to take, they assume I have a drug addiction. It's not an addiction—it's what keeps me functioning like a normal person. "I don't take hydrocodone unless I just came out of surgery, you idiot," is what I want to scream at the majority of them.

And then, there are the people who avoid you like you're contagious. You can't catch it. If you don't know what to say to me, tell me that so I can start the conversation. I'm not private about what I'm going through—I lay it out on the line for everyone to see and to know what I'm going through, because if it helps one person recognize a symptom or understand what so-and-so is going through, it is worth it to me.

I miss my friends most of all. People who I thought would be there through the hard times, even some family members, have turned their back on me. Some people don't want to face reality when it is staring them in the face, so they do the only thing they can: run, hide, and pretend nothing happened. I would like to know how they will feel when it's too late to talk to me, enjoy a cup of herbal tea together, or just take me to the park and sit with me.

*

RICK PHILLIPS
Rick was diagnosed with type 1 diabetes in 1974
at age 17 and rheumatoid arthritis in 1999 at age 42

I am always very concerned about people who pass those things along. I had a friend who attempted to wean himself off insulin so he could keep a job. He used a product that some well-meaning person had told him would act in a way that would allow him to stop using insulin. He talked to me about it and I did not point out the glaring error of his thinking. He died a few weeks later as a result of excessively high blood sugars. I decided right then I would never be silent again. The stakes are much too high to allow such nonsense. I doubt I could have changed his path, but if I had spoken up, at least I would feel better about the fact that I had warned him.

*

LESLIE ROTT
Leslie was diagnosed with lupus and
rheumatoid arthritis in 2008 at age 22

I don't handle well-meaning advice well, because it is usually uniformed and useless. Please don't try and sell me snake oil cures, or tell me to do this or take that. If it worked so well, wouldn't we all be doing it? I don't want to be sick, but since I am, I deal with it as best as possible, without others who aren't sick trying to tell me how I should live my life. I don't want to hear that your grandmother had arthritis, so you completely understand. You don't.

I wish people would realize that even though they are trying to be helpful, they aren't. It's hard to be sick when you're young and don't look sick most of the time. If you ask me how I am, I will probably tell you I'm fine, even if I'm not.

*

TIEN SYDNOR-CAMPBELL
Tien was diagnosed with autoimmune
rheumatoid disease in 2010 at age 40

When I come across well-meaning friends and family who truly only want me to get better, I have become stronger at letting them know I appreciate the concern and have an entire team of people working on the same thing, and I really would appreciate talking about something else. I do my best to let people know exactly where my pain or fatigue levels are on any particular day. I'm very lucky to have friends and family who respect when I don't answer the phone, or get off the phone due to feeling pain or fatigue that is too much to ignore.

If someone says, "I wish I could stay in bed all day," my response is, "As long as you're willing to have symptoms like the flu every day, you most certainly can!" Or, "If I could go back to work all day, I would definitely trade places with you!" These are my responses when I feel defensive about the assumption that it's not as bad as I think it is.

The one reaction that gets under my skin like no other is when someone asks about my issues, I proceed to tell them, and they respond by comparing their surgeries, illnesses, or pain to mine. It's not comforting and is really dismissive of my struggle. It's inconsiderate and I avoid people who do that whenever possible. However, I really appreciate it when people know someone who has had to manage rheumatoid arthritis upon meeting me or learning of my diagnosis. These compassionate souls seem to instantly understand that it's unbelievably difficult to manage, and offer verbal and physical support without judgment or comparison. Their grace is very comforting.

I would really love for people to understand that I can't predict when my body will simply cease to function. It's an everpresent issue that can change from minute to minute, hour to hour, day to day, etc. I would love to know when I get out of bed that my feet will not hurt upon touching the floor, and when I brush my teeth that it won't sap the energy out of me and require a nap before doing anything else.

If I was walking the day before, it's not uncommon for me to be unable to do that again for several days. This is very frustrating, especially if I was able to be more active for a few consecutive days the week before. When fatigue sets in, it's not uncommon for me to close my eyes and rest my head on my husband's shoulder, or curl up and nap on the couch while visiting family or friends. It's happened at weddings, funerals, and other gatherings that pull more energy than I have. That's when confusion is likely to come into play. Usually, a person is sick and then get better. They don't get sick, stay sick, get better, get sick, and get better multiple times within short periods of time. If everyone understood this, there would be less stigma attached.

My therapist and I worked on some responses to have handy when discussing my condition. When someone asks how I'm doing or asks for an update on my progress or lack thereof, my response is "If I talk about it, will you promise not to offer me any suggestions for medications, or cures, or diets that you heard might work?" When someone asks if there's anything that they can do for me, some of my possible responses are:

- If you really want to know, I'd really love some new company (or a ride) to my next infusion or appointment. But I want you to know it's chemo, so I may fall asleep on you. Is that okay?

- My family is doing such a great job taking care of me. I would appreciate them getting a break for a day or night and have you bring a meal over. I would really appreciate that.

- Sometimes I feel isolated since I'm not in the work world, and I don't get out of the house too often. I would love to get out of the house and do something around the city. When I find something interesting, like a jazz workshop or a paint party, would you go with me maybe once every month or two?

*

The good physician treats the disease; the great physician treats the patient who has the disease.

WILLIAM OSLER

*

CHAPTER EIGHT

Treatments & Therapies

When I'm resting on a flare day, I need to remember that I am not wasting the entire day doing nothing. I'm doing exactly what I need to do. -ANONYMOUS

Because the exact causes of autoimmune disorders remain largely unknown, treatments run the gamut and are not an exact science. What works for one many not work for another. What medical therapies have been offered? Which have you tried?

*

CHRISTINA AMES
Christina was diagnosed with rheumatoid arthritis in 1987
at age 20 and diagnosed with fibromyalgia in 2011 at age 43

I've been extremely fortunate so far in that virtually all my fifty-plus surgeries have been related to my birthdefect, not to RA. While the disease itself is undeniably active, so far I've not had to undergo any surgical procedures. Those surgeries may have been preparing me:

my surgeon had to break bones, insert and remove pins and staples, and use donor bones in reconstruction, all of which are used in disease related surgeries. I know what to look for if infection is present, and I know how to change dressings. If it ever happens, I'm so ready.

I do, however, wear a brace for my wrist on occasion. Pain comes in different forms for each person, as well as pain tolerance, and when I break out the brace, I know it's a high pain period. I also at times wear compression gloves, specific to arthritis. I use heating pads frequently, as heat for me is much more soothing than using ice.

I have also felt like a guinea pig. I think one of the hardest concepts for a layperson to grasp is that treatment is so varied and specialized for each person. If you have a headache, you take Tylenol, and it works for the vast percentage of people who try it. With RA, you might begin with a certain drug that has worked for many people. You might increase the dosage if it does not show results, or add another to it. All over a period of several months, not hours, as with a headache, or even days as with a sinus infection.

Many of the prescription drugs we try take months to produce results, needing time to build up in the system. During this time, we might still be in pain. And after this period of several months of trying a medication, lab work may show that the inflammation levels are still rising. So we go through the process of trying something else: do we keep our initial drug at the present levels and add a biologic? Or do we stop it completely to see if the biologic (hopefully) works? It truly is an endless roulette wheel of trying things.

But again, I feel fortunate. I went through two previous biologics before landing on the one I currently use, Simponi. It has been a wonderful fit for me. I take it along with methotrexate, which didn't work on its own or with the other two biologics I tried.

I wouldn't feel right if I didn't mention steroids, in particular prednisone. In the weeks following the Big Flare, it definitely was a wonder drug. I'd taken it before for various things, but never at such high doses for such an extended period. It does amazing things, but it is also horrible. It made me into the meanest shrew of a woman, picking fights and being snappish and short with people. That is not my normal personality, I assure you! I always have some on hand if I feel I need to take it, with the blessing of my doctor, but I hope I never need it. Ever.

*

J.G. CHAYKO
J.G. was diagnosed with
rheumatoid arthritis in 2010 at age 38

Medication was the first line of fire when I was diagnosed. I was started on a baseline DMARD (disease-modifying antirheumatic drug) that worked slowly in the body to reduce inflammation. I was diagnosed early, so x-rays showed no major damage and now the fight was on to keep it that way. I was one of those seronegative enigmas— my bloodwork showed no inflammation, but my warm marshmallow joints and hours of morning stiffness were more than enough evidence for a diagnosis. It would be four years before my bloodwork caught up to the rest of my body, finally revealing rising inflammation and reinforcing what I already learned. It was an odd relief to see those numbers. Despite the evidence burning through my days and nights, I always had a nagging doubt in the back of my mind that my symptoms could be psychosomatic. If only that were the case.

The first medication was about reducing inflammation and swelling, and getting me into a place where I could function. I learned it would take at least three months to notice improvement if there was to be any. Six months later there was no change, and so my rheumatologist increased the dose. Another few months went by and things still did not improve. I took each day one at a time, unclear of the level of wellness I was supposed to achieve. My years of dance training had provided me a high tolerance to pain. I rarely complained about physical ailments. I didn't want to be a high maintenance patient. I thought the daily onset of stiffness and swelling was part of the natural progression of the disease. I thought this was how I was supposed to feel. I didn't know I could strive to be better. It would take a couple of years to finally fall into step with the rhythm of RA, to understand the crescendos and diminuendos of my disease and know when I should ask for help.

One DMARD was not enough to control symptoms so I was given a second one. Now I was on two medications, taking several pills a day. I didn't like to take medication. I was stubborn, believing there were more natural ways to reduce pain. I was a child of aromatherapy, hot baths, soothing massage, ice, and body salts. But rheumatoid arthritis wasn't just a minor pain—it was relentless, hot, throbbing and damaging. Without proper defense, I ran the risk of developing irreversible joint damage. I was a dancer. My body had always flowed, and now under the direction of RA, it was slowly rusting from pain and swelling. And so I began my daily routine of medication.

The addition of the second DMARD helped for a time. It was hard to determine if it was the medication relieving my symptoms or the weather. It was a hot dry summer, and I enjoyed an unusual period of increased energy. I swam, went for walks along the beach, and traveled. Long days capped with inky twilights soon dwindled into early crimson sunsets with fresh dew beading the patio railings. With the swift arrival of fall, I relapsed into the early days of my disease. My second DMARD dose was increased. Again, I enjoyed a brief period where everything seemed tolerable. I even returned to the theatre to perform after a four year break. It felt good to get back on the stage and into the life I had always known.

Medication is only one line of treatment and it can only go so far. I had to find other ways to manage and maintain my quality of life. I was referred to an arthritis program that included physiotherapy and occupational therapy. The physiotherapist recommended range of motion exercises to help with morning stiffness and suggested low-impact exercise, such as swimming and walking to keep moving. I continued with gentle yoga to keep my muscles flexible and supple. I was told to try to engage in at least twenty minutes of continual activity every day. The inflammation from rheumatoid arthritis could put me at risk for cardiovascular complications, such as heart attack and stroke, so not only was it important to maintain muscle strength and flexibility but to stay as active as possible. There are days when I'm not motivated to exercise. I'm sore, I'm tired, and my joints are burning, but I do my best to keep moving. I set goals to reach a certain amount of steps every day. If I'm at the desk for long periods of time, I make myself get up a go for a walk at least once or twice every hour.

I was on the maximum dose with two DMARDS. They helped me reclaim a bit of my former life, but as before, their effectiveness wore thin. Once again I struggled with swelling, pain and fatigue. I fell off the exercise wagon. During this time labs showed a bold increase in inflammation. My rheumatologist added a third DMARD, and I became a patient of triple therapy. Triple therapy was being endorsed in the rheumatoid world as one of the most effective treatments for controlling symptoms. I was hoping to be one of the success stories. Tired of juggling several pills a day, I opted for a weekly injection for the third medication. I saw dramatic improvement in only four weeks. My morning stiffness was greatly reduced, and lasted less than thirty minutes. I woke up feeling more fluid, less like a tinman and more like a mermaid. I was amazed at the difference. My fingers shrunk, I had more energy, and while there was always lingering tenderness, I didn't suffer the burning that used to consume my joints. I spent another summer swimming, walking, and even enjoyed my first hike in several years along the lush trails of our west coast rainforest. Triple therapy had made a big difference to the quality of my life.

Occupational therapy had also supplied me with amazing little gadgets that helped me function at work and at home. I had braces for my wrists to support my joints while doing simple tasks like handwriting or housework. I switched to a light canister vacuum that was easy to maneuver so that my quest for perpetual neatness could be satisfied. I have some nifty kitchen gadgets such as a sturdy multi-sized jar opener to help reduce the pressure on my hands and a battery operated can opener. I wear a pair of finger splints every day. I love my finger splints. They support my joints, hugging them like a gentle massage and preventing me from putting too much pressure on them.

One of the most useful things I learned in occupational therapy was voice dictation for writing. On those sore and swollen days when my fingers are thick and puffy, typing is difficult. With a voice dictation program, I can give my fingers a break and keep right on working. Voice dictation does not come without its challenges. In the beginning the program is just getting used to your voice, and there may be some words it does not recognize, causing me to go back to do some major editing. As with all things, voice dictation takes time and practice. The more you use it, the easier it becomes and the program will begin to recognize your own unique diction and the melodic intonation that is your own unique voice.

Treatment and self-care is more than what your medical practitioner recommends. It's about taking time for yourself, allowing yourself to be selfish on those rough days, finding your own pace, and making the best decisions to nourish your life. It's about finding those joyful moments in each day. It's about shifting the particles of your life to fill the cracks with warmth and serenity. Always do what works best for you. It takes time to figure that out, so don't get discouraged. One day at a time, one hour at a time, one minute at a time. One day you'll look back and be pleasantly surprised at how far you've come.

*

JUDITH FLANAGAN
Judith was diagnosed with rheumatoid arthritis in 2012 at age 32
and fibromyalgia and polymyalgia rheumatic in 2014 at age 34

I have been on a steroid, prednisolone, which caused me to gain weight. It's a constant uphill battle to try to lose the weight. I have been on Humira which I self injected each week. It was my first biologic treatment but did absolutely nothing for me in any way, shape, or form. My rheumatologist changed me to the biologic Actemra, which I receive as an IV infusion. I also use various things like heat and ice to help with pain, and a TENS machine. I also use nonsteroidal anti-inflammatories. Humira was definitely the least helpful out of all the treatments I've tried. So far Actemra has been the most helpful. It gives me some relief for one to two weeks each month, but when chronically ill, we take what we can get.

*

SHELLEY FRITZ
Shelley was diagnosed with
rheumatoid arthritis in 2012 at age 42

When it comes to treating my rheumatoid disease, I've tried treatments ranging from heating pads to biologics. When first diagnosed, I started taking corticosteroids and nonsteroidal anti-inflammatory drugs along with methotrexate, a disease-modifying antirheumatic drug. Steroids decreased inflammation and reduced pain, but over time they caused me to want to eat my kitchen and made me irritable. Gaining forty pounds led to osteoarthritis in my feet. I still use steroids on occasion to get through a particularly rough patch, although I cringe when I open that medicine bottle. I've been on methotrexate for almost six years and although I'm not certain how much it has benefited me, I have had minimal joint damage. Weekly shots at home are no picnic, but I'm now immune to their pain.

*

BRENDA KLEINSASSER
Brenda was diagnosed with
rheumatoid arthritis in 1991 at age 31

I wore cock-up splints on my wrists for years until finally undergoing bilateral carpal tunnel surgery. The constant repetitive motions of my wrists starteded to cause numbness and pain. I also had to wear braces for tendonitis in both ankles. An MRI revealed torn tendons in my right ankle and I had to wear an aircast for six weeks, even to bed, so it could heal. I tried all kinds of nonsteroidal anti-inflammatory drugs, but most were too hard on my stomach. I also had steroid injections for shoulder bursitis, but I always ended up getting sick after a couple of days. Before I had cartilage removed for costochondritis, I had numerous steroid injections, but the pain returned as soon as they wore off. Even my knee was injected once, as it was so swollen walking became very difficult.

I've been taking a biologic for over sixteen years. That is truly the only therapy that has helped me get my life back and to continue working full-time. I am not pain-free by any means, but the biologic allows me to remain mobile and active.

The amount of pain medication over the years finally took its toll. An EGD procedure, an endoscopic procedure in which a flexible tube with a light and camera on the end was inserted down the throat, revealed two small stomach ulcers. It's not very pleasant to get ready for, as the spray has a horrible taste to it. Getting my IV ready for the procedure was the worst part. I had to have them take it out and try again, as it hurt so bad. As mentioned before, I'm not a good patient when it comes to having IVs drawn as my veins tend to collapse.

I used a cane in the beginning, as it was very difficult to walk. It helped me get around the apartment when I had problems with ankle tendonitis. The cock-up wrist splints were very helpful, but it was hard to deal with them all the time, especially at work. I wore them at night to help me sleep. For my ankles, I use a topical gel prescribed by my podiatrist. My wrists have been much better since I had the carpal tunnel surgery in 2010. You can hardly see my scars. I had to do physical therapy, but I was able to do that at home. I did contrast baths, which meant switching from warm to cold water in a pan for ten minutes at a time. I held Play-Doh in my hands for two minutes to help strengthen them. I had to massage my scars several times a day.

*

CHANTELLE MARCIAL
Chantelle was diagnosed with
rheumatoid arthritis in 1999 at age 19

I've been on biologics for quite some time, and was on methotrexate as well until I stopped it to try to get pregnant. I have taken steroids, NSAIDS and have had rheumatoid nodules removed from both elbows. I am fortunate that I am not on any prescription pain medication—the hoops patients have to go through to get them these days are insane! I find that my biologic does a great job managing my RA, but without the methotrexate it does wear off after three weeks instead of lasting the full month. That's tough because I get flares monthly now where before they were few and far between.

*

LAYNE MARTIN
Layne was diagnosed with
psoriatic arthritis in 2007 at age 47

Prior to my diagnosis, treatments were based on my complaints. Back in the late 1980s and 1990s, I had problems with hip pain, mostly on the right side. My primary doctor diagnosed hip bursitis and offered a steroid injection. It worked great! I was back on my feet and working my normal job as a nurse that very day. After three to four months the pain slowly returned and I'd get another steroid injection. This kept up for years. I knew the consequences of steroid injections and was mindful to make sure I never got more than four shots a year. However, I soon had trouble with my knees and shoulders, and each time I was offered a steroid shot, it always worked wonderfully. I tried hard to keep track of how many shots I was getting in a year. Sometimes an orthopedic doctor injected my knee or shoulder, other times my primary doctor gave me a shot of Kenolog during allergy season, and a couple of times my podiatrist gave me steroid shots into my feet. They certainly were not keeping track and I knew it was up to me to be mindful of how much cortisone I had injected into by body.

Eventually I couldn't take the right hip pain. Following an MRI, my orthopedic surgeon finally agreed I needed a total hip replacement. He had hoped to postpone it for as long as possible because I was only in my forties and he wanted it to last as long as possible. In 2007, I had a right total hip replacement. At the time, doctors thought it was from wear and tear from working twelve-hour shifts as a hospital nurse for twenty-seven years. But the pathology report of my hip suggested an autoimmune disease, and I was referred to a rheumatologist.

The rheumatologist diagnosed me right away, stating that my sausage toes, psoriasis of the scalp and spondylolysis of the spine were classic for psoriatic arthritis. I was sent for labs, a tuberculosis test, and x-rays that day, and started on Enbrel, a biologic. After a few months my white cell count dropped too low and I was switched to Humira. After four years, the Humira stopped working and due to insurance changes I was put on methotrexate. However, my disease progressed with the methotrexate and they tried several other disease-modifying drugs but so far we haven't found one that works. I was then put on Cimzia, another biological, but had terrible side effects and it was immediately discontinued.

I am left taking low-dose prednisone and daily naproxen. I also take fish oil, calcium, magnesium and vitamin D. I see a chiropractor monthly and go for acupuncture every other week. The acupuncture really helps with my anxiety and stress levels.

I also have a lot of different splints, braces, a cane, walker, and bars in my bathroom and around the toilet. The only devices I use daily are the bars to get in and out of the shower and on the toilet. The braces and splints I use only when certain joints are flaring. And, I have a TENS unit that I use every morning on my lower back. I often times have numbness in my feet and my back will be stiff so, the TEN's unit helps to wake up my nerves and relax my muscles.

*

KATHLEEN MEKAILEK
Kathleen was diagnosed with chronic regional pain
syndrome in 2005 at age 38, rheumatoid arthritis in
2014 at age 46, and ulcerative colitis in 2016 at age 49

What treatments have I endured for my RA? This question should read, which treatments haven't I endured for the treatment of my RA?

One thing not mentioned is all the testing that is done before any treatment can begin. I've had enough x-rays that I should glow in the dark from the radiation—my family's running joke. There have been too many CT scans and MRIs of various body parts to count. If I had copies of them all, I could make a collage of my body from head to toe. That being said, I guess I should start at the beginning and go from there. It started with me picking up a pitcher of tea and feeling a pop in my left wrist. I noticed my ulna was on top of my arm instead of being to the side. I decided a quick trip to the emergency room was in order. X-rays showed no broken bones but did reveale crystals. I was placed in a brace and referred to a hand specialist. He determined my triangular fibrocartilage complex was torn and that I needed a partial left wrist fusion which left me with forty percent range of motion and also removed three carpal bones, leaving me in a long shoulder-to-hand cast for four weeks and a short wrist cast for five weeks. The bones were lost, so a biopsy wasn't done which delayed my diagnosis.

Later that year I began having abdominal pain. It was determined that I had fast-growing fibroids measuring up to five inches in diametered. I needed a complete hysterectomy. A month later, I had trouble straightening my right elbow and saw an orthopedic surgeon, who after reviewing my MRI results, determined a laparoscopic surgery of my elbow was necessary to remove some fluid. He also did a debridement and a synovial and muscle tissue biopsy which showed "a few cells consistent with rheumatoid arthritis without the regular pattern that is usually observed."

In January 2015, the partial fusion of my left wrist was still not helping the pain, so after more testing it was determined that I should have a distal ulna head replacement, so I now have a titanium left wrist. This landed me in a cast for about a week and then directly into physical therapy for six weeks. It has helped the most with the pain, I guess since there is nothing left to attack.

I've also had so many steroid shots in my fingers that I'm at the point where I don't even get deadened for them, just stick the needle in, I'm good; it's just a pinch. It's amazing how much pain a body can endure when you are in a vast amount of pain to begin with. I was then able to go until October, when I started having issues with tingling in my lower arms and hands. After EEGs were performed on both arms, I underwent surgery on my cubital tunnels, first the left and then the right two weeks later. Six weeks later it was followed by the shortening of my right ulna, taking out over an inch of bone and using a six-inch plate and seven screws to put my arm back together. This put me in an exocast that could be removed for showering for six weeks, and then the use of a bone stimulator because the bone was healing at a glacial pace. To this day, the middle is still not healed and I would think that I should be able to feel a broken bone, but there are greater pains, so my body acknowledges this one as normal and just goes on. During this surgery, I also had my right wrist debrided and my triangular fibrocartilage complex fixed because it had some tears. I was told that this was just a temporary fix and might need to have the wrist replaced some time in the future if the pain continued.

Six weeks later, the pain in my right shoulder had caught up with me. I underwent surgery to shorten my clavicle at the acromio-clavicular joint and the coracoid process, along with debridement of the whole shoulder area and removal of any arthritic damage. I still continued to receive steroid shots in my hands and six months after shoulder surgery needed a steroid injection in it. This was the first time my bloodwork tested positive for rheumatoid factor, even though damage had been seen in all the surgeries.

In late August, I started having abdominal pain again. I waited two weeks and then finally went to the emergency room where I was told I needed my gallbladder removed. When it was taken out, it was shaped like a kidney with a stone blocking the duct, and the rest filled with stones. But the pain didn't stop. I was sent for a colonoscopy which revealed ulcerative colitis. I was referred back to the surgeon to look for signs of adhesive bowel disorder. Another laparoscopic surgery found no adhesives, but did find diverticuli on the outside of my colon, possibly explaining the abdominal pain.

I had been on prednisone, but it didn't do anything for me except make me swell up like a balloon and I think that was the least helpful for me. The most helpful was the wrist replacement because there is nothing left to da mage except the remaining tendons that are now started to give me twinges of pain every now and then. The steroid shots have been good temporary fixes when surgery is not warranted, but they are just temporary and have to be re-done every six months or so. The downside to them is that they also weaken tendons and combined with RA, I'm not sure how many my joints can endure before the tendons give out and the need for surgery will be there.

My regimen of nerve blockers, anti-inflammatories, and muscle relaxants seem to help me live a relatively normal life, and Plaquenil and methotrexate seem to be slowing the progression of the disease. I don't like the side effects of methotrexate, it makes me sleepy and nauseous for two days after taking it. So, I have now stopped taking it in the course of writing this, much to the chagrin of my rheumatologist. I am starting to have flares regularly and am noticing significant changes in my hands, so on my next visit, we will discuss biologics and I'm sure I will start a regimen with one. Besides shots, medications and surgeries to help pain, I also use heat and cold treatments. My favorite for my hands and feet is my hot paraffin wax bath/dip. I dip my hands or feet ten times to get a nice thick coat and then wrap them in a towel to hold the heat in. This helps with the stiffness and keeps my fingers and toes moving.I also have a TENS unit that I use on my arms, shoulders and back. It helps to relax my muscles when they spasm and keeps some pain at bay. I have learned biofeedback and use it daily to keep stress under control and to help breathe through the pain.After my diagnosis of ulcerative colitis, I have also switched to a sugar, gluten, soy, dairy and caffeine free diet. This also seems to help my RA. I have not had any alcohol since I began my treatments for RA, either.

*

RICK PHILLIPS
Rick was diagnosed with type 1 diabetes in 1974
at age 17 and rheumatoid arthritis in 1999 at age 42

I have used seven biological medications over seventeen years. That seems like a lot. But in looking at it a bit more closely, I used one medication, Remicade, for five years and have used my current biologic for three years. So the check off of medication occurred after I stopped Remicade and before I started using Rituxan.

139

In the case of my last TNF inhibitor, I had an adverse reaction which caused me to be hospitalized for five days because I developed what the doctor described as lupus-like syndrome. I was immobilized, had a high fever, and significant pain. The situation was resolved by massive IV doses of steroids and removal of the offending medication. I was told I could not return to using anti-TNF inhibitors.

Switching to the current biologic medication was a major decision. I was afraid of some of the side effects listed in the warnings. I believe I had good reason to have such a fear. I had an awful reaction to the previous medication, and the listed side effects of the new medication were troublesome. After three months of being off biologics I knew I could not stand to do nothing. I was having difficulty walking and even lifting my arms. I finally decided to begin the new medication and it has been a wonderful experience. I have also used several DMARDS including methotrexate.

I can't use steroids for prolonged periods due to tremendous increases in my blood sugar. Prednisone can increase my blood sugar way above the normal range. Even short-term use is damaging, so I have to carefully weigh the risks and benefits.

*

LESLIE ROTT
Leslie was diagnosed with lupus and
rheumatoid arthritis in 2008 at age 22

I've tried a variety of treatments and have been on steroids, biologics, and immunesuppressants. I have also had steroid injections in my hip as a result of severe bursitis. My current regimen, which has been the most successful, includes Flexeril, Imuran, and quinacrine.

I have not had any surgical procedures or joint replacements, but fear I may need them in the future. And that scares me. I've watched several of my chronic friends whom I've met through blogging and advocacy go through joint replacements. It seems like an endless cycle. If joint replacements last ten or even twenty years, and you get one in your thirties, the chance is high that you'll need another one. This is one of the things that scares me the most. I remember the first Arthritis Walk I went to. They had a vendor there with elbow replacements. My (non-chronically ill) friend got excited, and pointed them out to me. I didn't know it was even possible. It freaked me out.

*

TIEN SYDNOR-CAMPBELL
Tien was diagnosed with autoimmune
rheumatoid disease in 2010 at age 40

Over the course of the past six-plus years of actual diagnosis and treatment, I feel like I have been put through a never-ending stress test. It's the kind of ordeal that puts a tattoo on your soul. The treatments started relatively easy and initially I was instructed by a holistic physician to take some herbs and supplements, receive light therapy and chiropractic care. Simultaneously, I was also seeing a traditional or allopathic physician and he had me take some initial pain meds and one medication that was supposed to reduce inflammation and swelling. The combination of the two was never quite successful

141

enough because I continued to decline in activity, losing functions and activities of daily living. I have gone through acupuncture treatment which was successful to a point. If I could have gone to acupuncture a few days per week, I'm sure that I might have been able to manage the pain better, but that treatment is cost prohibitive to an empty wallet. I was gifted ten sessions that made my life better for the time I was able to receive the care. Out of everything that I have done, aside from getting full body massages, this is my preferred treatment.

Once I got deeper into the illness, it became an increasingly difficult to manage and started to take me out of work and into the hospital for various issues including pain and infections. I have taken all of the OTC medications available, as well as first level prescription pain medication and I was finally able to get opiate medication management. This is a very controversial issue because there is a very high risk of addiction to the medication, but I am confident in my care. I see this doctor bi-monthly and we talk each time about the reasons that my pain management drugs may not work during a time period. Rather than change the pain management protocol, we collaborate with my rheumatologist on ways to get the disease under some level of control or remission. Sometimes that means going on steroids in addition to all of the medications to control inflammation. This all has to be monitored because I have developed osteopenia from the long-term use of the steroids and that doesn't help my bones at all.

Biologics were introduced to my care approximately one year into a final diagnosis, due to other treatments not working for me. I have taken four different biologic medications over the course of five years. One other medication that I had a very bad allergic reaction to in the infusion suite is not among those four. I only had a small bit of the infusion before it had to be stopped and I was given medications to reverse the closing of my throat and eyes, and itching all over my body. What I know for sure is that I am unable to operate a self-injection medication. For one, it hurts my fingers and hands and for another, it hurts so I have to have someone else do it for me. If no one is around, the fear of the needle and hurting myself further will stop me from getting the medication I need to control the disease.

I have gone through several rounds of occupational and physical for my knees and wrists, worn splints and braces, treated with heat and ice, and attempted to exercise my way out of pain. All of which have ended in me "not making satisfactory medical progress." My physical and occupational therapists told my insurance company that nothing will work until my knees are replaced, and I undergo surgery to correct my wrist issues.

I underwent a bilateral knee replacement surgery—yes, that's both knees at the same time—a few years ago. I would love to say that the surgery corrected all of my problems, but it didn't and it actually highlighted other lesser known problems. I wouldn't have had my knees done if I had known or realized that I would be so dependent on my hands and arms to move my body. When everything hurts, turning over becomes a five-minute process. My shoulders finally were able to have their say in my pain problems, and it became obvious to me that my surgeries would be ongoing if I wanted a chance at some semblance of a normal existence.

I know I'm looking at several surgeries from damage that has already occurred in multiple joints, in addition to my lungs and vision. It's probably the most lonely that I have ever felt in my life. You are sure that no one else is experiencing these issues, until you meet others who have the same, less, and more physical, mental/emotional, and financial issues.

*

CHAPTER NINE

Narcotics & Opioids

There are things known and there are things
unknown. In between are the doors of perception.
-ALDOUS HUXLEY

When pain is overwhelming, use of narcotics/opioids can make all the
difference. But side effects and potential for addiction are considered
by many to be too steep a price. And this is where the argument for
and against begins. What are your feelings about using narcotics and
opioids for pain management of your disease?

*

CHRISTINA AMES
Christina was diagnosed with rheumatoid arthritis in 1987
at age 20 and diagnosed with fibromyalgia in 2011 at age 43

I think this is a sensitive subject for many people. I've taken a few
of the usual ones prescribed, but like the steroids, I never feel right
taking them. I'm not anti-narcotics by any means, I just prefer not to
take them. Yet for a good many patients, they are the only option.

Many are not able to take biologics because of liver problems. Or perhaps they are allergic to the components of a drug. I truly think it is a stigma, because these patients can appear to others as needing only pain pills to survive. And while I am sure there are some who become dependent upon narcotics, the majority need them and use them merely in order to get through the day. It is becoming more difficult now with all the regulations surrounding doctors and pain clinics, and I truly feel for those who must have them. I do believe that if you can find the right cocktail of medications specific to your symptoms of RA, that pain pills should not be necessary. This is my viewpoint, and it has been my experience; undoubtedly, there are differing ones.

*

J.G. CHAYKO
J.G. was diagnosed with
rheumatoid arthritis in 2010 at age 38

I always resisted medications. It started in childhood. Whenever I contracted one of those nasty congestive colds, my mother chased me around the house with a spoonful of vile-tasting medication. I detested the dreadful taste of "cherry" cough syrup; it tasted nothing like cherry. It was bitter and acidic, and in my childhood mind it tasted the way turpentine smelled. Then of course there were the frequent ear and throat infections. This brought a soothing pink concoction that coated a raw throat, tasting slightly sweet, like strawberries with a hint of chalk. After a few more bouts with this particular issue, I began to develop a distaste for that medication, too. And so began my resistance to taking any kind of medication.

Let's face it—medications aren't made to taste good. They're made to make us feel better, and rheumatoid medications are specifically designed to prevent damage by reducing inflammation. Until I had RA, I didn't take a lot of medicine. I didn't like the idea of filling my body with them, and my childhood memory of gagging on fake cherry liquid caused me to balk at the idea of ingesting pills. For colds and flu I turned to chicken soup and hot toddies. Only for particularly bad viruses did I resort to taking cold medication in order to have a restful night's sleep or survive the workday with as little misery as possible.

A diagnosis of rheumatoid arthritis changed all that. Whatever my resistance to taking medication was, I knew this was important to help control the symptoms and prevent irreversible damage to my joints. I complied with this new line of behavior because it was important for me to protect my joints and remain mobile. Although I no longer danced, I wished to maintain a certain level of fitness, and with damaged joints that would not be possible.

Rheumatoid pain was a constant, burning heat in my joints. While the DMARDS worked to decrease inflammation, I turned to NSAIDS (nonsteroidal anti-inflammatory drugs) to relieve the pain. The good thing about NSAIDS is that I only need to take them when needed. If I'm having a good day, I don't need to take them; but there are those rare times when I need to take them over a period of several days until the symptoms decrease.

I have never used narcotics for pain control. I'm not against them. I believe that there are people who benefit from them, but I'm exposed to the downside to these addictive substances every day. The infamous Downtown Eastside of Vancouver, B.C. deals with hundreds of deaths from overdose each year, giving opioids a bad reputation. Narcotics, opioids, fentanyl—whatever name you choose to give them—are powerful and highly addictive substances. They need to be strictly monitored to prevent overuse and overdose. Controls need to be put in place to check compliance.

Everyone has their limit and their own tolerance to pain, and not every pain medication will provide relief. I think healthcare providers should work with patients to do what's best for them. It all comes down to quality of life. We do what we have to do to achieve it.

*

JUDITH FLANAGAN
Judith was diagnosed with rheumatoid arthritis in 2012 at age 32
and fibromyalgia and polymyalgia rheumatic in 2014 at age 34

I wouldn't mind if I had to use opioids and they were prescribed to me, because there is a difference between dependency and addiction. Many patients have suffered because an opioid medication may have been the only thing they found helpful. I believe if it's generally helping the patient, then so be it—let them have it. I myself don't use opioid medication, but I would if it was needed. It makes me sad that the chronic pain community has suffered because of this issue.

*

SHELLEY FRITZ
Shelley was diagnosed with
rheumatoid arthritis in 2012 at age 42

Use of opioids has become a hot topic in the chronic pain world. I certainly hope there is never a generalized rule about who can use opioids because chronic pain is individualized in nature. No one can describe my pain but me, and no one can assess whether I have reached a point in needing to take a pain pill but me. My theory about pain is to seek the source of the pain first and try to control it. Today I am at a point of knowing my current medications are not controlling my joint damage and accompanying chronic pain so I will need to switch to a new biologic. Over the last month, I have tried using heating pads, adjusting my activity level, eating only healthy foods, and limiting stress all in an attempt to reduce debilitating pain levels. I'm waking up in the middle of the night in pain and struggling throughout the day with throbbing elbows, hands, knees and feet. It is impossible to think clearly when my mind is muddled with thinking about the pain I feel. Distractions at work and home can be helpful in getting through the day, but I know a can have a better quality of life than this. For several days now I have had to summon my husband to the bathroom to turn on the shower nozzle. Sometimes I just need to take pain pills to be able to function.

People who don't live with chronic pain, or with someone who lives with chronic pain, can sometimes be critical of those with pain. I see this come up in social media frequently and it been the topic of conversations on the political circuit as well. I get very emotional about hearing talk of limiting or even restricting use of opioids. While I do feel that taking opioids should never replace the quest to find a treatment for the pain, I know there are many of us treating our incurable disease but will still have ongoing pain. No one should live with pain when there exists a means to limit the pain.

*

BRENDA KLEINSASSER
Brenda was diagnosed with
rheumatoid arthritis in 1991 at age 31

I think that every person who lives with some type of rheumatic disease, or any other chronic disease for that matter, should have the right to anything that could help them feel better. I feel that drug-seekers are spoiling it for those who truly need this class of drugs. I'm also game for the chance to have medical marijuana prescribed. It was approved in my state of North Dakota during the general election. I know a lot of details need to be ironed out, but I think it is a very good start.

I do become angry when I hear stories about people going to their pharmacy and being told they can have only so many pills to get through the month. Most people I know take these medications responsibly and are not addicts. I've been prescribed narcotics on occasion but get sick as they are too strong for me to handle. But I have to be at my best when I am working. That's not to say that others should be denied because of the drugseekers.

I've also worked with my primary physician and rheumatologist about using alternative methods and supplements to help manage symptoms. Getting my vitamin D level back to normal has helped my pain level considerably. I live in North Dakota, so we don't see a lot of sun during winter months. My rheumatologist's nurse said that having low vitamin D can cause a lot more pain with rheumatoid arthritis. Since I am now off contraception for the endometriosis and am now postmenopausal, my pain levels were much worse until we discovered that low vitamin D was the culprit.

I also dealt with migraines for over thirty years. It was years before I correlated them to my monthly cycle. I believe the contraception could have been making them worse. The migraines stopped several months after I quit the pill for endometriosis. I was encouraged to try stronger medications for the migraines, but I need to be able to function at work. I feel that there are individuals out there who really need to take narcotics. Everyone deserves quality of life. It's different for each person.

*

CHANTELLE MARCIAL
Chantelle was diagnosed with
rheumatoid arthritis in 1999 at age 19

I feel that if a patient has exhausted all other treatments and opioid therapy helps them live a fuller life, give it to them! I think I have a different perspective on why this is such a sensitive topic these days. Back in the 1970s and 80s when the victims of opioid crises were of a different hue, there was no media coverage. No outcry when crack destroyed my community. But now that it has reached the suburbs— it's a crisis, a scourge...please. It's just changed demographic. But that's a different topic for another book.

*

LAYNE MARTIN
Layne was diagnosed with
psoriatic arthritis in 2007 at age 47

I feel that opioids and narcotics have a place when it comes to pain management but I tend to shy away from using them. I have found personally that walking and mild exercise have kept me more mobile than anything. When I do take a pain pill, they make me so groggy that I feel like I've wasted a whole day. I always try to weigh the benefit and only take them after I've tried either heat or ice, using my TENS unit, an Epsom salt bath, etc. I also find that they upset my stomach and make me so constipated that then I'm even more miserable. Lately, with my artificial hip failing I've had to resort to taking pain pills but try to only take them at bedtime.

I've actually found that xanax or ativan works better for me than narcotics. It might be because psoriatic arthritis attacks the tendons and ligaments in addition to the joints. So a lot of times my pain is actually from a swollen tendon. The benzodiazepines help relax the tendons and my pain is greatly diminished. They also help with anxiety which in turn tends to cause my arthritis to flare. So, if given a choice, I typically reach for a Xanax first before the pain pill.

When I first started having joint pain and stiffness, my drug of choice was alcohol. I would get home from work and my feet and lower back hurt so bad! I would pour a nice stiff drink with vodka to relax me, and eventually the pain would subside. Vodka became my drug of choice for the next ten years. But once I was diagnosed with psoriatic arthritis and realized I actually have a disease, I became much more mindful of what I put in my body. Some of the medications used to treat rheumatic illnesses can be hard on the liver and kidneys, so I rarely drink now and have my liver and kidney functions checked about every three to four months.

*

KATHLEEN MEKAILEK
Kathleen was diagnosed with chronic regional pain
syndrome in 2005 at age 38, rheumatoid arthritis in
2014 at age 46, and ulcerative colitis in 2016 at age 49

I used to hate taking medication of any kind and worried about becoming addicted. My chronic pain management specialist finally convinced me to take pain medication. He addressed my concerns with a simple answer: "If your body needs it, you cannot get addicted. Only overuse or not needing the medication can cause an addiction."

I don't know if this is true for everyone, but it is in my case. Even knowing this, I try not to use narcotics as daily treatment. I do use them for several weeks after surgery and when I have extreme flares. To me, I am more worried about damage to my kidneys and liver because of all the other medications I take on a daily basis. I think if a person needs them, they should be allowed to have them prescribed, as long as it is a reasonable amount and they are not abusing them. I'm upfront with all the doctors I see, and won't take prescriptions from them because I've a signed contract with my chronic pain management specialist. I will even refuse morphine in the emergency room and in surgery unless they call him and have it charted in my file.

When people hear you have narcotics, they automatically assume you are a druggie or junkie. Because rheumatoid pain is invisible for the most part, others don't see how some days it can be too painful to move and additional medication is needed for those occasions. I used to try to keep the amount of medications I was on a secret, but realized that people needed to understand exactly what it took for me to function every day. Now I'm up front with my regimen that includes muscle relaxants, nerve blockers, pain killers, anti-inflammatories, etc. When people ask why I don't drive, I ask them, "Knowing all the medications I take on a daily basis, would you want to be on the road with someone taking all those?" Their answer is always, "No!"

I think a lot of people don't want others to know the amount of medication it takes to live a relatively normal life. Many keep it to themselves for fear of people thinking they have a drug problem. I have actually found it liberating to let people know everything I take. It often opens the door to more questions that I willingly answer, and makes more people aware of the daily struggles that I face.

*

RICK PHILLIPS
Rick was diagnosed with type 1 diabetes in 1974
at age 17 and rheumatoid arthritis in 1999 at age 42

I use hydrocodone occasionally, but not often. My mother had painful neuropathy as the result of type 1 diabetes when I was a young man. I saw both the devastation that pain and the over prescription of narcotics can visit upon a person. I am determined to have neither. So I am very careful about using an opioid and if I error, I error on the side of not using the medication. When it comes to the prescription, my rheumatologist has indicated that I'm on the smallest dose available and it's more ibuprofen than hydrocodone. I am hopeful that at some point we will find a better way to treat pain than using narcotics.

*

LESLIE ROTT
Leslie was diagnosed with lupus and
rheumatoid arthritis in 2008 at age 22

I've never been on narcotics or opioids and am glad for it, but I believe those who need them should have access. I feel that those who oppose the use of such medications are those who are healthy and do not have an idea or understand the kind of pain that comes with many rheumatic diseases. I get very frustrated when those who are not sick judge those who are when they do not have the first clue about what it is like to be us. Treatment is a choice. None of the medications available to treat lupus or rheumatoid arthritis are a walk in the park. All of the medications we take come with risks. And unfortunately, a risk that comes with pain medications is dependence and addiction.

*

TIEN SYDNOR-CAMPBELL
Tien was diagnosed with autoimmune
rheumatoid disease in 2010 at age 40

Before I was diagnosed with rheumatoid arthritis, I was a very physically active person who made use of the city's walkways, running trails, and bike paths. I was also a clinical counselor at a methadone clinic where I created and ran a weekly pain management and addiction group therapy program. My perspective was somewhat unique because I had talked with a few hundred patients whose journey to addiction started with opiate pain medication abuse.

I myself had pain and injuries many times over the years and was very familiar with opiate medications for acute pain. I had taken them after surgeries and once the pain subsided, I no longer needed them. I never had a reason to take them long term until my rheumatoid arthritis affected me so badly that it was a last resort.

One of the last things I had endured before starting opioid pain management was a spinal procedure where they injected medication into multiple spaces in the lumbosacral spine to help numb the nerves. It was an extremely painful procedure, and unfortunately it didn't work. This was the point at which I began using narcotics for pain management. It was also the first time in several years that I had experienced a lessening of pain that was significant enough to allow me to do light household activity without enduring pain that was often excruciating.

I can honestly say that this pain is like no other. I told my physician that I would rather give a natural birth every month if I didn't have to endure this invisible pain all day, every day. He was the first person to truly act as though he understood exactly what I was talking about, and treated me for the pain I was experiencing.

My feelings are concrete about the fact that there are people who take opiates because of their illness of addiction, in addition to the fact that there is likely a somatic level of pain that has not been addressed. As a clinician, I worked to help people identify the triggers to opiate abuse, which was very often, a physical one. I gave them several tools to help manage these triggers, in addition to guided meditations to connect their minds and bodies.

I know there are many who have lost family members to the disease of addiction, and they feel very strongly about keeping the drugs out of the hands of people who abuse them. I feel deeply for their misery, but I think that they're frustration with physicians that overprescribe or run pill mills is affecting innocent patients. When I'm in pain, it is very frustrating to ride all over town trying to get your prescription filled. If you're thinking that my regular pharmacy should know I'm coming, I thought so too, but no, they can't, don't, or won't. Unfortunately, I know those who want to make it more difficult to obtain have little to no consideration for how those rules are an extreme inconvenience to people with legitimate chronic pain conditions managed by opiate pain medication. The times I have had to take my prescription all over town in order to get it filled have been too numerous to count. Why am I doing this? Because pharmacies aren't allowed to say if they have it in stock over the phone. The doctors aren't allowed to give out more than one month's worth at a time, so you have to see the physician for the same issue every single month as opposed to once every three to six months.

If your prescription renewal lands on Friday, they're out of stock (because goodness forbid they keep enough handy), and there's a holiday on Monday. The next shipment won't come until Tuesday, and you are already approximately four days without medication. Go back and read that sentence one more time. You cannot get this prescription filled until two days prior to running out. Those are just the rules I've encountered. I understand that some people have to drive two hours in order to get their prescription filled. I count myself lucky that I live in a major metropolitan city.

Overall, I get frustrated with the opiate pain medication debates being had in government. They make rules based on the complaints of the citizens affected by the crisis in opiate addiction, but fighting for the right to have access to pain medication is very disheartening. It's as though everyone who doesn't have a stake in my pain wants to rule out the ways I can be treated. The same goes for medicinal marijuana. The states that allow it have an easier time with chronic pain patients care, because the natural alternative is extremely effective. The states where this is not an option make all kinds of treatment difficult.

*

CHAPTER TEN

Biologic Therapies

He who studies medicine without books sails an uncharted sea, but he who studies medicine without patients does not go to sea at all. -WILLIAM OSLER

Biologic drugs entered the market in 1998. Genetically modified living cells, they are engineered to reduce inflammation by acting like natural proteins in your immune system. The downfall is that biologics can lead to secondary damage and higher risk of life-threatening infection. Have you tried biologics for treatment of your rheumatic disease?

*

CHRISTINA AMES
Christina was diagnosed with rheumatoid arthritis in 1987 at age 20 and fibromyalgia in 2011 at age 43

I was initially hesitant to begin biologic therapy, but it truly has been wonderful. I feel better now than I have in several years. I did my research on them, including the reading of all the package inserts.

159

Amusing side note, the package insert that comes with my Simponi covers my kitchen table completely. They are long and full of medical-ese, but I feel all education is key, even reading those. My doctor offered several choices after the first one I had to try, Enbrel. This is due to an abhorrent practice call "fail first." Many insurance companies require a patient to try a particular drug, often the cheapest, for a given condition and must fail it before they can move on to the next. Known as step therapy, this practice often prevents a patient from getting the correct medication. I personally know many people who have benefitted from Enbrel, and in no way am I suggesting it is a bad drug. It simply did not work for me. In the meantime, a patient's condition can worsen if they cannot get the most beneficial medication.

As far as side effects, mine are currently minimal. The injection doesn't hurt, and although I don't usually bleed, I like to have a bandaid over the injection site. I try to buy fun ones; last time I had a Star Wars bandaid. I'm just silly like that. I take mine at night, but sometimes I do feel out of it the next day. I might stay in bed longer or try to nap more. Either way, I consider this a small price to pay to feel better!

*

J.G. CHAYKO
J.G. was diagnosed with
rheumatoid arthritis in 2010 at age 38

I'm fortunate to live in a time when so much progress is being made to treat rheumatic disease. There are so many treatment options. Biologics is one class of medication that have given many people back their lives, pulling them from the mire of rheumatic disease.

I haven't tried a biologic. I'm currently managing well on triple therapy so I don't see the need for a biologic at this time. Would I take that route if my current regime failed? Probably. My only reluctance to taking biologics is not the side effects but the cost. I am only a part-time worker, my salary is not substantial. I have coverage through my partner's insurance plan, but none of my own. I have carved out a happy life living within limited means, but unfortunately my budget does not include the hundreds of extra dollars to spend on a biologic medication. For me the financial burden is the biggest obstacle for using biologics. I am hopeful that my triple therapy will remain effective for many years to come.

I've known many who achieved great success on treatment with biologics, but it seems for every one success, there follows ten failures. Medications do not work the same way in each person. It takes time to find the right combination to control disease. Having a chronic illness requires immense patience, because everything slows down. Sometimes while testing out various treatments, we can feel like guinea pigs trying to sniff our way through the maze. Biologic therapy is only one portion of that maze, but for some, it's the one thing that leads them to the exit.

*

JUDITH FLANAGAN
Judith was diagnosed with rheumatoid arthritis in 2012 at age 32
and fibromyalgia and polymyalgia rheumatic in 2014 at age 34

I have been on two biologics and am currently taking one. I follow my medical team's treatment plan, and always have. I trust them to look after me; if they don't, I will find a new team. If you aren't happy, move on. I occasionally get a headache and feel tired the day after the infusion, so I tend to have a really good rest day or "me" day, as I like to call it. Other than that, I don't have too many side effects.

*

SHELLEY FRITZ
Shelley was diagnosed with
rheumatoid arthritis in 2012 at age 42

Over the years, I tried four different biologics and found very little success with any. The first was etanercept (Enbrel), a TNF inhibitor, which targets an inflammation-causing tumor necrosis factor. I stayed on that biologic for about six months and noticed very little difference in daily inflammation and pain. My rheumatologist and I discussed quality of life and other treatment options, including the possibility of a research study. I switched to a different TNF inhibitor biologic, adalimumab (Humira) as part of step therapy, better known as fail first. After nearly a year of monthly infusions with biologic number two, I told my doctor it was not helping.

At that point I had a Vectra DA blood test done to determine my disease activity level, which revealed my disease was in the moderate to severe category. Research has always been a big component to deciding what treatment to use, so after extensive research on biologics and available research studies, I opted to switch to a third biologic, toclizumab (Actemra). After one infusion, I felt much better. I really felt like it was more effective for impacting my disease than its predecessors. Shortly after the second infusion I began having unbelievable fatigue, fever, muscle aches, and bright red bumpy rashes when I went outside in the sunlight. I was diagnosed with drug-induced lupus, and ordered to immediately halt any further toclizumab infusions. A few weeks later my odd symptoms disappeared and I was left without a biologic.

Enter biologic number four: abatacept (Orencia). Success was limited but I didn't feel worse than I had while taking other biologics, so I continued monthly infusions at my doctor's office for two years. Switching to new medicine is a monstrous ordeal with insurance. I wonder how many of us stay on a medication that isn't working well just to avoid battling the insurance company. When I reached the tipping point with Orencia not working, I moved to the janus kinase inhibitor tofacitinib (Xeljanz). Within a month I felt some relief. I had hope that this was the medicine for me but, as with its predecessors, Xeljanz was not the one. My immune system outsmarted the medicine, and took me back to square one.

The Great Biologic Experiment Game is frustrating. I feel like a laboratory mouse in my own research study. My rheumatologist and I had another lengthy discussion about medications and at his recommendation, I opted to start Rituxan infusions. I will be getting two five-hour infusions two weeks apart and then go through a second round four to six months later. I'll continue with that process. Please let this be the road to feeling better.

*

BRENDA KLEINSASSER
Brenda was diagnosed with
rheumatoid arthritis in 1991 at age 31

I have been on only one biologic, Enbrel, for over sixteen years. During the first month I had a few side effects including nausea, slight headache, and redness at the injection site. I really did not know anything about administering it. My nurse showed me how the first few times and then I started doing it at home each week, and have been doing it ever since.

Back in the beginning it was quite a process. Enbrel was the first FDA-approved biologic in 1998. I started taking it on April 20, 2001, almost ten years after my rheumatoid diagnosis. The FDA approved 25 mg injections in one site every three to four days. It had to be drawn up with a syringe but since my fingers were affected by rheumatoid disease, that was pretty difficult. Thank goodness they provided a tray. I set the bottle of Enbrel into the tray and then drew it into the syringe. I would then choose a site—either my upper arm, upper thigh or abdomen. Because it was a subcutaneous injection, underneath the skin, I had to squeeze the skin with the opposite hand and inject with the other. The FDA then allowed 50 mg on the same day but not in the same area. That meant still drawing it up with the help of the tray at 25 mg twice. There were many steps, and this process took at least thirty minutes.

Living with rheumatoid arthritis, you would think they would make it easier for the patient, right? It took years but I was finally offered the SureClick Autoinjector with the whole 50 mg approved by the FDA. I didn't hesitate to make the change. All you do is set it out for at least fifteen to twenty minutes. I would set a timer. It now takes less than five minutes to complete the injection. It stings for a bit, but that dissipates quickly. Another change has been made in that you can now leave Enbrel out at temperatures of 68 to 77° for two weeks, so now I set it out the night before my injection. That change is also great, because I now have Enbrel shipped to my place of employment. I bring the bag that Enbrel support provided me with, and use the cold pack from the pharmacy, so that is very convenient.

I used to get it dispensed at my local pharmacy which was in the same building as my work, but last year a change was made with my insurance company and the Enbrel now has to be dispensed by a specialty pharmacy. One of my friends at CreakyJoints suggested I have it sent to my place of employment. Working at a medical clinic has been a great advantage. I tried to get the other pharmacy to ship it to my previous pharmacy, but they refused. As I write this, Senate Bill 2301 was passed by the Senate. If it gets passed by the House, that means I could have Enbrel dispensed at the pharmacy I've used for decades. It would prevent the pharmacy benefit managers from telling a pharmacy they cannot dispense a medication that the same pharmacy has been dispensing for decades. It was actually my pharmacist who told me about this bill and even gave me the information. He knows I am an advocate for the Global Healthy Living Foundation aka CreakyJoints, so I really appreciated him sharing that with me.

Enbrel has truly changed my life. I never gave up, and did my research. My biggest hurdle was whether the insurance company would cover it. I can't take it when I have any type of virus or infection because it can deplete your immune system. I had been taking shark cartilage with the doctor's blessing even before I started the biologic, which helps boost my immune system. I never take any supplement without discussing it with my medical team first. When biosimilars are available, the whole process of administering will probably go back to the dark ages, as there is no way an autoinjector would be the first choice they would use to inject. It will be back to square one.

I thought it important to share these steps of administering a biologic so you can understand what a person living with rheumatic disease has to go through. At least when I go to my pharmacy, in the future he has to tell me if I am receiving a biologic or biosimilar. My state of North Dakota passed Senate Bill 2190, that I testified on behalf of, on March 11, 2013. That protects patients like me who live with inflammatory diseases. Being able to take a biologic all these years has allowed me to remain employed full time and functional. That's important to me!

*

CHANTELLE MARCIAL
Chantelle was diagnosed with
rheumatoid arthritis in 1999 at age 19

I'm a huge advocate for folks giving biologics a shot. I love that there has been advancement in the field as well, so there are more choices than there were twenty years ago, and more coming!

*

LAYNE MARTIN
Layne was diagnosed with
psoriatic arthritis in 2007 at age 47

I've used bilologicals off and on over the years. The first biological caused my white cell count to drop too low, so the rheumatologist switched me to another. I was on the second one for about four years, but due to a divorce I ended up losing my insurance coverage and I could no longer afford the new insurance's six-hundred-dollar copay.

Eventually I was able to get patient assistance and went back on it but I started having numbness first in my face and then down the whole left side of my body. My doctor sent me for an emergency CT of the head, fearing a stroke, but it was normal. He said it was just stress from my divorce and gave me a prescription for the anxiety.

The numbness persisted and some days were worse than others. Some nights I'd go to bed wondering if I'd wake in the morning. I felt so crummy and unhealthy that I actually thought I was going to die. I never thought about it being the biological, because my doctor told me it was all stress induced. Eventually the patient assistance program ran out and I had to reapply. This time it was not free and I had a copay larger than I could afford so I stopped the biological. Slowly, over the course of four to five months I started to feel better and the numbness gradually when away. I just assumed that with time and distance from the divorce, my stress level was coming down. I then moved and my new rheumatologist wanted me back on a biological. He prescribed one that was fairly new and I was able to get a year's worth for free through the patient assistance program. I did great after the first injection but after the second shot I started to get the numbness in my face. After the third dose I had numbness down my whole left side again and I felt like crap! All of the symptoms were that of multiple sclerosis, and my rheumatologist immediately had me stop the biological. It took about six weeks for the symptoms to resolve, and he said I can never take biologicals again.

I've recently read some studies showing that biologicals can cause demyelinating disorders in some individuals. Apparently, I am one of those individuals. Thankfully, my symptoms have all resolved and I was not left with any long term consequences.

*

KATHLEEN MEKAILEK
Kathleen was diagnosed with chronic regional pain
syndrome in 2005 at age 38, rheumatoid arthritis in
2014 at age 46, and ulcerative colitis in 2016 at age 49

I have not tried biologics yet as treatment, as my doctors have not yet recommended them. I started with prednisone and plaquinel and when I was weaned off the steroids, methotrexate was added. I have been on etodolac since 2005 for complex regional pain syndrome. I'm not at the maximum dosage of methotrexate yet since I haven't been diagnosed for long. My etodolac has been increased along with my methotrexate over time. Two and a half years might seem like a long period to some, but with each new medication or change in dosage, it takes a few months to see if it works and whether there are any side effects. Since I stopped taking methotrexate, my rheumatologist is waiting to see if I have flares (which I have been) and what my lab results show at my next visit. My red and white blood counts are low from the methotrexate and recent surgeries, plus the methotrexate was keeping me from healing properly. The subject of biologics and journey to find one that works will be starting soon. I just hope I find one that reduces the flares and pain without making me feel miserable.

*

RICK PHILLIPS
Rick was diagnosed with type 1 diabetes in 1974 at
age 17 and rheumatoid arthritis in 1999 at age 42

I am using my seventh biologic medication, and it has been a godsend for my RA. I believe that since I was diagnosed in a time with biologic medicines and my doctor was willing to use them, I have been saved lots of pain and loss of function. When I first saw my rheumatologist about the diagnosis I was left little choice but to opt as soon as possible to use a biologic medication. I began a treatment of methotrexate that very day and I was told that he would switch me to the first biologic treatment as soon as insurance approved the medication, about six months. The medication worked magnificently. I had no idea how bad off I was at that point. I used this first biologic medication for five years before it lost effectiveness.

*

LESLIE ROTT
Leslie was diagnosed with lupus and
rheumatoid arthritis in 2008 at age 22

I have tried biologics. Unfortunately, because I have both lupus and rheumatoid arthritis, this makes the treatments I can be on quite tricky. One biologic to treat my rheumatoid arthritis caused my lupus to flare. I was bedbound for two weeks and at first couldn't figure out why. As a result, most biologics are off the table for me. This is unfortunate, but I guess that's what happens when you have multiple rheumatic diagnoses.

*

TIEN SYDNOR-CAMPBELL
Tien was diagnosed with autoimmune
rheumatoid disease in 2010 at age 40

I was diagnosed with a fairly aggressive and severe form of rheumatoid arthritis and I have taken several biologics or DMARDs over the years. The first time I was prescribed a drug dispensed by an autoinjector and while it was slightly helpful, it was not too long before my rheumatologist changed me over to a drug dispensed through an infusion. Both the autoinjector and first infusion were quite scary because I didn't know what to expect. By the time I started the second biologic, I was more at ease and the medication seemed to do more work than the others. I remained on that medication until my insurance was cut off and went for several months without any medication, losing all of the progress I had made. The relief disappeared over a few weeks after the first missed monthly infusion. My hands immediately became swollen, tender, and the deformities that were dissipating returned quickly as well. Once I was able to get on public assisted insurance, I had to see a new doctor who decided to have me start another medication that he thought was superior, so I took that for quite some time. Now seeing my third rheumatologist and having taken yet another biologic, that I had an immediate allergic reaction to, I am currently only taking immunosuppressive medications.

As far as side effects go, I didn't have a great deal of them. I experience nausea and irritable bowels more than anything else with each biologic medication. I had to take an anti-nausea medication in order to tolerate each and every treatment with biologic medicines. Other than that, my biggest concerns are the effects on my vision, which can be a another effect of the disease, medications, or both.

*

Being in control of your life and having realistic
expectations about your day-to-day challenges
are the keys to stress management.

MARILU HENNER

*

CHAPTER ELEVEN

Managing Triggers

Your genetics load the gun. Your lifestyle pulls the
trigger. -DR. MEHMET OZ

Although the exact cause remains unknown, there is a plethora of
triggers unique to each patient. For some, its certain foods. For others
it's hormones or physical activity. But before we can manage the
triggers, we must first discover what they are. What triggers have you
correlated to a flare of symptoms?

*

CHRISTINA AMES
Christina was diagnosed with rheumatoid arthritis
in 1987 at age 20 and fibromyalgia in 2011 at age 43

I'm fortunate to have very few triggers. Mine are either hormonal
changes or weather related. I haven't seen many studies on this, but as
I go along on my rheumatoid journey, I meet more women who have
the same problem: The strain of rheumatoid arthritis that we have has

either been brought about by a massive influx of hormones such as childbirth, or a hysterectomy, or it rises and falls with the changes of our bodies at times of puberty or pregnancy. I fall into the latter category. I was in my teens when I started showing symptoms, and surprisingly still hadn't finished puberty when I started college. I believe this is why I had the initial diagnosis of juvenile rheumatoid arthritis.

These hormonal changes have dictated my RA, as the periods of highest disease activity, or lack of activity, have revolved around them. I'm turning fifty this year, and am smack in the middle of the stages of menopause. This has caused my latest period of high disease activity.

I also am very sensitive to weather changes, especially during cold weather. I live in Maryland, and while we don't have the harshest of winters, it still can get cold and damp. I always can feel a weather front coming through.

The way I've learned to deal with flares is to pay attention to what my body is telling me. If I'm suddenly tired, I know I need to rest more. If my fingers ache, I use compression gloves, and braces as needed. I also use over-the-counter menthol rubs on my larger joints, and that helps as well. Being warm is something that helps me so I nearly always wear sweaters, or have a cardigan close if I need it. I also use heating pads, and hot water therapy.

*

J.G. CHAYKO
J.G. was diagnosed with
rheumatoid arthritis in 2010 at age 38

The warm and gentle evening faded into the glow of a blushing sunset. Dark clouds gathered in the distance, cloaking the last remnants of daylight. Sometime in the wee hours I woke to the spatter of rain against my window. I pulled back the curtain and watched the tiny pinpricks of starlight disappear beneath the swollen rainclouds. I pressed my hot hands against the cold window pane, trying to douse the fire the rainclouds had ignited once again.

Trying to explain a flare to someone who has never experienced one is challenging. I've described them like a cluster of fireworks exploding in my joints, or a slow flow of scorching lava cascading into the porous crevices and sitting there, simmering. I often compare the feeling to the smoldering electricity in storm clouds jamming up my joints with a hot crushing density. In the midst of this heat, I can only describe feeling unwell. My stomach might feel unsettled as if I ingested a glass of sour milk. My head is fuzzy, I feel lethargic and drowsy, and my hands hot and puffy. The flare is an ambiguous sensation that only someone with chronic illness learns to recognize. The way rheumatic disease works in the body is so diverse that we all have our own unique warning signs and triggers.

Changing weather conditions is a big trigger for my flares. Our west coast weather is impulsive. Sometimes we can experience three types of weather in a single twenty-four-hour period, and that swiftly changing pressure churns the storm front in my joints. I can feel the shift in the air, and I'm not alone. I've known many people who experience a change in wellness along with the shift in weather. Nobody really knows why. I like to think that our bodies are tuned with the pulse of the earth, and that we roll, flow and shake with the water, the ground, and the air. Whatever the reason, a cold rainy day will blow up my joints like an evil clown filling helium balloons at a child's birthday party with hot magma. Not pretty.

Stress, lack of sleep, diet, and over-indulgence of alcohol or certain foods—all these things have the potential to open floodgates to a flare. And when my joints start burning, it's time to find a way to put the fire out. One of my favorite ways to soothe a flare is a hot bubble bath. I love to sink my body into the comforting scent of vanilla or lavender salts and enjoy the sensation of the tepid water wrapping around me. This is particularly helpful when my joints are sore and aching. On those days when they're hot and burning, I crush an ice pack between my hands, and the loud crackling that ensues is like the snapping and popping of icebergs breaking apart in the North Pole.

I'm always amazed at the heat my body can produce during a rheumatoid flare. I'm cold most of the time (my mother always said I had no blood), so I always know when a flare is coming on when that heat starts to travel through my body like a fever. I do the medicinal things when necessary, like NSAIDs and anti-inflammatory creams, but I find that the creams don't penetrate enough to really make any difference. I also find them messy, and that doesn't really complement my inclination toward an obsession of cleanliness, and some of them smell like the bitter antiseptic scent that lingers in hospitals and care homes. Not my kind of perfume.

On the neater side, my occupational therapist has fitted me with finger wraps and finger splints. The stretchy material of the wraps fit my fingers like a glove, and the gentle pressure relieves the pain and helps reduce swelling. In fact I'm wearing one right now as I type. I never leave the house without my finger splints. I love the way they hug my joints, preventing me from putting too much pressure on them or overextending them. They're like little spiral rings, except made of hard plastic instead of glittering silver. I do have the option of having them designed in stainless steel for a more cosmetic effect, and perhaps one day I may. But for now it doesn't lessen their effectiveness, and if I happen to lose one, they're more cost effective to replace in plastic.

But of all the things that I can do to manage my flare, the art of distraction is my favorite. There's nothing like focusing on something I enjoy that takes me out of the moment, putting me into a more favorable place. I have constructed my own emergency kit for flare days: books, hot water bottles, snug blankets, fragrant teas, Epsom salts and aromatherapy.

I see a flare day as a message from my body that it's time to take a break. I can pause and take pleasure in the little joys I don't always have time for. Anything that can mentally engage me and shift my focus, such as writing, putting on my favorite movie, or reclining on a comfy cushion with a hot cup of tea and getting lost in the pages of a book. I take this time to focus on me, and not on the all things that are waiting for my attention. It is part of a new rhythm in my life with RA.

*

JUDITH FLANAGAN
Judith was diagnosed with rheumatoid arthritis in 2012 at age 32
and fibromyalgia and polymyalgia rheumatic in 2014 at age 34

Mostly the hot weather seasons trigger my flares. I personally prefer the cooler seasons, but everyone is different. I manage my flares with ice packs, heat packs, TENS machine, warm bath with Epson salts, and also eye masks.

*

SHELLEY FRITZ
Shelley was diagnosed with
rheumatoid arthritis in 2012 at age 42

I feel like every day is part of a big flare. In the almost six years since my diagnosis, I have rarely felt exceptionally well. Sometimes I wake up and everything hurts worse than normal. This situation is usually triggered by stress, weather, or poor food choices. I make sure to minimize consumption of nightshade vegetables like potatoes which cause inflammation and aggravate my pain. If I eat poorly, I feel worse, although when I feel bad that five minutes of comfort food sure does give me a temporary fix. If I have a pack of Methylprednisolone on hand or available at the pharmacy, I'll take that corticosteroid for six days. That boost will usually get me through the rough patch. I use prednisone occasionally but sparingly. I have therapeutic beads I heat up in the microwave and place on very painful areas like elbows, ankles, and knees. On an extreme pain day, I've been known to have four or five heating pads on at once.

In warm months, I use the swimming pool for therapy. I feel absolutely no pain when I'm floating or stretching in the pool. Being weightless lets me move my joints flexibly without pain. The down side to aqua therapy is getting out of the pool when my true body weight catches up with me ten-fold. Those first few steps on land feel like I'm dragging a ton of bricks. When I have trouble walking well and the pain is intolerable, I take pain medication and try to distract myself by going about my routine. There have been days, however, when the only solution to a flare is to stay home from work and rest.

*

BRENDA KLEINSASSER
Brenda was diagnosed with
rheumatoid arthritis in 1991 at age 31

My flares are triggered mainly by stress. It's important for someone with a chronic illness to alleviate as much stress as possible. Triggers also include a change in weather, especially the barometric pressure going up or down. You would be surprised by what a slight change can do. Sometimes I even notice a flare if I eat something salty such as certain kinds of pizza or pastas. It doesn't happen all the time, so it's really hard to gage. When I'm bombarded by people wanting me to accomplish something, without having a chance to evaluate the situation first, the stress can cause anxiety and even a flare.

The worst place for me to experience a flare is definitely my shoulders. That makes it so much harder to move in bed. Getting dressed can also be a challenge. Raising my arms while in excruciating pain is extremely difficult. I have experienced flares in pretty much most areas of my body. Even my cervix has been attacked by rheumatoid arthritis after undergoing a colposcopy thanks to several abnormal pap smears. The procedure involved obtaining a tissue sample from the cervix, and was very painful. My gynecologist could not understand why I was experiencing so much pain. After the results came back, he apologized and informed me that what I experienced was cervicitis. My rheumatoid arthritis had actually attacked my cervix. It explained why inserting tampons was such a challenge. One of the first things I noticed after I started my biologic was that it was much easier to insert tampons.

My ankles are another area that have been attacked. I was diagnosed with tendonitis in both ankles, with my right being the worst. I actually ended up with torn tendons in my right ankle and had to wear an aircast. It did resolve the problem, but I may need to have surgical repair down the road.

My wrists are also involved—a result of wear and tear from performing my job duties. I underwent bilateral carpal tunnel release in 2010. You can hardly see my scars. I sometimes have to wear a wrist splint to bed if I am experiencing a flare. I also use topical ointments, such as Tiger Balm, which is very soothing. I also experience problems with my lower back, as I have a bulging disc in my lumbosacral spine.

In 1988, I was diagnosed by the Mayo Clinic with degenerative arthritis of the spine—this was almost three years before my rheumatoid diagnosis. My jaws have even been involved. I was told I had TMJ, but that wasn't the case. My jaws sometimes flare because of the halo I wore during my craniotomy.

Funny how this all seems to be connected. My life is truly like a roadmap, or connect the dots, if you will. Even my teeth have been involved. I have had at least six root canals and two crowns. All of those teeth have been extracted. The two that had root canals and crowns became infected many years later. A root canal was performed because the nerve was dying. Once the nerves dies, there should be no more pain, but that wasn't the case in my situation. I dealt with these two teeth on and off for almost ten years. When I finally saw another specialist, he said that I was a ticking time bomb, as the infection could have gone to my neck. The plan was to have the teeth extracted by an oral surgeon and then have implants done several months later. When the oral surgeon realized that these teeth were in the back, he said the implants were not necessary. I was fine with that. He performed the extractions with only a local anesthetic so I didn't have to be put out. He said I didn't even flinch. I told him I was tough. You have to be, living with this disease. You cannot let it beat you. I insisted on looking at those teeth, which he had to take out in pieces. They were ugly. We talked about the fact that this ended up happening because I live with an autoimmune or inflammatory disease, such as rheumatoid arthritis. He agreed. It was great to have that validated.

That was not the end of that saga though, as I ended up getting a dry socket like I did after my wisdom teeth were extracted. I truly believe that anything that goes wrong with my body—and the fact that it is constantly attacking itself—is the main reason why everything turns out to be such a big deal.

I also deal with a lump behind my right knee which sometimes gets to be the size of an egg and can be very painful. I experience left knee pain from a childhood injury when I tore ligaments. That seems to be more osteoarthritis than rheumatoid arthritis, because Tylenol seems to help. Moving even a little during a flare can actually help quite a bit, as does taking a warm shower if I have the energy. I was told by my physician that if either the cold or warm pack works right away, to stick with that particular one. It is different for everyone.

*

CHANTELLE MARCIAL
Chantelle was diagnosed with
rheumatoid arthritis in 1999 at age 19

I basically only get flares when my biologic is wearing off—about every third week after I inject. Since I've stopped taking methotrexate to try for a pregnancy, the biologic doesn't last as long. I usually just bear it unless there is a flare of my uveitis, in which case I add steroid eyedrops and sometimes bridge with prednisone until my shot is administered and takes effect. I'm generally not triggered by anything else besides occasionally around my period, but that depends on when I have had my injection as well. Thanks goodness for apps and calendars!

182

*

LAYNE MARTIN
Layne was diagnosed with
psoriatic arthritis in 2007 at age 47

The biggest flare for me is anxiety! I tend to be a worrier and I take on other people's worries and problems. I'm a nurse by trade so I have always been in a caregiver role. I genuinely care about other people and try to help them and "fix" them. But, it has taken me a lot of years to realize that I need to take care of myself too. With this disease I know I need to put myself first, but I'm not very good at that. I tend to put my kids and family's needs before my own and I find myself taking on their problems. I love the saying "not my circus, not my monkey." I have to remind myself of that almost daily!

To keep myself grounded I try to get outside with nature daily. Sometimes it's just a matter of sitting on the patio but being outside really helps me to stay calm. I limit my time on the internet, Facebook, Twitter, etc. I just can't take the negative stories that people post. I also find that even watching the news can cause me anxiety. I think its because I worked ten years with an ambulance service going on medical calls and twenty-five years as an emergency room nurse. I saw so much trauma, abuse, pain and suffering that I really think I suffer from posttraumatic stress disorder. To cope, I read a daily devotional and my bible daily. This also helps me to keep things in perspective and it gives me a sense of calm. And, I have a circle of friends from my church that I get together with weekly for fellowship. I listen to music and I love to watch comedy or feel good movies.

In addition to stress I have found some food triggers that cause me to flare. The main one is any foods in the nightshade family like tomatoes, potatoes, peppers, and eggplant. I can eat them in limited quantity, if they are cooked fully but, if I eat a raw tomatoes then I flare. The joints in my hands will become so inflamed that I can't turn a doorknob. It usually takes about five days for the inflammation and swelling to go down.

I've tried several elimination diets, which take months to do properly. Nightshade is by far my biggest trigger along with some dairy products. I don't do well with yogurt, milk and soft cheeses. But the dairy mostly affects my irritable bowel syndrome and not the psoriatic arthritis.

*

KATHLEEN MEKAILEK
Kathleen was diagnosed with chronic regional pain
syndrome in 2005 at age 38, rheumatoid arthritis in
2014 at age 46, and ulcerative colitis in 2016 at age 49

What triggers my flares? That's a good question, and I wish I had an answer. The truth is it seems everything triggers a flare—walking, standing, sitting, and just normal everyday activities people take for granted. I can wake up in the middle of the night from the pain of a flare. Was I sleeping wrong? Did one of my dogs lay on me? Why?

When I can go to one of my art show openings, I tend to arrive late and leave early because I know I'll pay for it over the next couple of days with fatigue, swelling, and pain not just in my feet and ankles, but in my hips, shoulders, and wrists, too. I attended one two days ago and am still suffering for it, but I can't just stay in bed all day. That doesn't do any good, I want to live my life, I want people to enjoy my work and I want to interact with my collectors.

To keep flares to a minimum, I keep a regular schedule with my medications and even schedule in an afternoon nap, which can range anywhere from two to eight hours depending on what I did that day, the day before, or the day before that. I have found that heat tends to help my abdomen and lower extremities while ice packs help my upper extremities. I can't explain why they react to the different changes in temperatures, just like I can't explain what will cause a flare.

Sometimes I will get moody or emotional when a flare is getting ready to set in. I will cry and just not feel good all over. I try not to take narcotics unless the flare is so bad that I can't move. I do take muscle relaxants and nerve blockers, and will take a higher dosage (still within prescribed limits) when a flare is becoming bad but before it becomes unbearable.

Since I also have CRPS, for me it is sometimes hard to distinguish between the two, especially if it's in the right upper quadrant of my body. I just realized that I tend to refer to my body in terms much like that of a machine. It's almost as though the "before" me is looking at the "after" me, and describing my body as parts of a device that I survive in, rather than something that is a part of me.

*

RICK PHILLIPS
Rick was diagnosed with type 1 diabetes in 1974
at age 17 and rheumatoid arthritis in 1999 at age 42

There are only two things I can associate with flares: lack of sleep and stress. Either or both might cause a flare, but they are just as likely not to cause any issue. I wish I could find a pattern or associate it with something, but truthfully I cannot. All I can say is that they come and disappear without warning or understanding.

*

LESLIE ROTT
Leslie was diagnosed with lupus and
rheumatoid arthritis in 2008 at age 22

Sometimes the weather triggers my flares. Most often, when I know what triggered it, it is emotional stress. However, most of the time, I do not really know what triggered a flare. That's what makes it tough. I have had emotional upheavals that I firmly believed would trigger a flare and didn't. Then I have had other events that have been much less traumatic that have seemed to cause a flare. Before I was on birth control, I used to flare every month when I got my period. Sometimes I just try and work through the flare, depending on how bad it is. I had a medication-induced flare, which caused me to be bedbound for two weeks, so it is very situational.

*

TIEN SYDNOR-CAMPBELL
Tien was diagnosed with autoimmune
rheumatoid disease in 2010 at age 40

It's been six years since my official diagnosis, and I haven't yet been able to identify a trigger for my flares. They start at random times and last for just as random periods. I have noticed, however, that my worst flares start in the evening after the sun goes down. I have many occurrences of having to lie in bed, use all of my tools, and still end up crying in ten to fifteen-minute waves for a few hours. I don't know if anyone else goes through this, but I don't have more morning stiffness and increased pain, like the majority of rheumatoid patients.

Sometimes I think that I am not taken as seriously because of this evening stiffness and increased pain. I have not been able to isolate any food that contributes to it to the point of having breakfast or lunch for dinner and vice-versa.

When these flares occur, they are also in random areas. For instance, my pain is in every joint, and some more than others. I also experience more severe flares in joints that most of my daily pain is attempting to manage.

As far as management goes, I have several different tools and assistance at my disposal. My initial reaction to a flare is to start paying attention to my breathing and slow that down as much as possible to keep myself calm. If the flare continues to escalate, I check the time to ensure that I have taken pain management medications and whether I can take a breakthrough medication. I typically try to lay down, no matter where I am. Of course if it's in public, I get to a place where I can sit still; ideally, that may mean going to the car. This is an example of how you start to fit your life around the pain. I no longer go to places that will keep me too far from the safety of a comfortable space. I have been known to ask a store employee to get a chair for me because of flares affecting my ability to stand or walk.

I keep a topical gel with me at all times and apply it to affected joints as soon as possible to calm the pain. The gel helps, but isn't really effective without other supportive measures. I keep my headphones attached to my phone for easier listening and communication though holding the phone is problematic due to pain in my hands and wrists in nearly all positions. Fortunately, on my phone I have a playlist of guided meditations for pain management that are between ten to forty-five minutes in length. I start one of those if I feel it will help ease the pain. Once in a while, I shake uncontrollably which is soothed by a heating pad. I travel with my heating pad now, even to Caribbean vacation spots. My heating pad is as essential as pain medications.

*

CHAPTER TWELVE

Affordability of care

Health is a state of complete physical, mental, and
social well-being, and not merely the absence of
disease. -WORLD HEALTH ORGANIZATION

Patients are consumers in the healthcare industry comprised of
pharmaceuticals and other for-profit businesses who operate to keep
profit margins healthy and shareholders happy. What challenges have
you faced with regards to affordability of care and medication?

*

CHRISTINA AMES
Christina was diagnosed with rheumatoid arthritis
in 1987 at age 20 and fibromyalgia in 2011 at age 43

I have medical insurance through my husband's job, and for the
most part, it has been pretty good. We've always opted for the higher
tier of coverage, so we aren't required to get referrals. They were
initially resistant in approving my biologics, even with my history, and

that was an issue, but now I don't have problems. It is, of course, expensive, but it would be more expensive to not have insurance, so for now, I am thankful we do. And I'm extremely grateful that we will continue to have medical insurance for both of us after he retires; not all agencies do this.

The company we have has many resources, things like auto delivery of prescriptions, and tracking your health with nurses are two of the programs that come to mind. I prefer not to use these, as I do things like this myself. They may be helpful to a newbie who has just received a diagnosis, but truthfully, I've dealt with my issues for so long, I just don't feel I need them.

As far as affordability, biologics are not cheap. The first one I was on, Enbrel, I paid the copay my insurance company dictated; I didn't know about any assistance programs. My doctor never told me. But after that, his nursing staff mentioned it, and I have applied for the assistance through the drug companies that manufacture whichever one I am taking. Most require a few minutes of your time to participate in surveys, but I feel that is a small price to pay for getting a smaller price to pay.

*

J.G. CHAYKO
J.G. was diagnosed with
rheumatoid arthritis in 2010 at age 38

I work part time, a choice I made so I could find a balance that worked for me while managing a full-time disease. There are advantages and disadvantages to this choice. I have more time to take care of myself and the people I love, and can still feel that I am contributing to a working life. The downside to this happy balance is that my salary is decreased and because I am not a full-time employee, I am not eligible for health benefits through work. I am fortunate that I am covered on my partner's work plan as a dependent, so a percentage of my medication cost is returned to me.

It's funny, this perception that Canada has free healthcare. Universal healthcare is another way it has been described, and that's true—every citizen in Canada is entitled to healthcare. But make no mistake, it's not free. We pay for it through our personal and business income taxes and in British Columbia we are billed extra premiums to supplement basic healthcare such as a doctor's appointment, a trip to the hospital, and minor investigations like lab tests and medical imaging. Our government has a program called Pharmacare that covers a portion of certain medications based on our yearly income. We pay out a deductible every year for this privilege. Private health plans can be purchased to cover extra medication costs, and private services such as physiotherapy, massage and occupational therapy.

I could easily find more pleasurable things on which to spend my money, but I can't complain too much—my medical expenses are moderate. My pay fluctuates from week to week based on the hours I work, so I have to pay attention to my budget and make adjustments, but I usually don't find myself struggling. The occasional physio-therapy session, and tools such as braces and finger splints are not beyond my resources. I'm grateful for that. I have modified my lifestyle and sacrificed some superfluous luxuries to make it work, but I don't regret it because I have gained more riches in my life than anything I could ever buy.

*

JUDITH FLANAGAN
Judith was diagnosed with rheumatoid arthritis in 2012 at age 32
and fibromyalgia and polymyalgia rheumatic in 2014 at age 34

I live in Australia. My doctor will mostly bulk bill me and I won't have to pay, but sometimes it can be close to eighty dollars per visit. Medicare usually subsidizes my medications as well as my biologic infusion vials of Actemra. Hospital visits are covered by Medicare on the public system, as I am on disability. I can't imagine what would happen if I couldn't afford care and Medicare wasn't available. I probably wouldn't be here, so for that I am very grateful to have Medicare. I also have an infusion nurse allocated to me through a company called Lifescreen who administers my Actemra once a month via IV.

*

SHELLEY FRITZ
Shelley was diagnosed with
rheumatoid arthritis in 2012 at age 42

Every time I switch medications, I face a battle with my insurance provider. I have had to fight to ensure that I get approval for the medicine my doctor and I believe is the next best step. Fortunately, I have a rheumatologist who fights on my behalf and his persistent staff

192

will continue to appeal until I can get approval. All this takes time and I am often left without adequate treatment for many weeks until the new medicine is approved.

I refer to the month of March as "big money month" because that's about the time I reach my deductible. The medications I take total more than my child's annual college tuition. Once a hefty deductible is met I can worry slightly less about my budget, especially after reaching my out-of-pocket maximum. I have copay assistance for some of my medicines to lessen the cost. Copay assistance cards often have a maximum benefit amount so it is important to research and ask questions.

If I weren't on my husband's insurance through his company, I would be in a heap of trouble with medication costs and doctors. The insurance plan offered through my own employer is limited to network providers, a group that does not include my rheumatologist, primary doctor, or endocrinologist. The biologics I have taken are not covered either under that plan. Therefore, we have opted to pay more to add me to my husband's insurance plan in exchange for access to the doctors and medications I need. Is it affordable? I shudder thinking about what my path would have been and what condition I would be in without the options I have had for doctors and treatment.

My family must prioritize health and education costs over other things like house repairs, entertainment, and travel. Medications, like biologics, are extraordinarily overpriced. It's incredible to think that I am taking these medications out of necessity in order to prevent additional joint and organ damage from my immune system attacking my body, yet I'm imprisoned by the insurance company who holds my fate in their hands. I pray a lot. I pray for more affordable medicines and for a cure.

*

BRENDA KLEINSASSER
Brenda was diagnosed with
rheumatoid arthritis in 1991 at age 31

My biologic is very expensive. I have a high deductible insurance plan where I am employed. My deductible is usually met before the end of January, as I have to come up with the whole amount before I can receive the first box of the biologic. I am already saving for next year. It is a challenge. My monthly insurance premium is higher but with the lower deductible, even though it is high, is much more manageable with my situation. I have a great medical team, and they are cognizant of what I am up against.

I am especially concerned if I were forced to go on disability, or even early retirement, how I would manage to stay on the biologic. It really is something I try not to think about too much, but it is always in the back of my mind. I also have eye and teeth issues as mentioned before, and that gets paid by my health savings account, which is before taxes and is a great help. I also contribute a small amount to help it continue to grow.

*

CHANTELLE MARCIAL
Chantelle was diagnosed with
rheumatoid arthritis in 1999 at age 19

I am fortunate that, for the most part, I have always held private insurance through my employer or that I purchased myself. I use a copay card for my monthly injectable biologic and that's super helpful! I have been prescribed physical therapy but I feel like the copays and time away from work are too much of a financial toll. I wish there was a way you could just get the instructions and then just check in quarterly, but no luck on that—yet!

*

LAYNE MARTIN
Layne was diagnosed with
psoriatic arthritis in 2007 at age 47

My biggest challenge is affording medications. When I retired at age forty-nine, I went on medical disability. With that came Medicare as my primary insurance. Then I went through a divorce and found myself living strictly off the disability. I've had to make some hard choices with regards to medications and treatment options. I can buy groceries and pay rent, but there's not a lot left over each month for medical care.

I had been on Humira for four years when my Medicare coverage kicked in. Suddenly my copay went from twenty dollars to six hundred dollars a month. I could not afford it. When the pharmacist told me the cost, I started to cry right there in the store. I was dumbfounded and angry! I knew my disease was going to progress. I was mad at the pharmaceutical company! How was I going to survive? What was I supposed to do? What do other people do? I had always had access to good healthcare and getting the medications I needed. Suddenly I felt alone. I felt like nobody cared!

That was also a defining moment for me. I became a patient advocate and started writing blogs. I became involved with Grief Diaries, CreakyJoints, and now Real Life Diaries. I now know about patient assistant programs and have taken advantage of the programs on several occasions.

*

KATHLEEN MEKAILEK
Kathleen was diagnosed with chronic regional pain
syndrome in 2005 at age 38, rheumatoid arthritis in
2014 at age 46, and ulcerative colitis in 2016 at age 49

My orthopedic surgeon said it best at my last visit: "Unfortunately you have a nasty, awful disease that is expensive to treat." I have had twelve surgeries in three years. Each year I meet my deductible and out-of-pocket expenses but living on two pensions doesn't leave much room for extras. Unfortunately, my surgeries are often the last to get paid. We have to pay the doctors, because I have to be able to see them. So, we don't eat out, ever. One meal out equals one doctor visit.

We cut coupons, shop sales and only buy the bare necessities. This year, we didn't have a Christmas. Well, we had a little one. I got my husband a new pair of pajama bottoms and he got me a new and bigger heating pad. Our phone rings constantly from the hospital,

MRI center (which just wiped out part of our budget—I had to pay them off because I needed another MRI). When one medication cost more than two hundred dollars even with insurance, you scour the internet to see if the pharmaceutical company has a program or a coupon. You cringe as your husband plans a week's worth of dinners with one ham or chicken, using that one protein for him and your diabetic teenage son, because it's near the end of the month and you have doctor visits coming up.

When your children don't ask for Christmas or birthday presents, and don't expect anything because they hear the conversations about how much everything costs, it forces them to grow up faster than they should. It also helps them take care of you. It makes them hug you and put their heads in your lap because they are afraid of losing you and understand the tough choices that are being made.

I have cancelled and rescheduled doctor visits for when I know we will have money for the copay. I have gone a day or two without at least one of my prescriptions, hoping and praying I won't have a flare and that we will be able to afford the generic soon. I haven't tried a biologic yet, because I am relatively new to being diagnosed and my doctors are trying the "normal" course of treatments first. But each time I go in, my medications get increased, making me wonder how much longer before something else is tried and then wondering how to cover the cost of added treatment.

Fortunately, most of my doctors just expect the copay and some swallow the rest of the bill, while others work out a payment plan with me. I have what I would consider good insurance, a lot better than what others are offered. I often wonder what happens to patients who have no insurance, or the bare minimum. If we are sacrificing this much just to get by, what do they do? What do they go without?

*

RICK PHILLIPS
Rick was diagnosed with type 1 diabetes in 1974
at age 17 and rheumatoid arthritis in 1999 at age 42

I have not faced significant issues. I have excellent insurance at this point (one never knows when that might change) and I work hard to maximize payment on my part. I watch my costs relentlessly and I take every opportunity to save money as I can.

*

LESLIE ROTT
Leslie was diagnosed with lupus and
rheumatoid arthritis in 2008 at age 22

When I first got sick, but was not yet diagnosed, I did not have health insurance. When I started graduate school and realized that something was very wrong, I was lucky to have amazing insurance. I had basic copays for medication, but never had to ask how much a procedure or anything like that would cost. I was very, very lucky. Without insurance, I would not have been able to afford my medication. Since that time, I have had standard student insurance, insurance through the marketplace, Medicaid, and now employer-based health insurance. So my experience has run the gamut. I do worry, now more than ever, about being able to afford my medication, care, and insurance. The only reason I can work and do what I do is because I am faithful about taking my medication and seeing doctors when I need to. It certainly stretches my wallet, and I would love to have the kind of disposable income that some people my age have where I could actually do something fun rather than socking away my extra money for my health.

When I first saw my rheumatologist, he told me I should quit school and move back home with my parents. The fatal flaw of that suggestion was that my parents didn't have health insurance. With talks of healthcare reform, I always wonder about those who are eligible to stay on their parents' insurance, but their parents don't have insurance. For me, it gave a whole new meaning to "stay in school."

Unfortunately, being sick comes with sacrifices, and that means staying in a less than ideal situation because of insurance. While no one should have to do that, it is a reality that I believe many of us face at one time or another on our illness journey. While there were other reasons why quitting school was not an option for me—mainly that it was who I was, it was my whole identity—having insurance versus not having insurance was a pretty big factor in that decision.

*

TIEN SYDNOR-CAMPBELL
Tien was diagnosed with autoimmune
rheumatoid disease in 2010 at age 40

My care has run a bit of a triathlon since my diagnosis over six years ago. I was working full-time and was afforded medical benefits that covered some, but not all, of my care. That first year I ended up spending over twenty percent of my gross pay in copays, deductibles, medications, and transportation. The medical plan I had was really designed for people who rarely get sick, and definitely not for anyone with a chronic condition. Eventually I was no longer able to work due to multiple surgeries, constant pain, and missed work due to illness and doctor appointments. It was at this point that I slipped through a crack of not having insurance when I desperately needed it. Cobra coverage was not an option we could afford. I was ineligible for medical assistance because my husband made more than the minimum each month to qualify. To understand that better, my state did not accept the terms of the Affordable Care Act.

During the time when I received no care for my condition, it affected my health immediately. That was a very scary few months. When I was finally able to enroll in a healthcare plan, it was through medical assistance due to my chronic condition—a partial blessing, because I was able to get all of the care and medications that I needed but due to the strict guidelines for medical assistance, I was unable to work. This was the state of my healthcare for a few years. It was a relief not to worry about medical bills, but it was also worrisome due to my household operating with my income being primary. This disease has affected everything in me and my family's lives.

I will say that Medicaid was absolutely the best in terms of helping me get the help and care I needed. I am now a recipient of Medicare due to being totally and permanently disabled by federal guidelines.

This has been an adjustment because this insurance does not cover every aspect of my care. My specific need is locating the appropriate vision and dental plans, and it has been very interesting and time consuming trying to figure out the best options to cover my needs. My vision has been affected and my dental history lends itself to future problems that can be very expensive to manage. The money I receive as a medical retiree is not so great that affording comprehensive coverage will be possible. I am looking at my options very carefully, but I sure wish Medicare would not need giant books to tell me what's covered, and not have any information about where I can locate what I do need covered.

*

The moment you accept yourself,
you become beautiful.

OSHO

*

CHAPTER THIRTEEN

Toolbox of Alternatives

Being able to walk pain-free is a blessing. Being
able to walk without showing the pain is a skill.
KYLIE MCPHERSON

Many autoimmune patients find traditional therapy isn't enough, and seek alternative and naturopathic remedies to augment medical treatment. Ranging from omega-3, magnets, herbal tinctures and acupuncture to yoga, Reiki, and medicinal marijuana, the list of options is broad. Which alternative treatments have you tried?

*

CHRISTINA AMES
Christina was diagnosed with rheumatoid arthritis
in 1987 at age 20 and fibromyalgia in 2011 at age 43

I have tried a couple of alternative treatments, and my doctor is open to whatever works for his patients. I have compression gloves with copper in them, and while they are comfortable and make my hands feel better, I cannot tell if it is the sensation of tightness that is helping, or the copper dots.

I also tried acupuncture. It was different. It was a very generalized session at a local clinic that had moved into a larger space, so they were offering a free half hour. While it wasn't painful, after about twenty minutes I could feel the needles. It's just me, I know. I can't stand anything like that on me for that long. The owner told me they can customize a program for various diseases, but I haven't been back. If it lasted only a few minutes, I might consider it, but with my predisposition to feel freaked out, I'd have to think about it.

My neighbor is very interested in essential oils, and has had success with them. She gave me some to try for the pain I have on the soles of my feet. I did not have relief, nor did my husband when he tried a blend for his sinus issues.

I would probably try different treatments, if there was one that appealed to me; I'm not anti-alternative medicine. I've just had more luck with Western medicine, and I hesitate to upset the balance I have.

*

J.G. CHAYKO
J.G. was diagnosed with
rheumatoid arthritis in 2010 at age 38

I was the all-natural girl in my youth. I avoided aluminum in my deodorants, used only baking soda based cleaning products, and relieved minor ailments with aromatherapy, hot baths, massage and soothing lavender wraps. This all changed with the onset of RA.

Nothing in my aromatic collection was strong enough to control the inflammation in my body or prevent damage. I didn't know enough about natural alternatives and so I trusted my rheumatologist to guide me, and to date he hasn't steered me wrong. That's not to say I wouldn't be open to trying a few things.

I recently acquired a Himalayan salt lamp. I had always been intrigued by them, although I can't really define the reason. I find them soothing—there's nothing quite like a soft warm glow illuminating the room, accompanied perhaps by some smooth jazz and perhaps a splash of brandy, to calm the mood. Do I really believe in all of the extraordinary benefits the salt lamp is supposed to provide? Cleanse the air? Reduce allergy symptoms? Increase energy? Improve mood? I'm not sure. It makes sense that my mood can be altered by its soft radiance, but that's really all I can say about it—so far no miracle cure for my arthritis.

One brilliant weekend in the middle of winter we traveled up to a resort not far from our home to spend a couple of luxurious days in a little lakefront town nestled in the mountains called Harrison Hot Springs. We went to indulge in the natural hot springs that have been bubbling there for hundreds of years. The natives used to call them Warum Chuck and believed the springs had magical abilities to cure many ailments, including rheumatism.

It was an enchanting weekend. We lounged in three alluring pools beneath clear frosty skies, intoxicated by the slight scent of sulfur in the steam that curled its way skyward. Every swollen joint was lulled into a winter's nap. I indulge in hot baths in my own home throughout the week, but this experience was unique. It was Mother Nature in all her restorative glory stripping away the discomfort of arthritis. It was like dipping my body in a hot paraffin dip, the sulfurous heat coated inflamed joints and dulled the relentless throb. I emerged feeling years younger, reveling in the tingling of a renewed energy flowing through my body. It is an experience I intend to repeat. It's a temporary fix, certainly, but for those few precious days I was restored to the body I knew before the arrival of RA.

I treat myself to a hot stone massage when finances allow. There's no feeling quite like the soothing heat of warm stones penetrating my muscles, while a masseuse rubs my tender joints with lavender and peppermint oil. I recommend them as often as financially possible— and don't forget to take time to relax in the lounge beside a waterfall cascading over a wall of stonework with a glass of champagne in hand.

I tried acupuncture once years before the onset of RA. It was part of my treatment after being hit by a car. My physiotherapist was having a hard time getting my muscles in my right hip and backside to release, so he thought perhaps a round of acupuncture might be helpful. I can't say I was thrilled with the suggestion—the idea of my body getting poked with a multitude of needles was not appealing— but I went along with it. For six sessions I lay on the table feeling like a pincushion from someone's sewing room and in the end there was no improvement. I have not tried it again.

I've had many suggestions over the years on natural remedies. I'm sure they hold great benefit for many people, but the trouble is that most medical doctors don't usually have a lot of knowledge on herbal medications. There's always the risk that some conventional medication will have an adverse reaction to natural treatments. I'm always open to new ways to relieve the symptoms of RA. I may not always agree with them or try them, but I'm always willing to listen to how they work (or not) with the people who use them. In the end, it's always about finding the best route to a life of wellness.

*

JUDITH FLANAGAN
Judith was diagnosed with rheumatoid arthritis in 2012 at age 32
and fibromyalgia and polymyalgia rheumatic in 2014 at age 34

I take omega-3 and other herbal and natural tablets. I would like to try acupuncture and other treatments as well. I believe a mixture of both can be beneficial. The only thing that has stopped me is price, but I will try them when I have the money. I am very interested in trying hot rocks for my spinal pain, shoulder pain, neck pain and migraines.

*

SHELLEY FRITZ
Shelley was diagnosed with
rheumatoid arthritis in 2012 at age 42

When I was diagnosed, I searched through online blogs, books, and research for information to guide me in how to best treat my rheumatoid arthritis symptoms. I hoped that the slew of medicines I took would adequately curb my symptoms, but over time I realized I needed to look into alternative treatments. Therapeutic heating pads help ease pain in sore joints and tendons. Paraffin wax soothes my aching hands and even feet via microwavable wax-filled booties. I have tried copper gloves and magnetic jewelry, to no avail.

A few girlfriends suggested we take a Tai Chi class together since the art has been helpful for others in relaxation, building strength, concentration, and balance. The class was a bit out of reach for me but not for the reasons I suspected. I thought it might be too physically rigorous but the real struggle was remembering all of the similar, but slightly different, moves in the sequence. Rather than continue with live classes, I purchased a Tai Chi DVD for rheumatoid arthritis patients that I can view at home. I also utilize an online yoga routine designed for people with arthritis. The stretching involved in yoga is relaxing and beneficial in soothing muscle and joint pain. Monthly massages were helpful for a few months until my nerve pain returned and prevented more massages.

Although I was skeptical of magic lotions and supplements that advertise that they cure arthritis, I have tried many of them out of sheer desperation. Sometimes I get very temporary relief from these, but they certainly are not a cure and neither my disease activity or pain level have decreased from using them. I am interested in using acupuncture as I have heard it can be helpful to many people with rheumatoid arthritis. It is not covered by my insurance so should I find it to be effective, I am not sure if I will be able to continue with the acupuncture sessions if I am paying out-of-pocket.

*

BRENDA KLEINSASSER
Brenda was diagnosed with
rheumatoid arthritis in 1991 at age 31

I take several kinds of supplements, all with my primary care physician's blessing. I never try anything without consulting him first. Just because it's natural doesn't mean it doesn't interfere with other medications. I take shark cartilage to boost my immune system. My other supplements include vitamin B12, biotin, calcium with vitamin D, and a multivitamin to ensure I am getting everything I need. The biotin helps with skin, nails, and even my hair, and I've been able to grow it out and get a new hairstyle. That is huge for me.

I was taking ginger root for nausea issues but had to cut back because it started causing heartburn. It also works like a blood thinner, which I don't need. I did some physical therapy for a short time but found that doing the exercises at home worked just as well. When you live with a chronic illness, you are not left with a lot of funds at times. You save where you can. My biologic has helped a great deal, but as mentioned before, is extremely costly.

*

CHANTELLE MARCIAL
Chantelle was diagnosed with
rheumatoid arthritis in 1999 at age 19

I had a gastric bypass so I have been on vitamins ever since daily. I try to add things like turmeric to my diet but haven't had any marked improvement because of any supplement I've tried in the past. Same for trying alternative diets. I felt good overall but they had no impact on my rheumatoid arthritis. A lot of the other things like massage, reiki, acupuncture, are out of my budget for regular treatment.

*

LAYNE MARTIN
Layne was diagnosed with
psoriatic arthritis in 2007 at age 47

I've tried several different types of alternative medicines. I was very fortunate in that my first rheumatologist had a naturopathic doctor working with his practice. I was introduced to alternative medicine soon after being diagnosed with psoriatic arthritis. I have probably tried everything out there but the only ones I've stayed with and find that work best for me are acupuncture, chiropractor, TENS unit, and eating a clean diet. The acupuncture has really helped with my stress and anxiety levels. And, it has helped to calm down some of the smaller joints. It is not something that works overnight and my insurance doesn't pay for it so I have pay out-of-pocket. I go twice a month and find it very helpful. It's been worth the investment for me. I also find that the chiropractor has been very beneficial. Because I have two old compression fractures in my back due to osteoporosis, they don't do the traditional manipulations on me. My chiropractor uses a handheld device called an Activator. It works great! I'm typically a little sore after and have to go home and ice but by the next day my pain is relived significantly.

I bought a TENS unit at the recommendation of my chiropractor a few years ago. That is the single most valuable piece of equipment I own even those it only cost about twenty-five dollars. I use it daily on my lower back but it can be used on any joint or muscle that is causing pain. I love it and take it with me when I travel.

I also try to eat a clean diet. I rarely eat processed or fast foods. If I am traveling or it's a special occasion I try to make the best choices I can. If I know I'm going out to a restaurant than I look up the menu ahead of time and try to find things that are lowest in sodium, not fried, and don't contain things in the nightshade family.

I've tried taking different supplements like turmeric, ginger, and eating tart cherries. I can't say that I've found any benefit in any of these and most of them caused me such bad heartburn that I had to stop. I do take a daily multiple vitamin and vitamin D daily. I was taking fish oil but had to stop it for an upcoming hip revision surgery, it can promote blood thinning and increase bleeding during surgery.

That takes me to one of my many soapboxes! Do your research before jumping on the latest craze wagon! Some of these supplements have great benefits but they also can have some side effects and may not mix well with your current medications. Always do your research!

*

KATHLEEN MEKAILEK
Kathleen was diagnosed with chronic regional pain
syndrome in 2005 at age 38, rheumatoid arthritis in
2014 at age 46, and ulcerative colitis in 2016 at age 49

Because I also have chronic regional pain syndrome along with rheumatoid arthritis, most alternative procedures would do more harm to me. Massages, acupuncture would most likely cause flares to my CRPS which in turn could cause a rheumatoid flare. My body is extremely sensitive to touch, so people, even my family, have learned to side hug me from the left or let me lead. Sometimes it's not a hug at all, just arms outstretched in the air without touching. I do take multivitamins, calcium with vitamin D, zinc, vitamin C, iron because of anemia from microbleeds due to ulcerative colitis, and B12 to help with symptoms and ensure I get essential nutrients.

I've also switched to a diet free from gluten, sugar, soy, and dairy. I do not drink alcohol or consume any red meats, greasy or fried foods, or anything high in fat. It is actually easier to list the foods that I can have rather than what I can't. This is mostly due to ulcerative colitis, but seems to have helped my RA and CRPS at the same time.

We have an organic garden and greenhouse where we grow fruit and vegetables year round. What we can't grow and preserve by canning or freezing, we try to buy organic. It was a really easy switch for me because I had been so sick with ulcerative colitis that I had basically been on a liquid diet for two and a half months before getting it under control. I use a lot of tumeric, ginger and cinnamon in my cooking. They are supposed to be good for inflammation and for ulcerative colitis. I don't know if they are helping or not, but considering they are the only seasonings my body can tolerate, I will use them regardless.

The body is truly amazing if you listen to it. I can tell by the smell whether something has a trigger in it that will set me off. The more spices or sugar something has in it, the more offensive it is. Most people talk about withdrawals from caffeine, alcohol or sugar; I experienced none of that. It was like a relief for my body, and its way of saying thanks. It also lets me know when I try a new food that doesn't agree with me—if the smell doesn't get me, it feels like a bunch of little nails in my stomach. I can then feel it making its way through my intestines, and then get out of my way, because it's a race to the restroom! I have learned to carry a change of underwear and wipes in my purse. At first I felt self conscious about it, but now it is just another part of my life that I've grown to accept.

I also use a TENS unit on my sore muscles and joints, and that gives some relief. A wax paraffin dip does wonders for swollen, aching hands and feet, plus it forces me to just sit and relax for thirty minutes which helps to control stress.

Overall, the one alternative treatment that has helped the most is learning biofeedback techniques. By being able to visualize my body relaxing, I can actually feel my muscles softening and the stress leaving my body. I will always be grateful that my chronic pain management specialist had this option available and that my insurance covered it.

*

RICK PHILLIPS
Rick was diagnosed with type 1 diabetes in 1974
at age 17 and rheumatoid arthritis in 1999 at age 42

I've never tried such treatments, but I might try acupuncture. I have seen many people discuss how much it has done for them and while I am not confident it works, I would try it. So what is stopping me? Cost and access. While there are some acupuncture clinics in my area, they are mostly associated with chiropractic offices which do not specialize in the practice. But even if I found someone whom I could trust, I then have to figure out how to pay for it. My health insurance does not pay for the service and I cannot justify purchase of the service with so little promise that it would offer benefit.

*

LESLIE ROTT
Leslie was diagnosed with lupus and
rheumatoid arthritis in 2008 at age 22

I haven't really tried any alternative remedies. I have been heavily reliant on modern medicine. And for the most part, it has worked for me. My body is very sensitive, so I get worried about trying things that are considered alternative. I'll admit that it is a personal bias and not necessarily a correct one. Maybe one day I will open myself up to trying different things. And If I don't, maybe one day I will regret that I didn't. But it is a personal choice.

*

TIEN SYDNOR-CAMPBELL
Tien was diagnosed with autoimmune
rheumatoid disease in 2010 at age 40

I manage my pain from the perspective of over twenty-five years of experience as a medical massage therapist and educator, and over six years as a body-centered psychotherapist with a specialty in chronic pain and posttraumatic stress.

I was introduced to holistic medical care in the very beginning of my journey, and was very familiar with different options to care for chronic pain. My experience is likely different than others because I was an expert on options for self-care. I have found this to be the most frustrating aspect of my self-care and ability to prevent flares from occurring.

I am a Reiki Master and still do the work on myself, in addition to my healing community sending me positive, healing energy. I was able to receive acupuncture because ten sessions were gifted to me and that was an awesome experience. I was only able to have those sessions and unable to continue due to not having the funds to pay for it. Even community acupuncture was more than my household could afford. The out-of-pocket costs for herbal or supplemental support are also too high for a family with limited income.

If there was truly a disease that has to be attended to on several fronts, it's RA. It affects and assaults so many aspects of the body, mind, and spirit that even doctors don't recommend relying on traditional medical attention alone. At a minimum, attention to diet, managing stress, obtaining and maintaining supportive environments are all essential. If I could have it my way, I would see an acupuncturist, naturopath, and chiropractor in addition to my rheumatologist, pain doc, psychiatrist, therapist, and pharmacist. It would be even more awesome if all of them worked together like they do in many cancer centers who see the benefits of holistic care.

True compassion means not only feeling another's
pain but also being moved to help relieve it.

DANIEL GOLEMAN

*

CHAPTER FOURTEEN

The Pain Brain

It's not just pain. It's a complete physical, mental, and emotional assault on your body. -JAMIE WINGO

The pain-brain connection is an established and widely accepted theory that chronic pain signals can make us more susceptible to mental struggles. Further, the brain may not be able to attend to other tasks efficiently because it's preoccupied with pain signals. What mental struggles do you experience as a result of your disease?

*

CHRISTINA AMES
Christina was diagnosed with rheumatoid arthritis in 1987 at age 20 and diagnosed with fibromyalgia in 2011 at age 43

Like most people, I have experienced many of these mental struggles from time to time, such as depression and feeling hopeless. In having a chronic disease such as RA, however, these feelings can be devastating. During periods of flaring, depression and hopelessness are quite common. I especially had these feelings when I was going through my Big Flare. I went from feeling fairly well to being an invalid within only a few months, and since my symptoms were so different from what I'd experienced previously, I was frightened. What was this new monster coming to attack me? Was it something new, and even more dangerous? Then came frustration. Why couldn't anyone say what was wrong? Why couldn't I find a rheumatologist who would actually take me seriously?

I remember when I finally met with my current rheumatologist. When I explained my history and how I was so worried about these latest problems, he listened to me. After I was all talked out, he gently patted my hand and said, "We'll get this figured out." It was such a feeling of overwhelming reassurance. Even though I'd had this disease for so long and was dealing with something new and scary, here was another person who had my back.

I will say that I'm thankful these feelings do not dominate my life. I have them, acknowledge them, deal with them, and can move forward. I think that having a good support system helps more than anything else, at least for me. When I had the Big Flare, I had family and friends helping out constantly. My parents and neighbors brought food, my family kept up with the housekeeping, and my husband was an endless source of help and comfort, taking me to my many appointments. I'm very lucky.

While I do have an upbeat, hopeful personality, I do find that sometimes, having some time to process and recognize these feelings can help immensely. I take time to cry. Tears can be incredibly cathartic, literally washing away pain and sadness, and allowing you to move forward. General feelings of malaise and depression come and go, and I manage those as quickly as possible. I try to address them by doing something productive. For example, when I feel like I can't do something, I focus on all the activities I am still able to do,and I find that that helps me feel fulfilled.

*

J.G. CHAYKO
J.G. was diagnosed with
rheumatoid arthritis in 2010 at age 38

It was a shock for me to learn I had rheumatoid arthritis. How was that possible? I was a healthy and fit female in her thirties. The routine of my life was well established. I woke at the crack of dawn, exercised, had my morning coffee, and went off to work. In the evenings, I would attend dance classes, rehearsals and social gatherings. I was laying the foundation for the work that was the core of my existence and I was speeding along at high velocity.

When rheumatoid arthritis zipped in, the momentum of my life stalled. All the goals I had been racing toward became lost in the shadows of chronic illness. My world had been altered. I was unable to continue dancing, and rheumatoid arthritis stole the stamina I needed for hours of rehearsal and performance. Frustration replaced my drive and inspiration. I found myself irritated and cross with the slower pace of my life. I could no longer go from zero to sixty in thirty seconds. Instead, I went from sixty to zero. I felt empty and unfulfilled. I had been on what I thought was an unstoppable course, and now I was facing a deadend. I can't say my self-esteem suffered much. I had spent most my life toiling in an industry that cultivated low self-esteem—rejection is normal in a life with the arts. I developed a thick skin early on in order to survive in the competitive environment. My moments of self-esteem were fleeting, based on minor criticisms we all have about ourselves. It wasn't in my nature to wallow in melancholy over an unpublished story or a lost role. It was part of the life I had chosen. I just moved on to the next thing. I didn't let those setbacks stop me, and I wasn't about to let rheumatoid arthritis take a swipe at my self-confidence.

I learned a lesson in measured perseverance with RA. I took a step back while I tried to figure out a way to manage my disease and still nourish that creative desire in my soul. A hole had been ripped into my life, and I found myself standing on the edge of a growing chasm. I was determined to close the gap and find a way to the other side. Rheumatoid arthritis was destined to be permanent, so I had to look at it from a new perspective.

I embraced the new limitations of my world. I cut back on work and theatre commitments, and left the world of dance. I learned everything I could about my disease. I participated in research projects, physiotherapy and occupational therapy classes. I learned how to cope by focusing on the positive aspects of my life: my friends, my family, my unique talents, and all the little things that brought me pleasure. I gave myself permission to take time out for myself and not feel guilty. I could still live a rewarding life. I sought out new ways to stay active and enjoy activities to which I had grown accustomed.

Instead of aiming for long-term goals, I focused on day to day. Completing daily goals within my reach allowed me to gain control and gave me a sense of accomplishment. I recognized my new limitations, but I refused to be bound by them. Every few weeks, I took a few more steps beyond the new boundary of my life. I composed a new script to bring me back into the life I knew, even if it was on a smaller scale.

*

JUDITH FLANAGAN
Judith was diagnosed with rheumatoid arthritis in 2012 at age 32
and fibromyalgia and polymyalgia rheumatic in 2014 at age 34

Since 2012, and hearing news of the conditions I live with, I have often felt that I have let my nieces down because I'm unable to do what I once could. Before my diagnosis I could pick them up and run around with them, play on the floor, and many other things but had to give those things up after my diagnosis due to symptoms.

I cope by trying to realize this isn't my fault, and my nieces will understand as long as I can do somethings with them and compromise certain activities by doing them in different ways.

*

SHELLEY FRITZ
Shelley was diagnosed with
rheumatoid arthritis in 2012 at age 42

At least a few times a month I think I can't do this anymore. I reach a breaking point from unremitting pain, so I vent to my husband or have an ugly cry in the car. Sometimes I cry quietly in bed, praying this disease will go into remission so I can lead a normal life.

Day after day of unalleviated misery eats away at me. If I am in so much pain, how much destruction is the chronic inflammation causing my body? How long will it be before I can no longer use my hands or legs, or develop a serious lung or heart problem? How long will I be able to continue working? It's really fear of failure from this disease taking over. I don't like having to rely on others to open bottles and doors for me, or button my pants or zip my dress. When I get in the car and my wrists and hands are throbbing while I struggle to press my foot on the gas pedal without sheer agony, sometimes the outcome is sobbing from hopelessness. Since I work full-time, I can only take mild pain medication and only when absolutely necessary.

The steroids I often need cause me to gain weight, so it can be challenging to stay positive and have self-confidence when my clothes no longer fit right. Some days I am not comfortable in my own skin. Continuously being exhausted and achy takes a toll. I started taking an antidepressant after my mother died in the fall of 2016. With both parents lost to cancer and my body not responding to medicine to fight this disease, the antidepressant was needed.

222

Consider being late for work and jumping out of bed to take a quick shower, then throwing on clothes and heading out the door. This is not a reality in my world. I wake up an hour earlier than I used to when I didn't have rheumatoid arthritis. I wake up earlier so that I can take a pain pill and start a bizarre routine of stretching arms, ankles and feet just so I can get out of the bed and into the shower. My ridiculously unforgiving body does not care that I need to go to the bathroom, and I physically can't get up and walk without stretching. Getting ready takes twice as long as it used to, and is just exhausting. After a shower, I just want to fall back onto the bed and sleep. Self-affirming pep talks are what drive me to keep moving until I can get out the door, and get my child to school and myself to work. Every day is like that to some degree. Incessant pain and slow mobility lead to feelings of hopelessness.

*

BRENDA KLEINSASSER
Brenda was diagnosed with
rheumatoid arthritis in 1991 at age 31

I have definitely dealt with feelings of hopelessness. I did go to a counselor about four years after my diagnosis. She was very helpful and told me that I would not have to go long. I did the work and learned to write about my feelings, which helped a great deal. I got away from doing that but six months after the craniotomy I picked it up again and have done it every day since. It really does help, and I can go back to see how far I've come on the journey.

I also deal with low self-esteem at times. Things have never come easy for me. I always had to study harder than others. I am in a daily battle, and it can become discouraging at times. I know I am not alone, as I have a great community to lean on. Sometimes you need to be able to vent, and if crying alone helps to get it out, I see nothing wrong with that. I did a lot of crying in the beginning. I had no idea how this was going to play out and I was only thirty-one at the time. How was I going to continue working or even be able to accomplish day-to-day tasks? I feel that we need to be more open about feelings of depression. It is nothing to be ashamed of, and is more common that we realize. I've found that having a small circle of friends is much easier so you don't have to continue to rehash all the bad stuff with everybody you come in contact with. I simply do not possess the energy to do so.

I believe having a sense of humor is paramount to getting through times of hopelessness. You know the saying, "It's always darkest before dawn." I also find that walking while listening to soothing music helps to keep me calm and centered. It keeps me moving, and helps to unclutter my mind from all the things that can hold it hostage.

*

CHANTELLE MARCIAL
Chantelle was diagnosed with
rheumatoid arthritis in 1999 at age 19

Guess I'm goning to disappoint here, but none. I'm pretty level headed. Sure, after spending an hour on the phone with an insurer, I am peeved, but that's normal. I know a lot of folks deal with depression as a result of their chronic condition, but for me it's just never been an issue. I watched my mom and all but a couple of my very large family deal with RA, fibro, lupus, etc and I learned a lot. Some deal with depression and it's tough to watch. But I try to be an ear to listen and a hand to hold.

*

LAYNE MARTIN
Layne was diagnosed with
psoriatic arthritis in 2007 at age 47

The mental struggles fluctuate from day to day. In the beginning, when I was first diagnosed, I was in denial for a really long time so I pretty much ignored the fact that I had a chronic illness. I would shrug off my aches and pains and attribute them to my job or spending too much time outside doing yardwork. The biggest struggle came when I realized that I could no longer do my job. I had been a nurse for thirty years and absolutely loved my career! I felt like my whole sense of self and identity was being stripped from me. I struggled when people asked me what I did. What was I supposed to tell them? I was humiliated that I was only forty-nine and on medical disability. It was very degrading for me, and I felt ashamed that I no longer worked. I felt like I was no longer a productive member of society.

A neighbor one day asked me if I'd be interested in volunteering at our local thrift shop. It was an easy job of sorting through donated items and visiting with the customers. At various times I also helped out at the foodbank. I felt like I was contributing to society again and I was helping others. I started to feel my sense of self-worth returning.

Then, about three years after my retirement the unconceivable happened and my twenty-nine-year marriage dissolved. That sent me into a spiral. The shock of betrayal was excruciating and naturally I felt that, in some way, it was my fault because of my disease. I literally shut myself off from society for nearly two years. I did not engage in any social engagements and rarely left my apartment other than to go to the grocery store or to my daughter's house. The emotional pain was so great that I actually thought I was going to die. The grief was unbearable at times, I put up a pretty good facade during the day but by evening it consumed me.

With the stress of the divorce, the loss of my home and leaving my community (I moved to another state to be closer to my daughter), my arthritis flared. With increased joint swelling, stiffness and pain came more sorrow and hopelessness. Vodka became my solace. It all became a vicious unhealthy cycle.

Finally, I decided that I was going to die if I didn't take control of my life. My lifestyle was very unhealthy, my emotional and mental health was in havoc, and life was not very enjoyable. So, that was it, I made up my mind! I enjoyed a last few drinks of vodka and dumped the rest down the drain, crying as I did. The next day I started to eat healthy, mostly meats, vegetables and fruits, and I cut out all processed foods and anything artificial. The first week I was miserable as I detoxed my body. After a couple of weeks I was able to start an exercise program of walking. Within five months I had dropped seventy-five pounds and felt the best I had in years!

Eventually, I decided to interact with people again but I didn't really know how to start. I didn't have any friends because I had totally secluded myself for two long years. I had never attended church but a friend of my daughters invited us to go one Sunday. It took a lot of courage and I tried to back out at the last minute but, I also knew I needed to go for my mental health. It was by far the best decision I've ever made! The people were so nice and welcoming. I soon became involved and joined a community group, then a bible study group and I now volunteer my time to serve coffee from time to time.

As I write this, I am now facing a total hip revision surgery in a few weeks. I have friends now that I can rely on, they check in with me several times a week to see how I am doing. They pray over me and bring me meals when they know I'm not able to prepare a meal. I feel very blessed and glad that I can share my story to offer hope.

*

KATHLEEN MEKAILEK
Kathleen was diagnosed with chronic regional pain
syndrome in 2005 at age 38, rheumatoid arthritis in
2014 at age 46, and ulcerative colitis in 2016 at age 49

There are two mental struggles that I have with my experience living with RA. The first is guilt. I wonder if my children or grand-children will develop it since mine has been traced to a genetic connection on my paternal side. If my babies develop this nasty disease in the future, I will bear the burden knowing that I passed it to them. That their suffering comes from me and that there is nothing I can do to prevent it. I hope everyday that this genetic curse ends with me.

So far, none of my cousins or their children have shown any signs and my brother has no sign, so maybe that means I am the lucky one to get the gene. If it stayed with me and didn't get passed, it ends with me. This is what gives me hope.

I also feel guilty because I often wonder if I didn't doom my youngest son, Jonathon to a life with type 1 diabetes. There is no genetic connection to diabetes on either side of his family (me, his mother, or his father). However, when he was born he had autoimmune thrombocytopenia purpua. After everything else was tried to restore his platelets, he was given a transfusion from me. It makes me wonder if my genetic factor for rheumatoid arthritis is somehow responsible for his development of juvenile diabetes. What does that mean for his future and developing RA? Sometimes this guilt is overpowering, and I pray that if I have to die young from the aggressive progression of this disease, that it please ends with me. I will take all the pain, shots, medications, surgeries, organ removals without complaining if it means saving my children and future generations from suffering and feeling what I feel.

I also feel guilty for putting my husband through this with me. I keep telling him that I will understand if he leaves because it is so much to handle and he has put so much on himself to help and take care of me. We do have discussions that he retire early when he has the opportunity so we can travel and do things together. We had one good year, then it all started. Because of my constant pain, I sleep on the couch and he sleeps in our bed. I have tried sleeping with him, but he is afraid to move. When he falls asleep, he instinctively puts his arm around me which usually causes me to wake up and have to leave. Or, I will move and wake myself up with a cry, which wakes him.

We have not had sex in over a year because he is afraid of hurting me. We were the couple who had the swing from the chandelier, get naked in the backyard, healthy type of sex life. Going from at least four times a week to gradually none has had an impact on me, and I know it has to affect him. I told him I would give him a free pass if he ever wanted to use it. I will ask if he wants to try and he will refuse because he has learned to read me and knows that I hurt and would just be doing it for him. Until we can both enjoy it, sex will be nonexistent in our relationship. That is also how I know that he loves me mentally, emotionally and spiritually, not just physically. I have to tell him when it is okay to hug, and I have to lead it and tell him where to place his hands and arms. This is definitely not what he signed up for when he said, "I do." He married a vibrant, outgoing, energetic, stay-up-and-party-all-night girl who, seeemingly in the blink of an eye, turn into a fatigued, hurting, smiling on the outside, partial person of myself.

The second mental status that I really struggle with is anger. Why me? Why so aggressive? Why do I have to have so many surgeries, so many complications, and why can't any doctors give me any real answers? Why do doctors look at me with pity and say, "Sorry, there is nothing we can do except help you control your pain."

"You have a nasty, expensive disease that I would not wish on anyone." Seriously! Doctors have said this!

I'm also angry with my parents from hiding the truth about my family's genetic background. For over a year, I asked and asked if anyone had rheumatoid arthritis or any genetic autoimmune diseases, and was repeatedly told no. It wasn't until I contacted a cousin who is a doctor and had copies of my paternal medical records who was able to confirm the diagnosis of late onset rheumatoid arthritis in both my grandfather and a great aunt. Facing my parents with this knowledge, and asking why they didn't tell me, was just met with them responding with ignorance that they didn't know. Later, my father gave me a copy of the paternal medical records, and there it was in black and white. How do you get past that feeling of anger and betrayal by your own parents? That knowledge could have gotten me on medication sooner, possibly saved me from a few surgeries, or had the surgeries sooner before there was so much damage done.

I don't feel hopeless. There is always hope. A remedy might not come for me, but I hope it is not needed in the future. I set goals six months at a time and strive for those goals every day. It might be an art show, my son's high school graduation, my daughter's college graduation, a vacation that Chuck and I have long been wanting to go on, but six months. I can see six months. If I survive six months, I can survive six more, then six more and six more.

*

RICK PHILLIPS
Rick was diagnosed with type 1 diabetes in 1974
at age 17 and rheumatoid arthritis in 1999 at age 42

I have suffered from depression for many years and rheumatoid arthritis has not helped the condition. I continue talk therapy and use medications to improve my situation. I have come to accept depression just as I have had to accept rheumatoid arthritis and diabetes. It is simply a part of me.

I choose to view my depression as a blessing. I know that sounds ridiculous but years ago my pain would have been so awful that I could have thought of nothing else. The beautiful thing about living in 2017, is that my rheumatoid arthritis is controlled enough to allow focus on other issues. I know the difficulties of depression and I can testify how severe uncontrolled depression can become. But I also know that I can only worry about depression as a result of my rheumatoid arthritis being in control. It is the same with diabetes. Years ago I would not have lived long enough to have seen my diagnosis of RA. So for me these are borrowed years and as such I cherish the opportunity I have to live each day and I face depression and rheumatoid arthritis head on with the tools available to me.

*

LESLIE ROTT
Leslie was diagnosed with lupus and
rheumatoid arthritis in 2008 at age 22

When I first got sick, and no one knew what was wrong with me, I had a lot of anxiety. I was in a lot of pain, and was afraid that if I went to sleep, I would not wake up. Needless to say, I had a lot of sleeping issues, which did not help my physical or emotional well-being. Along with anxiety, I did have some issues with depression and low self-esteem, but the longer I have lived with these illnesses, the better those issues seem to get, although they can be a struggle, at times. I was on medication for anxiety and depression for a while, and that did seem to help. I also have tried to make more time for relaxation and self-care, and that helps, as well.

*

TIEN SYDNOR-CAMPBELL
Tien was diagnosed with autoimmune
rheumatoid disease in 2010 at age 40

This questions brings so many thoughts and emotions that I feel like I'll only cover what I've experienced if I ask my therapist(s) and psychiatrist to write a summary. I am still struggling with the loss of my bodily functions and, quite frankly, feel like this mourning period has taken a really long time to get through. Somewhere in this work I may have mentioned completing a sprint triathlon a few months before I got the diagnosis at age forty. I have been physically active most of my life—working out, walking outdoors, skiing, swimming, softball and occasionally rollerskating and ice skating. I practiced yoga somewhat regularly for several years, and liked to take care of my health and body.

I wasn't obsessed, and really understand that pain isn't something to simply overcome when there is an actual issue. I was familiar with setbacks because my knees had given me problems my entire life. It is the fact that I took pride in taking care of my body that this disease has left me feeling terrible about not having control of function, pain, and especially deformities. It is more than depressing—it's completely devastating. When pain takes over the control for immediate attention, it's like having an internal toddler who cries and cries, falls out in tantrums, but can't say what hurts.

The worst part of the mental aspects of this disease is feeling like life is not worth living. Some days it looks like actively considering what it would be like if you could actually die from constant pain. Some days it's not having enough confidence in your ability to get in and out of the shower without slipping and cracking your skull. Sometimes it's seeing yourself dead at the bottom of the stairs. Some days it feels like you don't have enough motor control or strength while driving to prevent a car accident, because your strength disappears. It is the days when you can't hold a fork in either hand to eat dinner, that you feel hopeless and helpless. I have not given in to desperation or hunger and asked my loved ones to feed me, I simply wait it out and have eaten many cold dinners as a result. The thoughts of death and dying can become somewhat obsessive when you lose control of what you previously could.

I would not have been able to handle many of these mental health issues without prior, professional knowledge and experience. Taking advantage of my knowledge, I secured a psychiatrist and therapist. This was so that we could work, as a team, to help me get into a safe state-of-mind. Knowing that therapy requires a partnership, I try really hard to be honest about my thoughts and feelings. This way, I'm not the only one who knows how I'm feeling. I think this is one issue that everyone with a chronic disease experiences. Not knowing who to talk to, feeling afraid of sharing these very dark thoughts, and not knowing what to do with all of the mental and emotional aspects of depression. Especially because it's related to a medical condition.

The depression was the worst when my family was, financially, in dire straits. I felt incredibly insecure, worthless, and had more than one day of suicidal thoughts. I kept myself in check by talking about it with my family, friends and therapist when I was having these thoughts. It was the most vulnerable time I have ever felt in my life. I know it scared others as much as it scared me but I used every single resource I could to make it through, because the alternative was not going to be better for me or my family and friends. Keeping a sliver of hope alive inside is your light. It never goes out. I happen to think that we just have a tendency to let everything around distract us from seeing that. Without that little bit of light, you wouldn't be able to see all of the distractions. It's there, you just have to look for it and don't let it out of your sight. Most of all, you cannot get help if you don't ask for it. Asking for help, for some, is the worst aspect of rheumatoid arthritis. I have learned, through the many instances of random assistance, that people honestly want to help in any way that they are able. We just have to trust.

*

CHAPTER FIFTEEN

Socialization or Isolation

The worst thing you can do to a person with an invisible illness is make them feel like they need to prove how sick they are. -ANONYMOUS

Living with chronic pain and mobility struggles means changes to everyday lives and routines including socializing. But when pain and stiffness keep us from participating, some find alternative activities to enjoy while others prefer quiet solitude. What impact has your disease had on socialization and isolation?

*

CHRISTINA AMES
Christina was diagnosed with rheumatoid arthritis
in 1987 at age 20 and fibromyalgia in 2011 at age 43

When I was a child, I was extremely shy. It's difficult being different, and constantly having to explain yourself to new people. I'm naturally an introvert, and prefer to have a few good friends, rather than dozens of acquaintances. When I left home to attend college, I didn't know anyone. I sat in my single room, and decided that I wanted to change my attitude; I'd try to actively get to know people. It worked for me, and the friends I made in college are still friends to this day.

I also met some wonderful friends through my kids' activities. Most of them got a major dose of what I deal with when I had the Big Flare; most were unaware that I even had the disease. I felt bad at one point since I had to drop several of the activities that I enjoyed, but at the same time, I gained friends who understood.

Social media is also a blessing. I have made several friends whom I doubt I'll ever meet, but who understand what I go through and are there any time, day or night. I can understand them and their problems as well, and try to offer support.

*

J.G. CHAYKO
J.G. was diagnosed with
rheumatoid arthritis in 2010 at age 38

I can understand how chronic illness can create a sense of isolation. It can be difficult to connect to friends and family when you've been tossed into stormy seas with a dingy, and they're still cruising along in a yacht. It's difficult for them to understand why you don't want to go out, or why you keep cancelling, because most people with chronic illness don't always look sick. I tried to keep up with the previous pace of my life, but I found it exhausting always playing the role of wellness when I was consumed with inflammation and pain.

It took some time, but I learned to say no. I don't feel guilty or upset when I refuse an invitation; I make that decision because it is the best option for me at the time. I trust that my friends and family will extend another invite in the future. I make an effort not to segregate myself from life. I stay present, I stay in touch, and I take an active interest in their lives to keep them involved in mine. I simply won't let them forget about me. If I miss a few invitations here and there, I'm confident there'll be other opportunities in the future.

Part of my support system is a dependable, stable partner. He's always there for me, through the good, bad and ugly. He doesn't treat me like a person with chronic illness. He believes I can do anything I put my mind to. He allows me to take the lead. If I'm having a bad day or a hard time, it's up to me to let him know. When my stubborn personality takes over, he steps in and gently takes hold of the reins until I'm ready to take them back. Communication is vital. My partner, friends and family can't read my mind. They can't empathize with my situation if I don't talk to them about it. It's up to me to let them know when I need to. True family and friends will take time to listen.

I'm thankful in the face of disease that I still maintain strong relationships. Nothing has changed in that respect. I know many who face relationship changes when disease touches their lives, but that hasn't been my experience. I was always the first person to walk away from a relationship if it didn't suit my needs. It's enough that chronic illness takes my strength and vitality. It's not worth it if a relationship is taking it from me too.

*

JUDITH FLANAGAN
Judith was diagnosed with rheumatoid arthritis in 2012 at age 32
and fibromyalgia and polymyalgia rheumatic in 2014 at age 34

I would say my rheumatoid disease has had a massive impact on my socialization, and it does isolate me. I feel as though I don't want to burden anyone, and often won't go because I tire and get fatigued very easily and can't stay long. It has impacted my relationships, I am pretty sure. I know for certain that family and friends would like to see me more than they do.

*

SHELLEY FRITZ
Shelley was diagnosed with
rheumatoid arthritis in 2012 at age 42

I've lost a lot of friends since I was diagnosed. I remember the first time I passed an offer to join friends at a sip and paint establishment. After a full day of work and a bad pain day, I was absolutely exhausted and knew there was little chance I would enjoy painting or socializing, not to mention even physically being able to hold the brush to paint, so I did not join the group of women. I did not tell my friend why I could not attend, just said I was unable to go. That friend never asked me to join them again.

I never know when this disease will break me down to the point of having to cancel plans, so there have been many times I made plans only to have to back out at the last minute. Then guilt sets in. I'm not sure why I feel guilty over something completely out of my control, but the fact remains that I do. Maybe I could have made it to that party, but wouldn't have made it to the dog park with my family on Saturday. I have to prioritize plans and posting my whereabouts on social media causes confusion for friends who knew I cancelled Friday plans but then I went to dinner on Saturday, for example, but what friends might not consider is how relentless this disease is in tearing me apart one day and then backing off the next day allowing me to feel a bit better. I often find it easiest to invite others out last minute when I know I feel well enough to go and won't cancel.

When I started telling people about my autoimmune disease, the reaction was mixed. True friends asked questions and showed understanding of the unpredictability the disease brings. Some immediately offered advice without asking questions. I got plenty of warnings about using harmful medications and taking special herbs. One person shared how she knows someone with rheumatoid arthritis and that person is feeling great without any medication. If I look fine from the outside, I should be doing fine, right? I have tried to explain to others that rheumatoid disease has a different impact on each person and what works for one may or may not work for another.

I distance myself from toxic people and situation that cause stress. I attempt to educate others but if the other party is not interested in knowing more, I walk away. I am hesitant in telling people about my condition for a few reasons. I am not seeking sympathy. I really don't want others to see me as this disease because that has happened in the past and then my options for growth at work or for socializing become limited. If someone sees me struggling to walk or open a door and they ask me about it and press to know what is wrong, I share with them. Otherwise, it is far easier to go with the response of "Oh, I'm fine," or "I'm fantastic!" and keep moving. I've learned that people don't really want to know how you are feeling if you feel bad most of the time. It's a bit if a downer.

Aside from the physical aspects, this disease causes depression and anxiety when I can't do things I used to do. All this makes me feel angry at this disease and the notion that I used to be somebody else. Now I am somebody I'm still trying to get to know. With that said, others must be trying to figure me out, too.

It's isolating not having people to talk with who understand what I am going through. Over the last few years I've reached out to organizations to get involved in advocacy and events in my area. CreakyJoints, Arthritis Introspective, and the Arthritis Foundation have become my families filled with people who get me. I don't really need to explain when I say, "Today has been especially rough."

Social media groups give me a place to ask questions and sometimes vent about things I might not share with others. When I visit those sites online and talk with others in conference calls, I am reminded that I am not alone, that others have pain and problems, too. I try to be mindful of how frequently I fall on my husband's shoulder in expressing feelings of pain, anger, and frustration. When I feel overwhelmed, he gets frustrated, although he never tells me he doesn't want to hear about my issues. I just don't want this disease to define me! I want my relationship with my husband to be balanced by both of us sharing with each other, but sometimes my problems run so deep that they swallow up our conversations. He is a patient, caring man and incredibly supportive. Everyone has their limits though and I don't want him to resent me or be mad at the world because of the cards we've been dealt. Having this disease makes it my family's disease—it impacts everyone. If I don't feel well enough to go to dinner or a movie, I now make my husband and kids go out together anyway. Sometimes in turn they insist on picking up food for us at home or watching a movie at home instead, but I like for them to still have time together doing what we had planned to do so that my state of health does not stay in the forefront and they are impacted as little as possible.

Controlling pain to go to sleep can add to high fatigue levels, which can really hinder my physical relationship with my husband. This is something we are working on. Not feeling well much of the time makes me discouraged. One thing we have done to remedy the situation is plan small getaways in advance so that we have something to look forward to and we have a scheduled date night of sorts to devote to our relationship. At home our romantic time together is based on moments when I feel better than usual. It could be easy for couples to give up and be embittered. We love each other tremendously and will work endlessly to overcome obstacles. It's not easy though. We have really worked on communication and honesty in our feelings. For a good amount of time I faked feeling well when I felt horrible, but now I just say it like it is.

*

BRENDA KLEINSASSER
Brenda was diagnosed with
rheumatoid arthritis in 1991 at age 31

Living with rheumatoid arthritis has definitely had an impact on my personal relationships. Only my mother truly understood what I went through. It took for my sister to be diagnosed with colon cancer to finally realize that I was truly in a lifelong battle. Sadly, she ended up losing hers, but we definitely became closer during that time.

As far as friends who I've had for a long time, some have remained and others have sadly drifted away. I know that within myself, I had to adopt a different kind of attitude with how I was going to continue to live with rheumatoid arthritis. This did not happen overnight. It took years, even a couple of decades.

I told you that I struggle with some things more than others do. It actually took a person who I admire greatly to help me see the light. This person also lives with rheumatoid arthritis, and has truly been a champion when it comes to inspiration. When I finally figured out how to manage and live with rheumatoid arthritis, and adopt this new positive attitude, that is when things started to really change.

I also lost my mother that same year. I wanted to honor her and thought this was a good start. Instead of feeling sorry for myself, I decided to start taking risks. I have never really been a risktaker, being afraid of it not working out. So, what? I would have missed out on some wonderful opportunities if I hadn't at least tried. It has also helped me to emerge from my shell and become brave in speaking out.

I guess what I am trying to convey here is that this really did help with my socialization, as far as social media is concerned. I am much less social in the real world. There is so much that irritates me, and a lot has to do with my life as a brain tumor survivor. I can't separate the two. I had already lived with RA for over seventeen years, so I knew that was not going away anytime soon. I was a late bloomer, and still am in some regards. I may be older in most situations, but there are times when I feel like I have some catching up to do. All of this modern technology that I've tried to keep up with can be frustrating at times. I feel left out of certain situations, but again that's because of how I struggle with catching on to things. It is even more of a challenge since having gone through my brain saga.

Some of my family members are much more understanding now. That can happen when you end up sharing about your struggles in a book. I elude to *Grief Diaries: Loss of Health*, which was the first book in which I shared my rheumatoid arthritis and brain tumor journeys. If it took a book, so be it. I actually write much better than I talk. It is hard for me to express some things without coming across as angry or frustrated. It seems that seeing the written word can sometimes alleviate the misunderstandings.

I felt isolated a lot of times. I know some people think there are things I can't do, so they don't bother to ask. That may be true, but at least give me a chance. I have one friend who is great about including me in activities. She knows I love rock concerts. I actually told her recently that she is the only person who thinks about me when a situation like that comes up. It hurts to hear people making plans in your presence and not include you. I try to include everyone, but that is just me. My disease has certainly progressed and caused other issues over the years, which makes it difficult to be conistent with plans. Sometimes you have to cancel or postpone. Some people are understanding and others think you are blowing them off. I cannot worry about what everyone thinks. That will just cause more anxiety and even cause a flare.

*

CHANTELLE MARCIAL
Chantelle was diagnosed with
rheumatoid arthritis in 1999 at age 19

I work a very interactive job, have a huge family and friends I get to see regularly when our schedules jibe. There have been a few times when I didn't feel a hundred percent and couldn't make a dinner party or a cookout, but for the most part I'm there! I think living in the middle of the city helps too. I can't go too far without bumping into someone and having a conversation.

*

LAYNE MARTIN
Layne was diagnosed with
psoriatic arthritis in 2007 at age 47

This disease has had a huge impact on my socialization! I never know from day to day how I'm going to feel. I have good days and I have bad days. It actually gives me some anxiety when I get invites to social engagements because I am a very social person and I love going to events. I get very excited about going out and start thinking about what I will wear, who all is going to be there, etc.

With this disease I know that on the day of the event, I might have to cancel. It makes me frustrated and it can be discouraging. I worry that people might stop inviting me if I don't show up. Then I will be in total isolation again. It's a real worry and concern for me.

I also struggle with telling people that I just don't feel well, I find myself making up excuses. People don't understand the level of fatigue that comes with psoriatic arthritis and other chronic illnesses. It's not like I can just go lay down, take a nap, and wake feeling refreshed—it's not that kind of fatigue. It's not something you can explain. Unless a person has a chronic illness too, they just can't understand it.

*

KATHLEEN MEKAILEK
Kathleen was diagnosed with chronic regional pain
syndrome in 2005 at age 38, rheumatoid arthritis in
2014 at age 46, and ulcerative colitis in 2016 at age 49

When I was first diagnosed, it came after a few surgeries (when biopsies were finally done, because my bloodwork was always negative) and people would joke about me becoming bionic or always having something break. Chuck even asked me if I came with a warranty. I was always open about it, answering all the questions I could when people asked about the scars on my arms, wrists, elbows, and shoulders. The more I talked, the more I found out that a lot of my artist friends had invisible diseases also. Everything ranging from fibromyalgia, multiple sclerosis, and RA. They all said that theirs were not as bad as mine, and I couldn't understand why they would keep it a secret. Most of them told me that when friends found out they had a chronic condition, those friends would disappear. I could not believe that this could be true. I always see the good in people and try to make people happy and put out positive energy. I believe that the energy we put out into the world will come back to us.

There are times I'm negative—everyone has those dark days, and some days we deserve to have them. But I've found that by being positive, it seems to draw the best in people. I was in for a rude awakening. As long as I didn't look sick, people were happy to see me and I was invited to do things. People would stop by the gallery to talk. Then, I went through my abdominal issues. I looked sick. When doctors and nurses look at you with pity in their eyes, you know you don't look good. My "best" friends, or so I thought, could not make the time to send a text, email, personal message, phone call to let me know they were thinking about me. I didn't want cards or get-well gifts, just a simple "Hey, how are you?" or "I have a couple minutes, feel like getting out of the house?"

How I would have loved if one of them would have come over to just sit with me. No pressure, just sit and tell me about your day. Four months. Nothing. I saw pictures of them out doing things, partying, visiting each other, but I was avoided like the plague. But at the same time, something wonderful happened. People who I thought of as acquaintances, Facebook friends, fellow artists, and some who I was just starting friendships, with stepped forward. A card would come in the mail, usually on a bad day, like they knew it was needed; healing mantra necklaces and bracelets from blossoming friendships, a neighbor who told me to come over and we could cry together. We would share stories. I would tell her about how my day or week was, and she would let me cry it out so Chuck wouldn't have to see me, because he had enough on his shoulders. I would let her cry it out because she had just lost the love of her life. Even though death and chronic illness are not the same, they are intertwined. If you really stop to think about it, they both go through the same stages of grief, at least that is how I see it.

I have another friend who has nicknamed me Bubble Girl because he thinks I should be encased in bubble wrap so nothing else happens to me. He will send me a message every now and then just to say hi and make me smile.

My relationship with my husband, Chuck, has gone up and down like a rollercoaster ride. It's not all sunshine and rainbows. There are thunderstorms and times he just wants to be left alone with his own thoughts. He'll stand outside cussing and yelling at the world. He is allowed this. I am not living with rheumatoid arthritis by myself—it is a journey we are on together. I know that if I'm having thoughts about what might happen in the future, he must be having them, too.

I thought I would be sad about the loss of friendships, but it is actually a relief. I always felt something was off and that the friendship was not fully reciprocated. It took me struggling to get my life back to realize that I was trying to make something work that wasn't there. Other people were in the shadows holding my hand in their own way all the time. And I can't forget about the children! Our gallery has Mommy and Me Classes and summer art camps for older children. They drew me pictures, would come by the gallery when Chuck was there to check on me, and no matter how bad I looked or felt, if they saw me, there was always a huge smile and a hug. No matter how bad I might have been feeling, that genuine childlike innocence filled with love was enough to break through any darkness. Adults have a lot to learn from children.

*

RICK PHILLIPS
Rick was diagnosed with type 1 diabetes in 1974
at age 17 and rheumatoid arthritis in 1999 at age 42

Socialization is always a difficult proposition with any chronic condition. In my life, the issue is usually family members who do not understand rheumatoid arthritis or its treatments. I sometimes feel judged by those who do not understand that it is sometimes necessary to rest and take copious amounts of medications. The stress is not constant, rather it is an undercurrent in some family relationships.

People who only drop in and out of our life do not see the days of exhaustion and pain as well as days of laughter and joy. The brief glimpses they get are not the entire picture. My wife and I work hard to keep our life in balance. In some cases it might look too easy or too difficult. Whatever the impression, it is wrong. My wife and I are not perfect, and we have struggles with Diabetes and RA.

*

LESLIE ROTT
Leslie was diagnosed with lupus and
rheumatoid arthritis in 2008 at age 22

I have always been a homebody, and am happy to spend time at home. However, it is frustrating when I want to go out or do what normal people my age are doing but can't because I'm not feeling well or am in a flare.

Being chronically ill impacts dating. It's important to be open and honest, but scary to know your dating pool might be diminished because you are sick. Granted, it's better to find out right away if someone does not want to have a partner who is sick, but it's scary to know a relationship might end solely for that reason.

I try to stick to all of my commitments unless I absolutely cannot. Overall, my friends and family have been supportive. Those closest to me know that if I beg out of things, it's because I am truly unable to fulfill that commitment, but the rest of the world is not always that understanding.

The other thing is that I know getting pregnant is not going to be easy or spontaneous like it is for some. I worry that I might have trouble getting or staying pregnant. I think that these diseases have made me realize that more than anything else in my life, I want to have children and be a mother. But I realize that this may not look the same as it does for my healthy friends. What is often a point of connection for people my age may be more isolating for me than it is for others.

*

TIEN SYDNOR-CAMPBELL
Tien was diagnosed with autoimmune
rheumatoid disease in 2010 at age 40

Rheumatoid arthritis effectively obliterated my social butterfly status. I used to have many work relationships that had become very close personal friends. I socialized with these friends at least two days after work, one for the softball team, and the other for the end-of-week happy hour. This change took very little time. I went from playing, to barely being able to walk upright over less than a month's time. I could no longer enjoy happy hour because my medications. My meds are so taxing, to the liver, that my rheumatologist instructed me to cut back to one drink per month. Over time, my inability to drive got in the way of going where I wanted to go. I had to quit, two different part-time therapy jobs, because there were days that I didn't have enough energy to do anything. After two back-to-back surgeries that left me recovering at home, I was unable to return to work. I went from being alive and well to a sick at home shut-in in a very short period of time.

Initially the isolation was fine because I spent a lot of time feeling complete fatigue, and sleeping throughout the day. I still had Chase, my big, beautiful, Chesapeake Bay Black Lab, during this time. Chase was my buddy, alerted me to visitors, and laid next to my bed to keep me company all day long. He was a very big comfort for me when I was home alone. It wasn't until we lost Chase to cancer at age fourteen that I understood how much impact he had on my sense of safety. I had a disturbing knack for falling asleep during many conversations, both over the phone and in person. Chase did not care if I fell asleep. Dogs are wonderful like that. When he passed, I was unable to nap comfortably at home, alone, for a very long time. I recently made the decision to get another dog to, specifically, serve as emotional support and companionship. This time I want my dog to be small enough for me to walk without fear of being pulled through the park. Those cute, little squirrels are very tempting for a dog to chase.

There are still times that I do not sleep well, especially if I hear random noises. There are times when I don't leave the second floor of my home for several days. Having a major surgery that prevents you from walking is even more scary. I was so isolated that, for many days, I only saw my immediate family. I depended on them and a few close friends to do everything for me. Isolation isn't just physical. It impacts the mind and emotions just as much, if not more. Mentally, isolation filled me with anxiety. When I was unable to walk and had little strength I felt like I was not safe. Not from my family, but from potential intruders. The state of isolation is feeling like there is no one on earth that is experiencing the same problems as you. The isolation tells you that you will never have a life full of adventure again.

My familial relationships and friendships have either been strengthened by having this chronic illness, or I have lost them altogether. These are the times when you find out who cares enough to support and who gives lip service but no real service. You really find out how important you are to people when you're in the hospital for a few weeks. In my case, people who called to check on me were just as important as those who visited. Those who did not visit or call are no longer priorities to me. That has been very eye-opening. Some friends became even more important to me and others fell off. For a while I was slightly disappointed in some friends who I thought were very close to me. I remember getting depressed about one friend, in particular, who I felt should have lifted a finger but didn't. I am grateful for the role that they played in my life and time. It has made moving on, from expectations, much easier for me than it ever has.

My marriage, fortunately, has benefitted from my need for support. I might never have given up control of anything without this disease. I was one of those super-duper, strong women who could do everything under the sun and didn't need anyone's help. At least not until I needed incredible amounts of it anyway. My husband has been the most incredible source of compassion and care for me. It has been a beautiful thing to be a witness to how our relationship has grown closer. This is not to say that it's always easy and lovely, because we all know that everything in life takes effort. Today, I have an abundance of gratitude for him and my adult children.

*

CHAPTER SIXTEEN

Finding a Balance

The secret of change is to focus all your energy
not on fighting the old but on building the new.
SOCRATES

When you live with autoimmune disease, it means living with more than just a disorder. Daily fatigue, stiffnes, pain, and risk of infection means balancing the realities of the disease with everyday life. In what ways does your disease impact your lifestyle the most?

*

CHRISTINA AMES
Christina was diagnosed with rheumatoid arthritis in 1987
at age 20 and diagnosed with fibromyalgia in 2011 at age 43

Fatigue is definitely my biggest challenge. Managing pain is much easier: take a pill, and (hopefully) the pain goes away. Fatigue is such a fickle thing, especially since you can sleep well at night, and still awaken exhausted. In all the years I've had RA, I have yet to combat this aspect completely. What I have found are some things that help. Not eradicate it completely, but help. I found that showering at night is something that helps me unwind. A warm shower calms me, and is soothing. I often read before bed, and try to keep to a similar schedule in the evenings. I almost always have to nap during the day, or if I don't sleep, I lay down and rest. Sometimes, I have a crushing feeling of needing to rest, and I have learned to heed those feelings.

I recently began a campaign to eat more healthfully, and hopefully lose some weight in the process. My son has an event at his college this fall, and I wanted to look my best for it, and for the two graduation ceremonies we have next year. I am currently following a program that uses low glycemic index meals, and eliminates most sugars. Giving up sugar has helped immensely in my quest for a good night's sleep. I truly do feel as though I have made strides in breaking the insomnia chain, and that is huge in my mind. My problem was not falling asleep, but staying asleep. I'd wake up to use the bathroom, and be awake the rest of the night, or for several hours at least. Now, I still get up, but I am able to go back to sleep. My weight loss is very slow, but gaining sleep is a wonderful side effect that I never expected.

*

J.G. CHAYKO
J.G. was diagnosed with
rheumatoid arthritis in 2010 at age 38

The biggest impact rheumatoid arthritis has had on my life was the loss of my physical dexterity. I was a dancer. I lived to move and rheumatoid arthritis put a stop to that natural unfettered flow. Now instead of fluid and graceful, I was stilted and stiff. The fatigue made it difficult for me to endure an hour of dance class. Sore joints impeded the moves I once found so effortless. Dance partners, unaware of my illness, unwittingly aggravated my joints with their masterful lead. I stepped away from the studio. I felt empty, hollow, and unable to quench the desire to get up and dance to the music that still played on around me. My muscles deteriorated with the lack of training. I held onto the hope that once I got rheumatoid arthritis under control, I would be able to return to dance, and that the miracle of muscle memory would restore what I lost. But I had a long way to go before that happened.

My theatre life also took a hit. I had walked the stage since I was fourteen years old. When the high school drama teacher cast me in the school production of "I Was a Teenage Dracula," I found a home on the stage. Dance required muscle, stamina, and grit—so did theatre performances. Rehearsals could run two to three months, and performances anywhere between four to eight weeks. After a full day of work, rehearsals became more difficult to endure; the constant fluctuation of my disease was challenging. I couldn't confidently commit to a prolonged production schedule and so I sat in the wings and focused on uncovering the pattern of my disease.

Activity had always been a big part of my life. I was determined to keep moving. Exercise is important for people with RA. I needed to maintain muscle and bone strength, and keep my joints as fluid as possible. I attended physiotherapy classes and learned low-impact exercises that reduced pressure on my joints. It was difficult and frustrating at first. Exercises that were once easy to perform were tiring and difficult. It was disheartening to realize how much of an impact rheumatoid arthritis had on my body in only a few short years.

During this time, I was adjusting and adding medications, trying to find the right combination that would reduce my pain and swelling. The flow of my life was unpredictable. One good day might be followed by three bad days, and one bad day followed by two good. On the good days, I pushed myself to exercise more, only to be sidelined by bad flares and a few days of inactivity. This pattern was not ideal. I needed to find a regular program that allowed me to engage in a small amount of activity even during a flare, and that's where low-impact activities made a big difference.

I try to exercise every day. I do yoga to stretch and maintain my flexibility, adjusting it day to day depending on my pain level. My physiotherapist encouraged me to engage in activities to work my heart and lungs, as people with rheumatoid arthritis are more susceptible to cardiac complications. Swimming replaced dancing, allowing me to get a good cardio workout without extra pressure on the joints. I found that I loved the feeling of my body flowing through the water. I was able to move gracefully beneath the tepid ripples and choreograph a new routine. My partner and I went for walks every day when the weather was pleasant. I received a Fitbit for my birthday allowing me to set hourly and daily step goals.

It took almost four years to get my rheumatoid arthritis symptoms under control, and with that I could push a little bit more. This past summer, I went on my first hike in four years. It was amazing to feel the forest floor beneath my feet, to see the clear sky peeking through the tree tops, and reach the first crest, looking down to the sparkling cove below us. A few weeks later, my partner and I registered for a weekly ballroom dance class. Once again, I felt the hardwood floor beneath my feet and the sturdy wooden barre under my hand. It didn't matter that I wasn't the same proficient dancer I used to be. All that mattered was that in some small capacity, I was able to reclaim a piece of the life I used to know.

*

JUDITH FLANAGAN
Judith was diagnosed with rheumatoid arthritis in 2012 at age 32
and fibromyalgia and polymyalgia rheumatic in 2014 at age 34

Both the rheumatoid arthritis and fibromyalgia impact me due to fatigue. It is far more than being tired, because not even a nap can make the fatigue go away. It certainly is one of the hardest symptoms to deal with, along the chronic pain. The fatigue comes on at any time, and affects daily activities and the length of time I can do any physical activity like walking. To manage it, I plan what I need to do each day and allocate time for each task depending on the level of fatigue I feel that day. I also try to go to bed at a reasonable hour, though I can be tossing and turning for hours until I eventually fall asleep. I don't like having to cut an activity short, but often feel that when the fatigue strikes, it is out of my control.

257

*

SHELLEY FRITZ
Shelley was diagnosed with
rheumatoid arthritis in 2012 at age 42

Recurring nightmares include scenarios like this: I'm walking and a stranger is following me so I start to speed up and look for a hiding place. I try to run but my body I can barely move as if in slow motion. The stalker grabs me and I wake up in a sweat. It is difficult to get a good night's rest when my subconscious is harboring feelings of helplessness and fear of becoming disabled. What would happen if there was a true emergency and I needed to jump out of bed and run? Hopefully my adrenaline would kick in and I'd be able to get my family and pets out in time. I suppose worrying about a hypothetical fire, tornado or burglary is a bit neurotic, but I really wonder if my body would be able to keep up in the event of such an emergency.

I take medicine to help ease pain so I can sleep, but I must take it before 8:30 p.m. in order to get that deep sleep, since I wake at 5 a.m. I read a suggestion to wake an hour earlier than needed to take a pain pill, reset the alarm, and then go back to sleep. I woke up to take the pain pill and went back to sleep, and overslept by three hours. I need seven to eight hours of solid sleep to feel refreshed, so I try to do that, especially on work nights. Of course, every night when I go to sleep, I say a little prayer that tomorrow will be a day I can pop out of bed. Fatigue is my greatest nemesis. Naps are helpful after work or on a hammock on a beautiful weekend to provide me that energy needed to finish out the day. I can't always take a nap when I know I need to though like when I'm in the middle of the work day and I'd like to curl up on a carpet and sleep for thirty minutes. If you could see the filthy carpet I'm referring to, you'd appreciate just how much that nap is needed. Since I can't always take a nap, I will eat an apple or get up and move to get my blood flowing. Sometimes I need to resort to caffeine from a soda. I think the best way I am fighting fatigue is by placing myself in situations, like working full-time in a high movement type of work, where I am unable to surrender to exhaustion.

Lately I've been fighting off viruses—and losing the battle. Picture throwing a boomerang of germs into the wind and having it swing right back. Working in an elementary school harboring millions of germs doesn't help, but I wouldn't want to be anywhere else. I take tons of vitamins and lots of vitamin C to ward off intruders. Having a healthy supply of hand sanitizer is important, too. I have considered changing careers where I am not surrounded by potential infections, but I enjoy my job and I'm just not ready to give in to this disease.

I had another cold that manifested into acute bronchitis a while back but the cough and shortness of breath haven't yet gone away. I began researching rheumatoid disease and found rather scary statistics regarding how this disease affects the heart and lungs. The average rate of survival for someone who develops interstitial lung disease is about five years. That scares that pants off me. With a current Vectra DA score showing high disease activity, and not currently responding to the medicines I'm taking, I am concerned about developing rheumatoid arthritis-associated interstitial lung disease.

*

BRENDA KLEINSASSER
Brenda was diagnosed with
rheumatoid arthritis in 1991 at age 31

Fatigue is my worst enemy. There are days when I want to crash right on the floor. I've tried several things to combat it, but it has unfortunatley become much worse since brain surgery. My doctor told me it might be something I battle for the rest of my life. I do find that being around positive people or having a good laugh can make me feel better. It can actually give me a boost or even a little energy.

My sleep pattern has been awful for years. I sleep maybe two to four hours at a time, and then lay awake. In the beginning of my rheumatoid journey, I woke with pain throughout the night. My knee hurt bad because of the lump behind it. I now sleep with a pillow under my knees and that seems to help a great deal. Nights for me are still the hardest. I can easily take an afternoon nap, but during the week that doesn't work out so great if I want to sleep soundly that night.

I have dealt with my share of infections. If I get a cold or sinus infection, it takes me a lot longer to get over it than the average healthy person. I am still battling from a bad cold as I write this. I had to actually stop taking my biologic for several weeks. As mentioned before, anytime you experience an infection or the flu, you can't take the biologic which then leads to a flare of rheumatoid symptoms. I know my biologic is still working after sixteen years, because when I finally got to take it again after a headcold, I did experience some relief. It is not perfect by any means, but it does allow me to have a life.

I know that living with RA can be dangerous when it comes to other infections. I have had shingles four times, and my dermatologist said that the biologic could have depleted my immune system enough to cause the basal cell carcinoma on my nose. We will never know for sure, but the risk of developing it again is definitely higher now. I have yearly skin checks, and so far there has been no recurrence.

The pain is always hard to deal with. I never know from one day to the next what surprise is in store. I take it day by day. There are times when it simply gets to be too much. I have a good cry, find a funny DVD to watch, and all is then right with the world. I try to walk at least five times a week to work and home again. Most weeks it works but when weather conditions make it difficult, I then make other transportation arrangements and make up by exercising at home. My full range of motions exercises twice daily help a great deal. Motion is the best possible gift you can give yourself. Be good to yourself and if you cannot do as much, that is alright too.

I am doing the best I can and that is all that matters. I live with rheumatoid arthritis, not anyone else. When you look at it that way, you gain perspective.

*

CHANTELLE MARCIAL
Chantelle was diagnosed with
rheumatoid arthritis in 1999 at age 19

I do experience fatigue and occasionally take a day of rest, but otherwise I try to push through until I can't physically move. And that's fine for me; I've been doing it for years and it works. But it's certainly not for everyone. I used to run track and I do miss the ability to run and do the stairs. I've injured both knees, and rheumatoid arthritis has weakened my ankles. But I can still walk, and I do! This campus is beautiful and I am lucky to be in Boston, which is America's Walking City. You can go from neighborhood to neighborhood in no time, so I find myself wandering the town quite a bit. It's a great way to lube the joints and see new sites.

*

LAYNE MARTIN
Layne was diagnosed with
psoriatic arthritis in 2007 at age 47

The biggest impact in regards to my lifestyle was being able to work. I loved my profession almost as much as I love my family. I enjoyed going to work each day. Working in the emergency room was different every single day, it was never boring! I was good at what I did and was highly respected by my peers and the physicians. I had worked my way up into a management position and at one point was managing an emergency department with just over one hundred employees. I loved my staff and I loved the patients. I considered myself a working manager and every day I looked forward to the lunch hour so I could relieve the triage nurse and the charge nurse for their lunch breaks. It got me out of my office and I could interact with the patients. Early retirement was a difficult decision and certainly impacted the lifestyle that I had known for all of my adult life!

Now that I have finally come to terms with retirement and having to go on disability, my lifestyle has changed significantly. I am now able to listen to my body and care for myself in the way that I need to. I enjoy my morning cup of coffee while I read my morning devotional and as I get myself mentally prepared for the day. I am able to eat healthy and do gentle daily exercises, rather than grabbing something out of the break room and counting a twelve-hour shift on my feet as exercise. I'm able to go to the chiropractor and for acupuncture on a regular basis. I meet socially with my church family weekly. I am able to see my grandchildren daily and get hugs and snuggles whenever I need them. Life is good now that I've accepted this disease and finally come to terms with my reality.

*

KATHLEEN MEKAILEK
Kathleen was diagnosed with chronic regional pain
syndrome in 2005 at age 38, rheumatoid arthritis in
2014 at age 46, and ulcerative colitis in 2016 at age 49

I am an artist. I paint, do photography, weld, do wire and barbed wire sculptures and use a chainsaw and other tools to carve wood. It has been eight months since I have been able to wield a chainsaw and carve a sculpture. I don't know when or if I will be able to carve again. I miss it, but I turn to my other mediums on my good days to keep me busy. Being an artist means going to shows and openings, interacting with people, hugging, air kisses, handshakes, lots of pictures, staying awake for long hours into the night, staying focused on the conversation and being able to tell the stories behind your work—all while standing in four-inch heels, working the room, and most of all being able to keep a smile on your face. I loved this life! I loved going into the city, because we live in such a small town. It made me excited and high on life. It was what I lived for. I am an extrovert and the thought of no cocktail parties, openings, banquets was not something that I was willing to give up.

Early on, my counts were within normal range so it was common to see me at events with braces or casts after surgeries. I did not keep my rheumatoid arthritis a secret (and still don't), and often it became the start of a dialogue. Now, things are totally different. With my blood counts low, I worry about being in crowds and touching things that other people have. So we have devised some plans that work for us. Chuck opens all doors, takes programs as they are handed to me, and if someone approaches with their hand out, he takes the first handshake. I use antibacterial gel a lot during events. If someone looks like they are coming for a kiss or hug, I rotate so it is a side hug and then turn toward the front of them and start talking. That keeps the kisses away.

I carry a mask with me in my evening bag and at the first sneeze or cough, I pull it out and put it on. We also carry a small pack of alcohol wipes that can be used to wipe down chairs and tables where I might put my hands, and for when I enter and exit the ladies room.

Since I am on a gluten, soy, sugar, dairy-free diet and don't drink alcohol, sodas or juice, I usually have bottled water that Chuck will wipe down and unscrew the lid for me.

On days when I have events, I take my afternoon medication an hour early and make sure to get a nap in of at least two to four hours, depending on how much time I have to get ready and be there. Luckily, I have never had an issue falling asleep, I just put my head on the pillow, close my eyes and immediately asleep. All the above is for when I am considered stable, counts might be low, but not too low and I should be able to keep from getting sick. However, there are times, especially after surgeries, where the flares are too bad. I'm trying to heal and am just too tired and worn out to do anything. This past year, in one eight-week period I underwent two surgeries and one procedure in my abdomen. I was so tired and exhausted. My body was telling me to rest.

I was on a liquid and soft food diet for two and a half months before introducing food back into my system to see if I could handle them. I went from a size ten to two in that amount of time. I dropped over forty pounds. I was at my high school weight. None of my children had ever seen me that thin. My eyes had dark circles around them and looked sunk in. My husband said I looked like death.

One evening, he sat beside me on the couch and as I put my head in his lap, he asked me if I had given up, if I was just going to let myself die. I told him that my body needed rest, it had been traumatized and I was fighting on the inside even if it didn't look like it on the outside. We just held each other and cried. But after that I knew I needed to push myself harder, and I did. It took another month and I was able to start being myself again. I still have constant pain, and probably always will, but I push through it because I want to be an example for my children that no matter what obstacles stand in your way, no matter how badly it hurts, if you want to achieve it, you can. Just keep pushing and it will happen. Maybe not today or tomorrow, but somewhere down the road, you will get there.

*

RICK PHILLIPS
Rick was diagnosed with type 1 diabetes in 1974
at age 17 and rheumatoid arthritis in 1999 at age 42

There are so many ways that rheumatoid arthritis affects my life and I cannot say I even know them all. Of course there are the medical considerations. This past week I had a cortisone injection for a very inflamed elbow. I took pain medications for weeks until I was able to visit my doctor and then after the injection my blood sugar spiraled out of control. I was feeling the effects of the raging blood sugar and I grew frustrated with diabetes. But I have to remember it was not the diabetes that caused the issue, it was the underlying RA.

The management of RA, just like diabetes, tends to show up in every medical decision I have to make. I know that type 1 diabetes is often identified as a 24/7/365 condition, but so is RA. I have to make decisions about management of my body with an eye toward how it might impact RA. I use Rituxan once every four months, and that means I am either planning my next infusion or recovering from my last. There is really no in between times.

I plan everything—trips, walks, dates—around RA treatment. Can I take methotrexate today? When did you last take it? Can I afford a day of recovery in my schedule if I take methotrexate on Monday evening? Or do I need to move this appointment based on how I might feel? Who knows exactly how I might feel one week from today? One thing I have learned is that my schedule must be fluid.

*

LESLIE ROTT
Leslie was diagnosed with lupus and
rheumatoid arthritis in 2008 at age 22

For me, fatigue is the biggest issue. I work full time, so not being able to nap during the day is a challenge. I drink a lot of coffee, which probably isn't so good and doesn't always work. My sleep continues to be a challenge for me. I have also experienced firsthand the infection risk that having lupus and rheumatoid arthritis poses, and this definitely impacts my interactions with others, travel, etc. I would say that it doesn't limit me so much as I try to be more cognizant of when I am around other people who are sick or in other situations that put me at increased risk of getting sick.

It's frustrating to have to worry about things that other people don't have to, and I think that's the biggest thing that comes with these illnesses. There's always that twinge of wanting to be normal, and knowing that life will never be that way again.

*

TIEN SYDNOR-CAMPBELL
Tien was diagnosed with autoimmune
rheumatoid disease in 2010 at age 40

When I think about all of the ways that rheumatoid arthritis has impacted my lifestyle, I really don't know an area that it hasn't. I can't even name one problem that has affected me more than another. I can truthfully say that fatigue is the one that confuses me. For one, it's not easily described because there is no reference for it if you've never had it. Two, it's not just feeling low energy, it is as if you have been mummified alive. Trapped with my thoughts and unable to get enough strength to get up and walk around, finally brushing your teeth, and then needing a nap. Think about having the flu forever. I know that's hard to imagine because you, subconsciously, know you'll eventually come out of that. The only way that I have been able to manage that is to listen to my body and respect what it's telling me. I still have bouts of rebellion where I still push to get something done, and it always ends up with me unable to get out of bed and move around for a few days. I don't know if I'll ever give in completely, at this point I don't expect to do that anytime soon.

The pain is very much the same in magnitude. There is no frame of reference for this kind of relentless pain. It is impossible to describe feeling like you need to be in the hospital, yet knowing that there's nothing they can do. It is impossible to understand why someone with all of these problems is smiling and acting like everything is fine. The only thing that I can do when these moments come along, is to take everything down to a snail's pace. I have to slow my breathing. It helps to breathe slow and deep because breathing is key to managing anxiety. I also have to slow down my thinking, because my thoughts will run circular races with thoughts of new conditions.

The anxiety that envelops me when I wonder if my next, new medication infusion will or will not work. It could make me sick, but I won't know until I get sick. It might also make me even more fatigued for a few days. Knowing that I'm susceptible to infections is incredibly frustrating and fills me with anxiety every time I am out in public spaces. This is compounded exponentially if someone sneezes or coughs near me. My susceptibility is more likely to incapacitate me, instead of just catching whatever it is they have. It was extremely frustrating when one coworker didn't stay home from work because of an ear infection. Once it entered my system, not only did I get the infection, I ended up with vertigo so bad that I had to spend a few days in the hospital. The only way I have figured out to combat this fear is by wearing a filter/ mask when traveling by air, bus, and train. Moreso during the cold, winter months when the flu is likely in the air. Otherwise, I'm at the mercy of everyone around me. It kinda sucks.

*

All of life is peaks and valleys. Don't let the peaks get too high or the valleys too low.

JOHN WOODEN

*

CHAPTER SEVENTEEN

7acing Progression

She's standing on a line between giving up
and seeing how much more she can take.
ANONYMOUS

Autoimmune disorders are riddles wrapped in a mystery inside an enigma. They are orphan diseases that falls across several different medical specialties. At the root of it all is a person in pain who fears progression. Has your disease progressed?

*

CHRISTINA AMES
Christina was diagnosed with rheumatoid arthritis
in 1987 at age 20 and fibromyalgia in 2011 at age 43

After thirty years with this disease, I think it has most certainly progressed. Throughout my answers, however, I feel as though I have spoken about how lucky I feel, and this is no exception. I feel fortuitous to have a relatively minor degree of disease progression.

271

Don't get me wrong: I am most definitely aware of this disease, and it controls nearly every facet of my life. But in thirty years, I do not have the degree of disfigurement that others have with a much shorter time frame. I don't have the classic swan neck type of finger shifting, at least not yet. And I'm still pretty mobile, although sometimes I do have to rely on a cane to get around if I'm alone, and someone's arm if I'm not.

Disfigurement doesn't scare me, probably because I was born looking different. What does give me pause is the fact I might one day be less mobile, that I will need constant help. When I had the Big Flare, it gave me an inkling of what that life would be like, with needing help doing the most basic of tasks. I don't mind saying that it was pretty scary. I think we as a society take pride in doing everything ourselves, and I'm no different. I'm glad I can do everything (mostly) of what I set out to do. But loss of body function, and loss of independence are truly terrifying emotions.

Being active, both mentally and physically, are helpful, and as long as I can, I will do both. I will always make sure I'm seen by a rheumatologist, and be careful to follow my medication regime. The Big Flare taught me that I must never again lack for disease monitoring, and I owe it to my family to be proactive. I will never stop trying to work for a cure, and advocating for those who cannot. Forewarned is forearmed!

*

J.G. CHAYKO
J.G. was diagnosed with
rheumatoid arthritis in 2010 at age 38

Rheumatoid arthritis has its own pace. In some, it comes on like a hurricane leaving a wake of destruction in its path; in others, it stealthily creeps in, emerging in fits and starts, always unpredictable, and always altering the path it takes. I can never let my guard down in the face of RA. A flare can come on at any time and it can last a few hours to a couple of weeks.

It's challenging to determine the natural course of disease. The normal of my life has changed. Is daily pain the new standard? Is this what I should expect from here on in? How long should morning stiffness last? I have a high pain tolerance and a resistance to being vulnerable. I have always been that unwavering rock regardless of where life has led me. I found a strength early on in my life that drove me to every success. That makes it difficult to know when I should seek help. My disease has gradually progressed over the years. It takes its own time, waiting until I am stable, lulling me into a false sense of security before erupting.

I am a bit sluggish on those flare days. Something as simple as opening a jar or pouring a cup of tea becomes an arduous task. It's the little things that I take for granted that are most affected by rheumatoid disease like tying shoelaces, opening jars, turning keys, or picking up change—swollen fingers aren't that easily manipulated. I may break more cups and drop more plates on days like these, but they can be replaced. I fear the loss of things I can't replace. I fear not being able to move to the music like I did the first time I stepped on a dance floor. I fear not being able to play beneath the theatre lights, to swim under a summer sky, to stroll the lush west coast trails on an autumn day. I dread the idea that my joints will always be in the line of fire, that nothing will be able to control this flaming beast and my joints will be damaged beyond repair. That might never happen but it's the possibility that haunts me.

In six years, I have gone from a couple pills a day to the all-powerful triple therapy treatment—three medications working hard to keep the inflammation in my body in check. With each adjustment I do well for a while, and then rheumatoid arthritis returns a little stronger as it finds a way through the cracks. The older I get, the more it makes its presence known. I've grown used to its pattern. I am thankful that in spite of pain and fatigue, I still have my mobility. Maybe not the same as before—I'm certainly not as agile and dexterous as I used to be—but I can move, travel, and even get on stage every now and again.

I have settled into an understanding with RA. I don't spend much time worrying about something I can't control. I take one day at a time, and put as much of myself into that day as possible. I don't look to tomorrow, I look to the minute, to the hour, to the day. It's amazing how much one can accomplish by focusing on small goals. I celebrate the most irrelevant victories, simply because they are victories. They stretch the boundaries of life with RA a little more each day.

*

JUDITH FLANAGAN

Judith was diagnosed with rheumatoid arthritis in 2012 at age 32
and with fibromyalgia and polymyalgia rheumatic in 2014 at age 34

I am quite certain my rheumatoid arthritis has progressed some,
though not a lot as it was caught early. I do have a few extra symptoms,
but due to early diagnosis and treatment, I've been lucky not to have
any extreme damage, well, at least not external. I know that
progression is slowed by current treatments, but they don't cure the
damage already done. The part of progression I fear most is dying
young, and the ever-growing emotional toll the disease can have.

*

SHELLEY FRITZ

Shelley was diagnosed with
rheumatoid arthritis in 2012 at age 42

My disease has progressed rapidly over this year to the point that
my disease activity level was last measured at fifty-three when forty or
higher is considered severe. This came as no surprise to me since I
have been feeling terrible and noticed significant differences in how I
am able to walk and function daily compared to even six months ago.

I don't suppose I needed the lab work to tell me it's taking over
my body at the moment. Some differences are subtle such as how my
wrist and finger joints are impacting the way I write, type, and grip
objects. I have had too many days of hobbling down hallways because
of painful, stiff feet, a more noticeable attribute to other people I meet.
I know this is a progressive disease with no cure. It was difficult to

type that because it is so true, and I prefer not thinking about it too much. There isn't a day that goes by when I don't consider how to best take care of myself so that I will be here for my children for many years to come.

Currently I am not responding very well to medicines to slow disease progression and fight inflammation. Researching this disease can be helpful but it can fill me with excessive information, creating a poisonous view of my future. Since my diagnosis, I tried four biologics and several DMARDs. Methotrexate has been an ingredient in my treatment recipe since the onset of my disease. My doctor and I have tried different combinations of ingredients over time only to come to this point where I am looking for my next contender off a diminishing list of possible biologics.

When I was first diagnosed and I began researching rheumatoid arthritis, I was concerned about joints fusing and becoming confined to a wheelchair. That is still a long- term concern, but today I am much more alarmed by chronic inflammation of my lungs and heart. When I first began reading about rheumatoid arthritis, I focused heavily on the impact it would have on my joints but always thought the impact it could have on my organs was not a concern since I was confident I'd find medicine to control this. As time passes and I still do not have a medicine I'm responding well to, I am becoming increasingly concerned about my future. The physical changes with my joints can be addressed through medicine, physical therapy, orthopedics, or surgery, but when inflammation continues to occur in the heart or lungs, serious irreversible damage can result. Thinking about this, and all of the unfortunate possible ramifications my continued inflammation, makes my chest pound with fear. I've been noticing a difference in my hand grip that's affecting how I cut with a knife and fork. It's a small change, but an important one, that makes me wonder how quickly it will progress. I try not to dwell on what could be one day and just focus on what I can do at this moment to make the best decisions regarding my treatment. Worrying about future outcomes from my disease only creates anxiety, and anxiety can lead to flares. It is an endless cycle.

*

BRENDA KLEINSASSER
Brenda was diagnosed with
rheumatoid arthritis in 1991 at age 31

I've lived with rheumatoid arthritis for over twenty-six years and there have certainly been a lot of changes. I was told in the beginning that I would get worse. Wonderful to hear. As mentioned before, the deformity in my fingers cannot be fixed. Over the past several years, I've had more swelling and redness in my hands. I am concerned that if I had to stop taking a biologic, my disease would certainly get worse. Every time I have a holiday from the biologic because of an infection, things start happening. When I am allowed to go back on it, I notice improvement within a few days, so I know it's still working. I don't know how much longer this will be the case. I have taken the same biologic for over sixteen years. That is a long time.

I tried so many other classes of drugs and supplements before I was able to finally get on a biologic. In the beginning, I was terrified that I wouldn't be able to work or care for myself. I leaned on my parents a lot during that time. I actually went home for about a week, as I was not doing well at all. My disease was progressing rapidly in the beginning. The methotrexate did slow it down some, but I had so many other things happen including nausea and sores that I had to wean myself off.

For me, it's about taking it one day at a time. I cannot think about my whole life, or what will happen tomorrow. The fear is there, but strong faith has sustained me all these years. I'm a fighter and that was proven when I had to work hard at keeping my job. Here I am, still employed full-time after living with this disease for twenty-six years.

*

CHANTELLE MARCIAL
Chantelle was diagnosed with
rheumatoid arthritis in 1999 at age 19

My progression has been significantly slowed thanks to biologics. I have developed OA n my spine but always have had issues with my back since I was a kid so no surprise there. I'm confident that if I maintain good contact with my doctor and continue my treatment that I can have slow progression and live a very full life.

*

LAYNE MARTIN
Layne was diagnosed with
psoriatic arthritis in 2007 at age 47

My psoriatic arthritis has slowly progressed over the last twenty-plus years. A recent bone scan now shows arthritis in both knees, both hips, both ankles and my lower spine. The bone scan lit up like a Christmas tree. Unfortunately, I've had pretty significant reactions to the biological medications so I can no longer take those. We did try another class of drugs called disease-modifying drugs but my psoriatic arthritis progressed despite these. I understand that I probably won't live to be eighty or ninty, and that is fine with me. I have had a wonderful, full life and wouldn't change anything about it. I know this disease can affect my internal organs so I try to eat a healthy diet and exercise when I can, and do what I can to keep myself as healthy as possible. Currently, I just take it one day at a time. Some days I'm stiff as a board and others I'm fairly mobile. I try to find humor in life and enjoy the people I'm with and my surroundings. I don't see any point in moping around feeling sorry for myself. I didn't ask for this disease but there are far worse things so in some ways I consider myself lucky.

*

KATHLEEN MEKAILEK
Kathleen was diagnosed with chronic regional pain
syndrome in 2005 at age 38, rheumatoid arthritis in
2014 at age 46, and ulcerative colitis in 2016 at age 49

RA has hit me hard. I meet people who have had it for years, and they haven't had as many surgeries and procedures as I have. Mine is

279

very aggressive and seems to love settling in my organs, and I wonder where it's going next. Actaully, that's not true. With the ulcerative colitis, I am fairly certain that my colon will be next, but what organ after that? Will it attack the eyes, heart, kidneys, liver? Exactly how many organs can the body adapt to living without? I have given up all the good things in order to try to help my body naturally. I am sugar free, gluten free, soy free, dairy free, caffeine free, and alcohol went away when I started methotrexate.

The biggest emotion that comes up for me is guilt. Guilt for all the money spent on doctors, medications and tests. Guilt for all the time spent waiting to see doctors, get lab work, take x-rays, have MRIs and CTs. Guilt for the endless hours my husband has to spend driving me to all the different places. Guilt for the time I haven't been able to be there for my family... my kids, my grandkids, my parents, my in-laws. Guilt that I might not be here for my children's marriages, births of more grandchildren or great-grandchildren. Guilt that I won't be around to give them advice. Guilt that I just won't be here. In the meantime, I hide my feelings of guilt behind a smile and try to act like everything is normal while the inside of me is spinning out of control. And there is nothing that I have taken yet that can stop it.

*

RICK PHILLIPS
Rick was diagnosed with type 1 diabetes in 1974
at age 17 and rheumatoid arthritis in 1999 at age 42

Progression of the condition can best be judged by the list of biologic medications I've used and discarded. I'm currently on seventh biologic treatment and if I ever think that rheumatoid arthritis does not impact me, I only have to miss a treatment or take a break. I recall during my last switch I had to resort to using a mobile grocery cart. I was so stiff I could barely move. This served to remind me how fortunate I am to have access to these medications and doctors who are willing to use them.

Each new medication is like a mile post of how far I have come. But it is also a reminder that there are far fewer options in front of me at this time than at any other time in my life. I see rheumatoid arthritis as a race to come in last. A race I do not think I will win. The question is, can I keep rheumatoid arthritis suppressed long enough to not run out of options?

*

LESLIE ROTT
Leslie was diagnosed with lupus and
rheumatoid arthritis in 2008 at age 22

Right now, I would say that my diseases are managed, for the most part. I am much more stable than I used to be. However, I fear becoming incapacitated by my illnesses. I fear needing joint replacements at a young age, and I fear having children in the future and not being able to take care of them. That scares me the most. I have accepted the fact that I will have these illnesses forever and that they are never going away. But I fear the day when I lose more than I have already lost. I fear the day when I'm no longer able to do things I love to do completely, and not just with modifications.

*

TIEN SYDNOR-CAMPBELL
Tien was diagnosed with autoimmune
rheumatoid disease in 2010 at age 40

One questions I continue to ask myself and my rheumatologist is even if my bloodwork isn't showing disease activity, why am I still in such great pain around my initially compromised joints? I have a gut feeling it's because I need multiple surgeries in multiple joints. It feels like they are getting worse and worse. At one point I couldn't write a paragraph without tears welling up in my eyes. Thankfully, I am not there right now. However, it still pains me to do things with my fingers and it stops me from wearing clothes with buttons and zippers. My biggest fear with this is that I am losing my joints to the point where I can't move because nothing functions properly. I am really, really scared of that prospect.

I had, originally, also envisioned being able to write something special since I spend so much time at home. I have, since, found out that my fatigue and inability to think clearly keeps from even doing that. I didn't have dreams of being a writer, but I had some things that I wanted to write. I have ideas for so many things running through my mind. I have started several writing projects. I am so easily distracted by things that I will leave, something I started, and not pick it back up for three to six months. I am pleasantly surprised that I have neared completion of this writing project in the allotted time frame. I have scheduled myself time to write, but I can't seem to get into a groove without falling into my pain-fatigue-guilt-depression cycle.

This cycle of mine has not been easy to deal with, emotionally or mentally. I feel guilt for not working and contributing to the family budget. The guilt becomes exhaustion or fatigue, and I stay in bed until I feel guilty for staying in bed but when I try to go do something, I can't because of too much pain. Waiting for the pain to go away, I get depressed and feel empty and sometimes worthless. The progression can feel like it is eating my peace of mind and curious spirit away little by little. I keep smiling because I know I have that kind of heart, but some days it feels like my will might not be enough to keep going.

*

Learn from yesterday, live for today,
hope for tomorrow.

ALBERT EINSTEIN

*

CHAPTER EIGHTEEN

Importance of Hope

Be like the birds, sing after every storm.
BETH MENDE CONNY

Hope is the fuel that propels us forward, urges us to get out of bed each morning. It is the promise that tomorrow will be better than today. But living with a progressive disease has a way of redefining what hope means to each of us. What does hope mean to you today?

*

CHRISTINA AMES
Christina was diagnosed with rheumatoid arthritis
in 1987 at age 20 and fibromyalgia in 2011 at age 43

Hope has been defined as a feeling of trust, or a belief that a certain thing will happen. I believe this absolutely. I believe that there will be a cure for this wretched disease, and I expect it in my lifetime. I don't know how I can be sure, I only know that it will be.

285

You may read this and think that I have a rather Pollyanna-ish view of life, that things are all roses and song. Well, roses have thorns, and songs can be sung in the wrong key. I've definitely found myself being stabbed by the thorns, repeatedly, nastily, and sometimes even had my flesh torn open by them. But I also know the velvety softness of the petals, the depth of the colors, and the delicacy of the fragrance of the rose blossoms. It seems to me that the adage is true: You are given this life because you are strong enough to live it. Many people dismiss this, but for me it is true.

I am strong, and because of that strength, I have hope. I have always had hope, I will continue to have hope, I will never give up hope. Hope is one thing that defines us as looking toward the future with incredible expectations, both from our own making and relying on others to aid us in our journey. It is an emotion given to us for the most priceless of reasons, that because of hope, we may eventually experience joy.

*

J.G. CHAYKO
J.G. was diagnosed with
rheumatoid arthritis in 2010 at age 38

Where possibility exists, there is always hope. Our world and our lives are full of possibilities: the things that could be are always just in front of us. Sometimes they are within grasp, and sometimes it takes a long journey to reach them, but they are always there, just waiting. When I was first diagnosed with RA, it altered the life I built. I had to stop certain activities, and come to terms with the idea that I might not be able to return to some of them. But I discovered there is always more than one path, and was willing to travel any street, highway or lane that would bring me closer to the possibilities I never considered until the arrival of RA.

This is where hope thrives for me. Hope has been described as fleeting but I believe it is a tangible thing. It exists everywhere—in rainbows behind the mist, diamonds in the granite, and flowers in the mud. The smallest light can guide us through the darkness of our bleakest moments. Hope thrives in our own strength and endurance, in the will and ingenuity to reinvent our life. As long as there is possibility for change, hope will exist. Our lives are supposed to flow. Even when it feels like we are stagnant, the world around us keeps moving and we just need to watch and learn.

The world of rheumatoid arthritis and rheumatic disease is also constantly shifting. Today there are more choices for treatment than ever before. Medical practitioners are more knowledgeable, and it's not just medication. Physiotherapists and occupational therapists can give us the tools to manage so that we can take control of our own health. I can't sit on the sidelines waiting for someone to tell me what to do. Nobody knows my own body better than I. If I listen to my body, I can learn how to move with it, I can let it guide me alongside my treatments to find my best life.

Hope is the force behind our changing lives. Rheumatic arhtritis was not the end of my life—it was only the end of what was safe and familiar. It has driven me to take risks, seeking out all the unfamiliar and wonderful things waiting to take me in new directions. It has made my life a delightful, challenging and stimulating adventure filled with trials and achievements that build strength, resolve and, of course, hope.

*

JUDITH FLANAGAN
Judith was diagnosed with rheumatoid arthritis in 2012 at age 32
and fibromyalgia and polymyalgia rheumatic in 2014 at age 34

My definition of hope is holding on, getting through each day, being brave, determined and being understanding. It also means to come together with others and support each other. It means knowing that that nobody has to fight this alone. It means that I have your back, and together we have each other's back. It means hoping for a cure, hoping that the world will some day be rid of these awful diseases that are quite often misunderstood.

*

SHELLEY FRITZ
Shelley was diagnosed with
rheumatoid arthritis in 2012 at age 42

Hope can mean having the expectation and desire for something to happen and it can also be thought of as wanting something to happen. I cannot just wish for a cure and sit idly by; rather I need to stay involved in advocacy and keep abreast of research so that I can expect that we will find a cure. Hope is the driving force that keeps me from shutting down and curling up in a ball. It means getting up every day and being grateful for everything I am blessed with having in my life. I am thankful for not feeling any disease symptoms until I approached forty. At the time, it felt as if I was moving along on a game board and steering clear of any major health scares then BAM! Suddenly I was dealt a card that was a game changer.

If I had developed disease symptoms earlier in life, I wonder how it would have impacted my path. I see others become hardened by the cold truth of chronic illness. I have things to be bitter about but they are not things I can control, so I focus more on the things I am grateful for and I find that it's more productive. We cannot change many aspects of our future but I do believe that if we lose hope and stop trying to feel better, we will begin to feel worse very rapidly and then this disease will have taken over. I've learned a lot from having to face this battle every day. I look at people completely differently now and wonder what battles they face and how they overcome them to keep moving. As I speak with others who have chronic illnesses, I try to offer hope by listening to them and sharing my story. We all have to find a thread of hope to cling to or we face a dark road ahead.

*

BRENDA KLEINSASSER
Brenda was diagnosed with
rheumatoid arthritis in 1991 at age 31

Hope is one of my favorite words. It's something that I cling to every day. It gives me purpose to get out of bed every morning. I attempt to approach each day with the fact that hope will help me get through the rough patches. I've experienced a lot of dark times but I've always come back to hope, which constantly sustains me. If it were not for hope, I would have given up a long time ago.

I have a friend who describes hope like this: "It is something that you can wrap your arms around." It's like a big hug all day long, and a friend who'll never leave. You can always lean on hope. Hope is a smile when I would rather frown, and instantly turns my mood around. Hope is laughter when I sometimes feel like crying, and the tears suddenly turn to joy. Hope is how I cope with all the things that this disease has thrown at me. Hope will continue to sustain me until I die.

*

CHANTELLE MARCIAL
Chantelle was diagnosed with
rheumatoid arthritis in 1999 at age 19

I have RA—it does not have me. It does not define me. It is merely the piece of a very full and fortunate woman that I am. I am hopeful because there is so much conversation surrounding this disease and other auto immune disorders. I think it's great that research is ramping up and new treatments are being discovered. I'm very hopeful that it will be better controlled in the next generation, and the next.

*

LAYNE MARTIN
Layne was diagnosed with
psoriatic arthritis in 2007 at age 47

Hope is being able to love and, share that love and compassion with others. By writing my story and sharing my journey I am hopefulness that it will inspire others and give them encouragement that life can be enjoyable despite the obstacles we may all face. I wish I was disease free and able to live a normal healthy life but, this is my life and, in looking back I wouldn't do it any other way. I've been able to help so many people by walking this same walk alongside them and having compassion and understanding of how they may be feeling and what they are going through. My hope is to continue reaching out and offering comfort to others.

*

KATHLEEN MEKAILEK
Kathleen was diagnosed with chronic regional pain
syndrome in 2005 at age 38, rheumatoid arthritis in
2014 at age 46, and ulcerative colitis in 2016 at age 49

Hope is a four letter word to me. To me, hope is tied to guilt. I know my rheumatoid arthritis is genetic, so I hope the DNA strand dies with me, but I live with guilt that I might have passed it on to one of my children and even their children. I hope my kids and grandchildren never have to know this kind of pain and suffering.

I hope people become more knowledgeable about this disease, and understand more of what I go through on a daily basis. But then I would feel guilty letting them know my struggles, because there is nothing they can do for me. I have to struggle through on my own.

I hope that there is a cure for this awful disease. There are so many medications to help with remission, why not find a cure? I feel guilty when I see cure announcements for other diseases. Instead of being happy, I can only wonder, why not a cure for me, for us? I feel guilty because I think it is unfair. I ask the why me question, and then feel guilty because if it's not me, it would be someone else. So, I guess the only thing that I can hope for and not feel guilty is a better tomorrow, a better world, a better day—for everyone, not just me.

*

RICK PHILLIPS
Rick was diagnosed with type 1 diabetes in 1974
at age 17 and rheumatoid arthritis in 1999 at age 42

Hope, for me, is my grandchildren, and their children's children. I do not know why I have RA. Was it triggered by stress or other environmental factors? Perhaps it was not triggered by something on the outside, rather an internal body process. I may never know the truth, but it does not matter to me. But it might matter to the children in my life. I believe we are very close to understanding the body chemistry that happens when a person has RA. Once we know that, I am hopeful my grandchildren can avoid it, or if they're diagnosed, that we will have better ways of controlling that. I have no illusion of a cure for me. I don't even dream about it. What I do dream about is a cure for my grandchildren. Now that's hope.

*

LESLIE ROTT
Leslie was diagnosed with lupus and
rheumatoid arthritis in 2008 at age 22

My definition of hope means trying to live each day to the fullest, regardless of challenges; to remain positive, and continue to believe that a cure for rheumatic diseases will happen in my lifetime.

I hope that if I have children, they will not be burdened with these illnesses. If they are, I hope there are more successful treatments available to them.

Writing gives me hope. I hope that sharing my story gives others hope. As a blogger, I am seemingly sharing my story all the time. But it's hard to put it all together in a cogent way. I'm so grateful for this opportunity, and the chance to educate others about what living with rheumatic diseases is like.

*

TIEN SYDNOR-CAMPBELL
Tien was diagnosed with autoimmune
rheumatoid disease in 2010 at age 40

My hopes have changed since the moment I realized that my life was no longer going to look the way I had intended. This disease was a blind turn that went downhill really fast. Before I was diagnosed, I recall telling my clients that they have to fight to become more than their disease, to not let whatever chronic condition they have be their introduction to new people or experiences. I thought I understood chronic pain and how to fight through it, because I had been dealing with problematic knees my entire life. I took over-the-counter meds and unless it got really painful, stopped complaining to my doctors years earlier. I had hope that one day I would get a doctor who could fix my knees. I applied ice and heat as needed, and stretched before working out. I had hope then. I even had a little hope after my diagnosis and after my knees were fixed, everything would be alright.

My hopes, now, tend to be more momentary and immediate in nature. What that means for me is that I have small hopes, like; I will be able to walk several minutes and do some shopping, or; I am going to work on one of my arts or crafts projects. When those hopes have been met, I am better able to have some for the next day. I still make plans that take considerable time, such as a vacation, with the hopes that I will not be too sick to go. I had planned a vacation to Jamaica last year and unfortunately I was unable to go because I was having a really bad flare. I buy trip insurance for everything that I do these days. It's critical to my security that I don't lose the trip and the money at the same time.

My hope is limited. It does not go into thoughts or dreams of being free from this disease. It does not include hoping for a pain-free week. I used to hope for that a long time ago. I had this one time when I feeling fantastic for three entire days. I was sure that the new combination of medications was finally working for me. As the third day came to an end the pain slightly resurfaced, but I still felt like it was working. The next morning, I was back to nagging pain and by the end of the week my lovely, level four pain had returned to six and a half. This is where I hover, no matter what combination is in my system.

My grand scale hope is equivalent to wishing for world peace, but in my case it's hoping for a cure. I feel more hopeful of winning the lottery to be honest. Watching others deal with, and pass, due to complications from rheumatoid arthritis and other autoimmune diseases doesn't instill personal hope. I don't mean to seem down and out, if that is what it sounds like. It really is my truth. It changes and sounds more positive some days, worse on others. This is what I am feeling today. My hope is about maintaining my presence in the present. It is a gift, after all, isn't it?

*

Surround yourself with people who provide
you with support and love, and remember to
give back as much as you can in return.

KAREN KAIN

*

CHAPTER NINETEEN

Finding Peace on the Journey

I don't want my pain and struggle to make
me a victim. I want my battle to make
me someone else's hero. -ANONYMOUS

Every journey is unique as a fingerprint, for we experience different
beliefs, desires, needs, and we often walk different roads. Though we
may not see anyone else on the path, we are never truly alone, for
more walk behind, beside, and in front of us. In this chapter lies the
answers to the final question posed: What would you like the world
to know about your autoimmune journey?

*

CHRISTINA AMES
Christina was diagnosed with rheumatoid arthritis in 1987
at age 20 and diagnosed with fibromyalgia in 2011 at age 43

I will simply say that I am grateful for Lynda Cheldelin Fell for
the opportunity she provided, and the rest of the team for all their hard
work to bring this book to the public. I'd like to thank my family for

their continued support. I would like to thank the readers. I hope you enjoyed it, and gained something from it. To those on the same journey, be well, and stay courageous. Illegitimi non carborundum.

*

J.G. CHAYKO
J.G. was diagnosed with
rheumatoid arthritis in 2010 at age 38

Nobody expects to deal with chronic illness. I never thought about it until the day I turned a bend in my road and came face to face with RA. I was diagnosed at the peak of my theatrical life. I had barely finished the first act. Alexander Graham Bell said it best: "When one door closes another door opens." I used to think all my doors as being open. If I wanted to walk through one, I just turned the knob. When rheumatoid arthritis made its debut, doors slammed one by one down my proverbial corridor.

Rheumatoid arthritis changed my life. I lost and gained. I found a renewed determination, drive, perspective and understanding. I learned never to settle. I took for granted the things I had a natural proclivity for, always believing they would be at my fingertips. I never had to push beyond my boundaries. I wasn't about to let a chronic illness take away my dreams or the life I had built. I was sure there had to be a way to live the life I wanted, even if it meant taking a new path.

With chronic illness, boundaries shrink, and if you don't continue to push, stretch and protest, you'll end up suffocating at its hands. Chronic illness can consume us if we allow it. It puts us at the mercy

298

of medication, medical appointments, diet, exercise, inflammation and pain. It delays our plans and upsets our life. It can feel a bit out of our control but there are still elements of life with rheumatoid arthritis where I can take charge. I can't predict when a flare will come on, but I can decide how to manage it. A work day or a day of hiking sidelined by pain becomes a day of rest and recharge; perhaps time to finish the book I started weeks ago, time to snuggle into my heating blanket and review lines for my latest show, time to sip some tea and watch a favorite film. Sometimes little joys get lost in our demanding world, but life has a way of forcing us to slow down and rediscover them. It's never a waste of time if it's time to take care of me.

Rheumatoid arthritis was not the end of my life. In some ways it offered a new beginning. Life is meant to flow, shift, wilt and bloom. Rheumatoid disease forced me to look beyond the perimeter and seek opportunities I never would have explored without its presence. In those moments when I thought I'd never get back on the stage, I turned to words. While I couldn't manipulate my body, I could manipulate prose, text, poetry and story. Words ignited my imagination, revived an early aspiration and paved the way back to the creative life I always desired.

Rheumatoid arthritis took some things from my life, yet. But it couldn't take things I hadn't yet obtained, and that gave me power. Just because there are things I can no longer do doesn't mean there's nothing I can do. Rheumatoid arthritis forced me to leave some activities behind, but I was able to go back and collect the remnants. It took work, patience and time, but after four years I got back on the stage. I do one, maybe two shows a year; I go back to the dance studio on a limited basis with my partner; I paint pictures with words, create new worlds, and meet new characters.

Disease is not my life. It's a part of my life. Rheumatoid arthritis doesn't define me. I am a writer, an actress, a daughter, a sister, an aunt and a spouse. I learned to reinvent my life and change my new normal. There are always new goals to fill the old ones. Even when I try and fail, I find consolation in the effort. It's not in my nature to sit back and surrender. Every year I will find my time to bloom and thrive. And I will keep on thriving.

*

JUDITH FLANAGAN
Judith was diagnosed with rheumatoid arthritis in 2012 at age 32
and fibromyalgia and polymyalgia rheumatic in 2014 at age 34

I want the world to know that being supported by people I love can make a world of difference. A little understanding and compassion can go a long way. A person's life can change a lot from these diseases, and people sadly die. This is why I push to raise awareness alongside other patient leaders and advocates around the world. Compassion costs nothing. Come on people! Let's work together to make a difference in the world.

*

SHELLEY FRITZ
Shelley was diagnosed with
rheumatoid arthritis in 2012 at age 42

I've stopped questioning why I suffer with autoimmune diseases. It is what it is. I can choose to curl up and cry about it, but that does not change the fact that it is still here in my body. I went through phases of grief and now I am at the stage of acceptance. It wasn't my choice to live with this, but as I look around at the world, it puts life into perspective for me. It could have been a lot worse! There are millions of people suffering, many from birth, who probably feel like they want to give up each day. We shouldn't perseverate over why something was done to us, rather we should embrace it and find a way to make something productive come from it.

That isn't to say it doesn't hurt or bother me to have to deal with this every day. The weight of living with this disease can at times feel insurmountable. When I feel overwhelmed by the stresses of not being able to do the things I used to be able to do and from having chronic pain, I reach out to others through online communities and through support groups so that I can help others find resources and hope. Whether it's striking up a conversation with someone out in public or responding to a question on social media, I feel that having human contact with others who have rheumatoid arthritis is important. We all have information and ideas to share with one another and we need to be reminded that we have amazing support out there from others who understand.

For those newly diagnosed with a rheumatic disease, find hope through small gains you make, seek support from positive people, remove yourself from toxic situations, advocate for what is right, reach out to friends who have stopped calling, and find your tribe.

*

BRENDA KLEINSASSER
Brenda was diagnosed with
rheumatoid arthritis in 1991 at age 31

I guess what I would like everyone to know is that you can live and thrive with rheumatoid arthritis. It doesn't have to consume you. I am more than my disease, much more. I am a fighter, writer, advocate, and friend. Most of all, I live with rheumatoid arthritis but it doesn't own me.

I was told early on in this journey that I was stronger than this disease. That person was absolutely correct. I now possess the tools and confidence I didn't have during those early days. I cried the first month. I had no idea how to cope. I thought for sure that I was going to become someone I wouldn't recognize. It was a very scary time. I fought hard and started doing my research. I didn't have a computer, so going to the library to check out videos and read articles was all I really had to fall back on. Things are so much different today.

I did a lot of research before starting my biologic. I've always been an analytical person, and wanted to know exactly what I could be facing. I need to know why something is. You telling me just because does not cut it for me. I believe strongly in research because that is what will help us find a cure one day. I have that hope. My being able to take a biologic in the first place was because of research and a scientist who discovered the tumor necrosis factor, or TNF molecule. I will always be grateful for that discovery.

I have found that helping others is really helping yourself. It gets my mind off the disease and helps to focus on a possible solution. Rheumatoid arthritis is not an easy disease to navigate, by any means. It can even be hard to diagnose, as it was in my case—almost three years from the time when I started experiencing costochondritis, which was actually the rheumatoid disease cooking up all along.

There have been many advancements with treatment options. There were no biologics on the market when I was diagnosed in 1991. The first FDA-approved biologic came out in 1998, and I started it three years later. I will never forget that first day. I was not administering my injections yet, as I was being monitored very closely. Within a month I did my first injection, and have been doing them at home ever since. That is a huge thing for me. It helps to keep my independence. You lose so much when you live with a chronic illness. It's the one thing I own, and it means the world to me.

I keep a diary so I can make sure to rotate the areas of injection. It stings a little, but when I think of the relief I get, I can handle that little bit of pain. I also know my pain threshold is high. I don't want to say that you ever really get used to the pain, but I think there are times when you can block it out. When I have a cold, my RA is not really active, which seems strange. I am always grateful for the reprieve.

I never know on any given day what gifts rheumatoid arthritis may bring, so I always need to be prepared. That is why I get up early in the morning, to be able to do some stretching or full range of motion exercises. Moving helps me immensely. I have very little morning stiffness, especially since starting my biologic. That was not always the case. I remember hanging onto furniture so I wouldn't fall. I actually crawled on the floor once because I couldn't walk around my apartment. I fatigue quite easily, so pacing myself is paramount.

I don't get all my errands done in one day. I cannot go grocery shopping and then off to the mall. It's one or the other. Too much in one day means I pay for it the next day. It's not worth it if it doesn't need to be done. If I want to do something fun for an evening, then I make sure to rest up and maybe take a nap in the afternoon. If I have to cancel, please do not take it personal. I feel bad enough already for having to bail.

I guess my final thought is that I have decided to remain positive, hope for the best outcome, and hope that a cure will someday be found. I will never give up hope!

*

CHANTELLE MARCIAL
Chantelle was diagnosed with
rheumatoid arthritis in 1999 at age 19

I would like people to know that this disease is a piece of me, for sure, but that it is just a piece. I am proud that I get the opportunity to advocate for fellow patients and to educate others. It is truly an honor.

304

My life will be accented forever with these incredible opportunities to teach and to learn from other patients. I want to convey that I have hope and that this diagnosis made me realize something: I am worth it. All of it. So bring it on!

*

LAYNE MARTIN
Layne was diagnosed with
psoriatic arthritis in 2007 at age 47

I would like the world to know that rheumatic disease is no walk in the park. It's a daily struggle, and some days are worse. Some of the struggles are physical and some are emotional. The anxiety of fighting with insurance companies over authorization of medications or worrying about a loved one can cause the disease to flare. Trying to live a peaceful life is key as is eating healthy and doing some form of low-impact exercise but, it's no cure, it just helps the day to day issues.

There is a lot of research going on regarding rheumatic illnesses and the future looks bright in regards to controlling these diseases or even finding a cure. I don't know if it will happen in my lifetime but I am optimistic for future generations.

*

KATHLEEN MEKAILEK
Kathleen was diagnosed with chronic regional pain
syndrome in 2005 at age 38, rheumatoid arthritis in
2014 at age 46, and ulcerative colitis in 2016 at age 49

This has been my journey. It has been a short one, so I might not have as much to say, but it has been a vicious one. Those who are close

305

to me know I hurt every day, but I will always put on a smile and a brave front to protect those around me from knowing the truth.

Lately, I have been giving the world peeks into my journey through this messy, nasty, expensive disease (as one of my doctors called it). I use a lot of humor. It might be considered dark humor to some, but it helps get me through the rough patches. One of my favorites was something I wrote around Christmas 2016. Now the numbers are grossly under what they are in reality, but you get the basic idea.

TWELVE DAYS OF CHRONIC ILLNESS

Twelve meds daily

11 x-rays taken

10 steroid shots injected

9 surgeries sutured

8 scars in tummy

7 MRIs reading

6 CT scans scanning

5 hair clumps falling

4 organs missing

3 replacement parts

2 procedures planned

and a new shoulder in the next year!!!!!

Each person's journey through this disease, and life in general, is different. I'm not documenting my journey because I want pity or sympathy. Rather, I want you to have a glimpse into a portion of my life and be able to understand why I am the way I am. I am still me, not a disease. Just a living human being who wants to be accepted for who I am.

*

RICK PHILLIPS
Rick was diagnosed with type 1 diabetes in 1974
at age 17 and rheumatoid arthritis in 1999 at age 42

I am fortunate to have RA. I am not sure how else to describe it. No, I did not want nor seek out RA, it found me. But by the same token, in 1974 when I was diagnosed with diabetes, I did not expect to live beyond my mid-forties, which is around the same time RA entered my life. I am reminded that my mother, who passed at age forty-six from complications of diabetes, never had to deal with RA. So knowing I've now made it to age sixty, I have to say I am pretty darn happy to have these past years.

Yes, these last years have been filled with RA, a condition I was not expecting and knew nothing about until I was diagnosed, but all the same I am still alive. I am still going and I am now able to see my grandchildren grow up. So yes, I want the world to know I am happy to be here with RA. I am glad to be able to laugh and joke and meet new people. I am happy to live and make contributions. Because every single day I lived past age forty-five was a gift, and rheumatoid arthritis will not ruin the daily surprise of living.

*

LESLIE ROTT
Leslie was diagnosed with lupus and
rheumatoid arthritis in 2008 at age 22

Life is a journey, it's just more complicated with chronic illness or whatever challenges you face. As a young person, it's difficult to get other people to understand that young people can have arthritis. In spite of these diseases, I successfully completed my Ph.D. I also went on to get a second master's degree in health advocacy. This was a direct result of my illnesses. Without my experiences, many of them negative at the hands of the medical system, I would never have known all the gaps that exist for patients, especially the chronically ill. So in a roundabout way, my illnesses got me to where I am today.

*

TIEN SYDNOR-CAMPBELL
Tien was diagnosed with autoimmune
rheumatoid disease in 2010 at age 40

My journey has truly changed my outlook over the years. I don't know the exact moment that I felt a new purpose, but I can honestly say that I have found something to do with the all of the challenges I've faced. I have become an accidental advocate for patients who suffer from the effects of rheumatoid arthritis. I have joined two different advocacy groups over the last few years and have made many new friends across the country. One of these is CreakyJoints/Arthritis Power that promotes patient participation in research outcomes and measurements. I am currently serving as a Patient Partner in Research as well as a Patient Governor.

These roles have given me new friendships that are mainly across telecommunication devices, but that keeps me plugged in to the outside world a few hours a month. My motto has become "No more decisions for us or about us, without us." I am very excited about the possibilities of making life more bearable for arthritis sufferers.

The Arthritis Foundation is the other group that I belong to. This foundation has given me access to information and support from other arthritis sufferers in the form of annual conferences and small support groups. I have met some incredible people and shared their challenges through our social media outlets. It is another way that I stay in touch with others who are experiencing the same problems from the same disease.

The foundation has also facilitated my involvement in upcoming legislative projects such as speaking with members of Congress who make decisions that affect the rheumatoid community. Again, I follow my motto that there will be "No more decisions for us or about us, without us." If you, or someone you love, needs some support, I wholeheartedly endorse these groups to empower themselves and others.

*

Shared joy is doubled joy;
shared sorrow is half a sorrow.

SWEDISH PROVERB

*

CHAPTER TWENTY

MEET THE WRITERS

*

CHRISTINA AMES
Christina was diagnosed with rheumatoid arthritis
in 1987 at age 20 and fibromyalgia in 2011 at age 43
fpdcopswife@verizon.net

Christina Ames was born in Washington, DC, and raised in the Maryland suburbs. She attended Indiana University in Bloomington, and earned a bachelor's degree in French Education, which she has yet to truly utilize. After graduation, she returned to Maryland, and eventually met and married her husband, Doug, who is a police detective. They have two children: Donnie, who is a junior in college, and Lauren, who is a junior in high school. Christina opted to be a stay at home parent, and never regretted it. She was the consummate school volunteer, doing everything from reading helper to football mom. She was also very active as a Boy Scout volunteer in her son's troop, and continues to be an active volunteer in her church. Because of the strong need to be involved, she decided to become an advocate for the rheumatic disease patient. She is active in the Arthritis Foundation, and is on the Patient Council and 50 State Network advocacy groups for Global Healthy Living Foundation. She has also written for CreakyJoints, and has a blog, Christina's Rheum. She enjoys reading, writing, and traveling, and is a passionate college football and basketball fan.

*

J.G. CHAYKO
J.G. was diagnosed with
rheumatoid arthritis in 2010 at age 38
theoldladyinmybones.com

J.G. Chayko is a writer and actress from
Vancouver, Canada, who has published
poetry, fiction and creative nonfiction.
She is the author of two blogs: The Old
Lady in My Bones, a series of stories on
her experience living with rheumatoid
arthritis, and a writing blog called
Corkboards and Coffeehouses. She has
spent many years on the stage and has

guest blogged for other sites and contributed to health articles. In
addition to writing short stories and poetry, she is currently working
on a novel.

*

JUDITH FLANAGAN
Judith was diagnosed with rheumatoid arthritis in 2012 at age 32
and fibromyalgia and polymyalgia rheumatic in 2014 at age 34
UnitedAdvocacy Australia.wordpress.com | jfbegatafe@gmail.com

Judith Flanagan was born in Brisbane, Australia, and raised in Tasmania, until age eleven when she moved to Eden, on the coast of New South Wales. She attended Eden Primary School with her sister Kylie, and then Eden Marine High School. From there, Judith held various businesses administration jobs until 2007, when she attended a local vocational school to study childcare. Whilst there, she was offerered a job working one-on-one with two autistic boys. Judith happily accepted, and found the work very rewarding, as her kind nature was very calming for the two boys. The following year she had another childcare job in Merimbula. Judith loved working with children. She loved seeing their smiling faces, and enjoyed watching their creativity blossom because she too is a creative soul, and getting creative makes her happy. In 2010, Judith went back to vocational training to study business administration and web technologies.

*

SHELLEY FRITZ
Shelley was diagnosed with
rheumatoid arthritis in 2012 at age 42
rheumatoidarthritis.support | shelley.fritz@gmail.com

Shelley Fritz was born in Walnut Creek, California, in 1969. She moved around throughout her childhood, spending time in Texas, Aruba, and Florida. She studied at the University of Florida and earned a B.S. in Elementary Education from Florida International University, and M.S. in Educational Leadership from Nova Southeastern University. Shelley has been educating children for over twenty years and currently works as a math coach supporting teachers and students. She lives in the Tampa Bay area with her husband, two children, two cats, and dog.

As she approached her fortieth birthday, Shelley began having fatigue, joint stiffness and inflammation. After nearly two years of symptoms, Shelley was diagnosed with rheumatoid arthritis in 2012 at age forty-two. Getting a diagnosis came as a relief, although at the time she knew very little about rheumatic diseases. Shelley stays involved with the Arthritis Foundation, Arthritis Introspective, CreakyJoints and the Arthritis National Research Foundation, among others, to network with patients, doctors and researchers to promote awareness of different forms of arthritis and the importance of advocacy.

*

BRENDA L. KLEINSASSER
Brenda was diagnosed with
rheumatoid arthritis in 1991 at age 31
brendasbrainstormandtrevor.blogspot.com
creakyjoints.org | blkleinsasser@gmail.com

Brenda L. Kleinsasser resides in Bismarck, North Dakota. She has worked in various avenues of the medical field for over thirty years, and has served as editor of the CreakyJoints Poet's Corner (& Artists too), for three years. Brenda is a fierce patient advocate for both rheumatoid arthritis and brain tumors, as she is an eight-year brain  tumor survivor. Brenda has testified in her own state of North Dakota, representing the patient's voice on behalf of the Global Healthy Living Foundation, via the 50-State Network as a super advocate. Brenda also volunteers for CreakyJoints with Patient Partners in Research 50-State Network and Patient Council. Brenda authors a blog, Brenda's Brainstorm and Trevor, stories that are shared from a golden retriever's point of view. Brenda also enjoys reading, singing and journaling. Brenda coauthored "Real Life Diaries: Living with a Brain Injury," and contributed to "Grief Diaries: Loss of Health" and "Grief Diaries: How to Help the Newly Bereaved." Brenda also contributed to "Surviving Brain Injury: Stories of Strength and Inspiration."

*

CHANTELLE MARCIAL
Chantelle was diagnosed with
rheumatoid arthritis in 1999 at age 19

Chantelle is a proud Bostonian born and
bred. She works in the relocation field for a
major institute of higher learning. Chantelle
is an advocate for patients and has spoken at
a Congressional Sub-Committee in support
of patients' rights. She comes from a large
family with a strong history of autoimmune disease. In her spare time
she enjoys cooking, reading and spending time with her husband.

*

LAYNE MARTIN
Layne was diagnosed with
psoriatic arthritis in 2007 at age 47

Layne Martin was born and raised in
the beautiful Pacific Northwest. At a
young age she was captivated by
nurses. She loved everything about
them, their crisp white dress
uniforms, the white shoes and
nylons, even the large white hats that
they wore on their heads. Layne

pursued a degree as a registered nurse and quickly gained the respect
of fellow peers and physicians alike. She rapidly moved her way up the
ranks and eventually found her true passion working in emergency
medicine. As Layne continued to excel in her profession, she enjoyed
mentoring those new to the emergency department. At age forty-
seven, at the peak of her career, Layne's world came crashing down
when she was diagnosed with psoriatic arthritis, a destructive
autoimmune disease. Soon she was plagued with the debilitating
effects of the arthritis and was forced into early retirement, leaving a
profession that she dearly loved and was destined to do. Today, Layne
volunteers her time writing blogs as a regional outreach manager and
patient advocate for CreakyJoints. She also participates in the National
Arthritis Database and recently was featured in an article in Everyday
Health titled, "Managing Bad Days with Psoriatic Arthritis."

*

KATHLEEN MEKAILEK
Kathleen was diagnosed with chronic regional pain
syndrome in 2005 at age 38, rheumatoid arthritis in
2014 at age 46, and ulcerative colitis in 2016 at age 49
www.kammeartgallery.com | kamme_art@yahoo.com

From a young age, Kathleen (Wagner) Mekailek always new she wanted to be an artist. She took art classes in school and loved them, but her parents thought her intelligence would be better suited for a more traditional career such as a doctor or a CPA. Instead, Kathleen found herself being

a housewife with four children to raise, the youngest diagnosed with autism at the age of two. Like most marriages under this type of pressure, it fell apart. A few years later, Kathleen met the love of her life and the man she would come to depend on when medical issues started to arise. Kathleen married Charles (Chuck) Mekailek a few years later. For Mother's Day 2013, her youngest daughter, Sami, gave her everything she needed to start painting again, but there was no inspiration. Her husband then gave her an easel for her birthday in June—still nothing. Kathleen's oldest daughter, Krista, gave birth to a granddaughter and after holding her, inspiration poured in. She soon took up photography and sculpting. Then in 2014, a new reality took over: rheumatoid arthritis. Chuck opened a gallery for her to continue giving her inspiration to go on.

*

RICK PHILLIPS, Ph.D.
Rick was diagnosed with type 1 diabetes in 1974 at
age 17 and rheumatoid arthritis in 1999 at age 42
www.RADiabetes.com

Lawrence "Rick" Phillips lives with his wife Sheryl in Indiana. Married in 1977, they are blessed with two wonderful sons and grandchildren. Rick was diagnosed with type 1 diabetes while on a family vacation at Disney World in 1974, and released from the hospital on his seventeenth birthday. Rick, graduated from Indiana University in 1979 with a Bachelor's of Science of Public Affairs. He earned a Masters of Public Affairs in 1989 from Indiana University. Rick served the people of central Indiana as a city comptroller, development director, and city planner from 1980 until 1994. In 1994, Rick started his career as Director of Finance for two school districts in Indiana. In 1999, he was diagnosed with rheumatoid arthritis and forced to retire in 2008. Not content to retire, Rick pursued a doctorate of education from Nova Southeastern University and graduated in 2012. In 2013, he started writing for TUDiabetes followed by CreakyJoints and RADiabetes. Rick is the founder of the annual RABlog week. He is active in advocating for people with diabetes and arthritis.

321

*

LESLIE ROTT, Ph.D.
Leslie was diagnosed with lupus and
rheumatoid arthritis in 2008 at age 22
gettingclosertomyself.blogspot.com
gettingclosertomyself@gmail.com

Leslie Rott was born and raised in Michigan, where she currently resides, although she spent several years living in New York. She is an e-patient, health activist, patient advocate, and blogger. She authors the blog Getting Closer to Myself. She has a Ph.D. in sociology from the University of Michigan and a master's degree in health advocacy from Sarah Lawrence College. She has written for a variety of health-related websites, and currently works as a health data analyst and client liaison for a home healthcare company.

*

TIEN SYDNOR-CAMPBELL
Tien was diagnosed with autoimmune
rheumatoid disease in 2010 at age 40
www.bodymindconsult.com

Tien Sydnor-Campbell was born and raised in Kalamazoo, Michigan. Due to her medical condition, she is now a retired body-centered psychotherapist with over twenty-five years of clinical experience in helping others with chronic pain and recovery from trauma. She came into working with the body as a massage therapist, massage instructor, and massage school director for nearly  twenty years before going back to traditional education. She obtained a master's in mental health counseling in order to better facilitate healthy connections and empower others in managing psychosomatic imbalances. Tien has been the beneficiary of exceptional support from a very loving husband, as well as two fantastic and understanding adult children, ages eighteen and twenty-one, who had to step up and step in as responsible teenagers in order to keep the household running smoothly. The support of family and friends has been critically important to Tien because the medical interventions have not always worked well and the use of trial and error can be mentally and emotionally exhausting. It is her hope that her contributions to this work help others experiencing autoimmune rheumatoid disease.

323

THANK YOU

I am deeply indebted to the writers of *Real Life Diaries: Living with Rheumatic Diseases.* It's not easy penning such intimate details of one's life for the purpose of helping others, and the collective dedication to seeing this book project to the end is a legacy to be proud of. I'm especially grateful to coauthors Brenda Kleinsasser, and my sister Layne Martin, R.N., two inspiring ladies whom I greatly admire for their dedication to patient advocacy. With so little nonclinical information available, it is my sincere hope that readers who share the same path will find compassion, understanding, and hope, and family, friends and professionals will appreciate the candid insight.

It's been said that pictures alone, without the written word, leaves half the story untold. A good story invites us to go beyond the edge of our own life into the world of another where we discover, learn, find commonality and—perhaps most important—we leave with deeper understanding. That's what Real Life Diaries is all about.

Lynda Cheldelin Fell

There's a bright future for you at every turn,
even if you miss one.

*

LYNDA CHELDELIN FELL

Considered a pioneer in the field of inspirational hope in the aftermath of hardship and loss, Lynda Cheldelin Fell has a passion for storytelling and producing groundbreaking projects that create a legacy of help, healing, and hope. She is an international  bestselling author and creator of the award-winning book series Grief Diaries and Real Life Diaries. She has earned five patient advocacy award nominations for her work. Her repertoire of interviews include Dr. Martin Luther King's daughter, Trayvon Martin's mother, sisters of the late Nicole Brown Simpson, Pastor Todd Burpo of Heaven Is For Real, CNN commentator Dr. Ken Druck, and other societal newsmakers on finding healing and hope in the aftermath of life's harshest challenges.

Lynda's own story began in 2007, when she had an alarming dream about her young teenage daughter, Aly. In the dream, Aly was a backseat passenger in a car that veered off the road and landed in a lake. Aly sank with the car, leaving behind an open book floating face down on the water. Two years later, Lynda's dream became reality when her daughter was killed as a backseat passenger in a car accident while coming home from a swim meet. Overcome with grief, Lynda's forty-six-year-old husband suffered a major stroke that left him with severe disabilities, changing the family dynamics once again.

The following year, Lynda was invited to share her remarkable story about finding hope after loss, and she accepted. That cathartic experience inspired her to create groundbreaking projects spanning national events, radio, film and books to help others who share the same journey feel less alone. Now a dedicated story curator, educator, and speaker, Lynda is passionate about harnessing the power of storytelling to help raise awareness and foster understanding about the complexities of life.

lynda@lyndafell.com | www.lyndafell.com

ALYBLUE MEDIA TITLES

Real Life Diaries: Through the Eyes of a Funeral Director
Real Life Diaries: Living with Mental Illness
Real Life Diaries: Living with Endometriosis
Real Life Diaries: Living with Rheumatic Diseases
Real Life Diaries: Living with a Brain Injury
Real Life Diaries: Through the Eyes of DID
Real Life Diaries: Through the Eyes of an Eating Disorder
Real Life Diaries: Living with Gastroparesis
Grief Diaries: Surviving Loss of a Spouse
Grief Diaries: Surviving Loss of a Child
Grief Diaries: Surviving Loss of a Sibling
Grief Diaries: Surviving Loss of a Parent
Grief Diaries: Surviving Loss of an Infant
Grief Diaries: Surviving Loss of a Loved One
Grief Diaries: Surviving Loss by Suicide
Grief Diaries: Surviving Loss of Health
Grief Diaries: How to Help the Newly Bereaved
Grief Diaries: Surviving Loss by Impaired Driving
Grief Diaries: Surviving Loss by Homicide
Grief Diaries: Surviving Loss of a Pregnancy
Grief Diaries: Hello from Heaven
Grief Diaries: Grieving for the Living
Grief Diaries: Shattered
Grief Diaries: Project Cold Case
Grief Diaries: Poetry & Prose and More
Grief Diaries: Through the Eyes of Men
Grief Diaries: Will We Survive?
Grief Diaries: Hit by Impaired Driver
Grammy Visits From Heaven
Grandpa Visits From Heaven
Faith, Grief & Pass the Chocolate Pudding
Heaven Talks to Children
God's Gift of Love: After Death Communication
Color My Soul Whole
Grief Reiki

Humanity's legacy of stories and storytelling
is the most precious we have.

DORIS LESSING

*

To share your story, visit
www.griefdiaries.com
www.RealLifeDiaries.com

PUBLISHED BY ALYBLUE MEDIA
Inside every human is a story worth sharing.
www.AlyBlueMedia.com

Made in the USA
San Bernardino, CA
07 February 2018